Praise for
Capital Market Revolution

"This is a thought-provoking and even scary book – because revolutions upset and destroy established orders. It is well worth a read for anyone who wants to understand how current developments and progress in capital markets will punctuate the economic equilibrium and lead to new winners and massive creative destruction of the old order."
– Marc Faber, editor of the *Gloom, Boom & Doom Report* and author of *Riding the Millennial Storm*

"... reads like a great Thomas Clancy high tech adventure novel that is nearly impossible to put down."   – *Trading on Target*

"Patrick Young is one of today's visionaries and realists concerning the future of the global finance industry."
– Lisa Benjamin, *Swiss Derivatives Review*

"... the most entertaining treatment of a very real revolution. No one near a screen can afford to miss it."
– Rory Collins, ex-CIO, Australian Stock Exchange

"... it very effectively screams with all the compelling audacity of an Israelite trumpet, for the destruction of those traditional City walls. Bravo."   – Book of the Week, *The Independent*

"... simply compelling reading."   – Mike Stiller, CEO, Global Direct Dealing AG, former Deputy Chairman of LIFFE

"... a breathless tour of this brave new financial world."   – *Time*

The New Capital Market Revolution

The New
Capital Market Revolution

The Winners, the Losers, and
the Future of Finance

Patrick L. Young

TEXERE

New York • London

Copyright © 2003 by Patrick L. Young

Published in 2003 by

TEXERE LLC
55 East 52nd Street
New York, NY 10055

Tel: +1 (212) 317 5511
Fax: +1 (212) 317 5178
www.etexere.com

In the U.K.

TEXERE Publishing Limited
71–77 Leadenhall Street
London EC3A 3DE

Tel: +44 (0)20 7204 3644
Fax: +44 (0)20 7208 6701
www.etexere.co.uk

This publication is designed to provide accurate and authoritative information in
regard to the subject matter covered. It is sold with the understanding that the
publisher is not engaged in rendering legal, accounting, or other professional
services. If legal advice or other expert assistance is required, the services of a
competent professional person should be sought.

TEXERE books may be purchased for educational, business, or sales promotional
use. For more information please write to the Special Markets Department at the
TEXERE address in New York or London.

Designed and project managed by Macfarlane Production Services, Markyate,
Hertfordshire, England (e-mail: macfarl@aol.com).

Library of Congress Cataloging-in-Publication Data is available.

ISBN 1-58799-146-2

Printed in the United States of America.

This book is printed on acid-free paper.

10 9 8 7 6 5 4 3 2 1

This book is for my mother, Joan, with all my love.
PLY

At first, chips went into calculators and digital watches, and the world marveled. Eventually chips went into assembly lines, elevators, artificial pets, rocket ships and blenders. There seemed no limit to what they could do, and no danger of oversupply. The more things there were, the more people wanted them. Their uses are indeed endless, but that does not necessarily mean they are endlessly beneficial or profitable.

Steve Zwick, *Time*

The future is disorder. A door like this has cracked open five or six times since we got up on our hind legs. It is the best possible time to be alive, when almost everything you thought you knew is wrong.

Tom Stoppard, *Arcadia*

The Empires of the future are the Empires of the mind.

Winston Churchill

Contents

Foreword

Why should a change of paradigm be called a revolution?

from *The Structure of Scientific Revolution* by Thomas Kuhn, 1962

Forty years ago, Thomas Kuhn answered this question affirmatively as it relates to science. He noted that such a change "need seem revolutionary only to those whose paradigms are affected by them," a reality caused when "existing institutions have ceased adequately to meet the problems posed by an environment that they have in part created."

Winding the clock forward 40 years to the present time, I was in the City during London Derivatives Week, June 2002, to pay courtesy visits to my colleagues at the various international exchanges, marketplaces, clearing houses and end-users gathered for the annual event. I had just stepped down as Chairman of Chicago Mercantile Exchange Inc. after more than four years in the role.

On this occasion, I had the privilege to have lunch with Patrick Young. I look forward to our encounters, which usually coincide with an industry conference – possibly in London, Burgenstock, Chicago, Singapore or some other international venue – as I always learn something new from Patrick when we exchange views. Patrick, as you can tell from his writings, conference speeches and appearances on business television, has very strongly held, "revolutionary" (as defined by him in this book) beliefs about global capital markets. As a former market participant, his current journalist and business development modes keep him in constant touch with many key decision makers. We spoke at length of what the present and future hold and Patrick, true to form, pulled no punches.

It is not too often that Patrick catches me off guard, even if I am taking the other side of an issue under discussion. However, over our coffee he proceeded to do just that, by asking if I would write a foreword for this book! As one who is living (and so far, surviving) amidst the Capital Market Revolution predicted in Patrick's first book, I am honored by his request.

Indeed, during the summer of 1999, at the very time that *Capital Market Revolution* became available in bookstores and, quite appropriately, through Internet booksellers, my CME colleagues and I were living through most of the core challenges and developing strategies to unlock the opportunities highlighted in that important book.

So, before discussing Patrick's new book – *The New Capital Market Revolution* – allow me the opportunity to recap a bit of (now ancient) CME history, as I believe there are some lessons for the future in what I encountered along the way.

In the spring of 1998, I stood in front of hundreds of Chicago Mercantile Exchange members, the first time I had done so as Chairman. The world around us had been turned upside down and inside out, like something out of an M.C. Escher print. Dramatic changes were underway in London and the Continent. For example, LIFFE had just lost its battle with DTB (now EUREX) to hold onto its benchmark Bund contract, and MATIF (now Euronext) was in the process of closing its magnificent trading floor in favor of the screen. These changes were having a profound impact on our previously insulated world in the United States. The Chicago press was having a field day with stories quoting veteran Chicago market participants predicting the demise of the Chicago derivatives exchanges by year-end. CME's seat prices, which already had been falling before I took the helm in January, had indeed continued their descent. For many, the outlook appeared to be quite bleak.

I told our members that the first order of business would be to develop a comprehensive strategy for CME – one that would allow us not only to survive, but to thrive. I told them it was critical that they understand the competitive landscape that surrounded us, for only then would they understand the necessity of changing many of the ways in which we conducted business.

During the lengthy Q&A which followed, one very worried member rose to ask how long it would take to develop this strategy. My answer didn't comfort her. I said that because CME didn't currently have a strategic plan, it would take several months to complete the task and that we would report back to the members in the Fall. She said we didn't have enough time for this; we needed to do something (anything!!) immediately, and if we didn't, CME would be dead by August. I calmly responded that we would stay the course, and our team left the meeting to do just that.

With respect to CME's strategy, the rest is history, as the saying goes. True to our word, that Fall we announced a comprehensive strategy that included a strong investment in technology coupled with a complete reorganization that would see us demutualize and become a for-profit corporation, much like our European counterparts. An overwhelming 98% of our members voted to demutualize – the highest margin of approval in CME's history. Over the next couple of years, we became the largest derivatives exchange in the United States. As to the future, I will leave that to others to forecast.

I tell you the above, not to boast of CME's current success, but to lay the groundwork for the lessons one can glean from reading Patrick's newest work:

- The "usual suspects" driving change in the markets, technology and regulation, continue to keep global capital markets in flux. However, one should not doubt that the result will be a continued melding of exchange-traded and OTC derivatives, as well as (underlying) cash markets and derivatives.
- Customer demand for greater flexibility, deeper liquidity, improved front- and back-end technology, and increased capital efficiency, cross-product and cross-border access will continue to foster consolidation. If you don't give customers what they want, they will find a different venue that will.

- As the current debates rage about electronic versus open outcry trading, mutual versus for-profit market centers, and for-profit versus utility clearing, consolidation will continue unabated throughout the food chain, affecting exchanges, OTC markets, liquidity providers, intermediaries, infrastructure providers, clearing houses and others. The pace of this consolidation will surprise even the heartiest "revolutionary."
- Timing is often everything in trading, which is just as true for product and service providers. The organic ebb and flow of change, caused in large part by the above-mentioned drivers, necessitates that one step back far enough to see the bigger picture. The goal is to realize that during times of stress, patience sometimes is a virtue. Being an early adopter can cause just as poor an outcome as being too late.
- And a conclusion that will be intuitive to a "revolutionary" – in order to survive and thrive through the revolution's paradigm shifts, one must be willing to embrace change and turn challenge into opportunity.

After reading Patrick Young's *The New Capital Market Revolution*, I believe you will understand why Kuhn's metaphor applies itself to today's capital markets as readily as it did to the science of 40 years ago.

Scott Gordon
President and Chief Operating Officer, Tokyo-Mitsubishi Futures
and
Former Chairman, Chicago Mercantile Exchange Inc.
August 2002

Preface to *The New Capital Market Revolution*

O nce upon a time I wrote a book which suggested much upheaval in financial markets. Many people were scared, others opted not to talk to me. An official at the NYMEX exchange in New York had me thrown off the trading floor for the sin of trying to make people understand just what changes technology was wreaking in the financial markets. The Capital Market Revolution was under way and I found myself somewhat in the limelight as an inadvertent spokesman for the revolution throughout the world.

It is rare that a revolution can be toasted with champagne but that was precisely how James Henry, on behalf of Cargills Investor Services raised a glass at the British Library on July 1st, 1999 to launch the original book *Capital Market Revolution* from which this book has grown. At that time, the strong consensus viewpoint was that London's LIFFE exchange, despite heavyweight new management, would simply hemorrhage and die. Meanwhile, nobody seriously believed that an assault on the primacy of the American derivatives market's dominance was remotely plausible. Perhaps a brief "flash in the pan" but nothing more. Likewise, it seemed unthinkable that there was anything but upside and continued dominance for the American exchanges. Hedge funds were – as ever – a bubble on the verge of collapsing and few people seemed to have much concept of just how much danger the financial markets faced as a result of the radical restructuring being brought on by the impact of continued deregulation and the removal of middle men: disintermediation.

When it was first published, I vigorously championed what was then essentially a novelty product with no trading in Europe or Asia – the Exchange Traded Fund. Today, ETFs are well on the way to becoming the world's dominant core investment product. Meanwhile, many "experts" simply laughed at the idea that 500 basis point mutual fund entry fees would ever fall. In fact, they tumbled by 50–90% within the following year for most major funds.

In 2002, the American marketplace finally saw in October the launch of single stock futures. In the late 1990s nobody was even talking about such a concept, yet CMR pioneered their introduction ("it won't be long before a major derivatives exchange launches a concerted initiative to trade individual stock futures") and I was subsequently delighted to be involved with the launch of LIFFE's successful Universal Stock Futures product as well as with the Bourse de Montreal and other markets, having championed these markets for several years. In 1999, few people paid much attention to my noting:

> The prospects for a market such as NASDAQ to be linked with a major derivatives market outside the United States for instance would create a powerhouse exchange which would have clear global potential, a broad product range and huge potential to dominate large chunks of the securities markets.

Yet, in 2001 NASDAQ took the first steps in this strategy by linking up with the LIFFE marketplace to create a US joint venture to trade single stock futures.

Likewise, there was a general sense of bewilderment at the concept of a fully fledged exchange to trade sports. An official at one leading clearing house was intrigued but asked politely if perhaps I could come back in about five years time with such an idea. Somewhat in advance of this schedule, in 2001, Intrade (http://www.intrade.com) was duly launched. I was delighted to be a founder along with a group of dynamic Americans: Ron Bernstein, Basil Bourque, John McNamara and Sean McNamara as we created the world's first sports spread trading marketplace. Betdaq, Betfair, and Tradesports have also successfully established exchanges in the sports trading niche.

The usual incipient bearish wariness about hedge funds has grown if anything in the last few years, yet few folk were suggesting explosive growth for the industry by 2001. At the time of *CMR*, I noted the likely impending supply problems of too much money chasing too few managers: "Indeed, by 2001 there may already be significant bottlenecks in the system. This growth splurge will be simply explosive."

The one issue which has not been resolved as rapidly as I expected – and indeed is still the subject of debate in some parts of the US, has been the question of the continuation of open outcry trading on market floors. Having been educated in markets through the trading pits, I naturally feel saddened that this fascinating system is on the verge of extinction. However, as I hope this book shows, extinct is exactly what pit trading will become and if exchange managements don't get to grips with the closure of open outcry markets soon, they will shortly find their markets extinct too. *The New CMR* examines the issues in open outcry versus electronic trading with a renewed interest. Alas, my conclusions will not please those specialists who believe the NYSE floor will live forever, nor those locals who think they have a divine right to trade on a floor within the Loop in Chicago. The death of floor trading remains imminent and, indeed, in many respects the financial markets are in danger of being held up if an orderly closure of floors cannot be undertaken in the near future. I retain a love for the futures pits as amazing places without which the development of capitalism would have been undoubtedly stunted. Alas, not everybody can afford hand-built motor cars, so most drive mass-produced vehicles instead. Likewise, in a commoditised technological world, pit trading has become a luxury capitalism can no longer afford. Schumpeter was right, creative destruction will reign supreme.

Perhaps the most gratifying issue is that *Capital Market Revolution* was simply so far ahead of its time at initial publication that the cores of its arguments remain as valid and important today as they did then. Having said that, there is a wealth of new information in this book which I hope will be of interest to old and new revolutionaries alike. The revolution is gaining pace as I write and too many folk have become used to the idea that they will be around for ever. During the period 2003–2005, we are going to see some remarkable twists and turns which will likely leave at least one of America's centenarian exchanges in tatters – if not completely sunk. The prospects are remarkable and the likely results destructive in a measure only Schumpeter again would have championed. Nevertheless, amidst the remarkable chaos which is being unleashed on the structure of markets everywhere, as ever in capitalism, the opportunities are sufficient to provide remarkable opportunities for traders the world over.

Welcome to *The New Capital Market Revolution*

Patrick L. Young (patrick@erivatives.com)
Monaco, October 2002

Introduction
Nowhere to Hide, Nowhere to Run

Explaining the new way of doing computers and networks is difficult. It's like expecting people in a feudal society to know what it would be like to live in a capitalistic society. It's just too hard to imagine until you're in it.

Bill Joy, Sun Microsystems.

There is nowhere to hide from capital markets. Nobody is safe from the Capital Market Revolution. The Capital Market Revolution presents the greatest upheaval ever seen in the fabric of financial markets. The Capital Market Revolution is born of new technology and is driven by new technology; and it will ultimately change the lives of every individual on the globe.

As the driving force behind the revolution burst on the scene, exchanges thought this new technology would secure their future through wider product bases and increased access to their products. Institutions saw it as a means to create great economies of scale in ever larger multinational frameworks. Brokers even saw computerization as a means to bolster pressurized margins. None saw the reality. The power of information technology threatening to destroy them all. That, very simply is the message of the Capital Market Revolution.

No broker, no banker, no middleman can count his position as being safe from the revolution. This is not an uprising which will be driven by the masses spilling spontaneously onto the streets. However, this is a revolution so profound in its global consequences for every single man, woman and child on Earth that it can (and likely will) bring masses onto the streets within a decade to overthrow the large lumbering government bureaucracies should they fail to appreciate the paradigm shift in world finance.

Revolutionaries, reactionaries or Luddites?

Throughout the text of this book, we will refer to those espousing the Capital Market Revolution as revolutionaries and those who are against it as Luddites. Why not reactionaries? Well, reaction is a mild-mannered pursuit becoming of country gentlemen or Christian Democrat politicians which is normally not vastly harmful but not greatly beneficial either. In the Capital Market Revolution, those seeking to uphold the status quo, or even vaguely tinker with it around the edges will be trampled underfoot with barely a whimper of their arguments against electronic markets being audible. This revolution will simply blow reactionaries away. Any person or organization eschewing the attitudes, attributes and skill sets required for the digital trading revolution, or even aspiring very gently to set the clock back, will at best end up driving a suburban minicab and at worst will face destitution.

Therefore, as reactionaries are too mild to sustain any opposition to the dynamic forces of the Capital Market Revolution I have chosen to refer to those against the whole process as Luddites. Ned Lud apparently broke into a house in a village somewhere in Leicestershire, England in 1779 and (according to the *Oxford English Dictionary*) "in a fit of insane rage" destroyed two knitting machines. As word spread about Lud's response, all such acts of industrial-age vandalism were greeted with the phrase "Lud must have been here." Bands of Luddites flourished in Britain from about 1811 until 1816. Groups of masked men, swore allegiance to "king Ludd" while destroying textile machinery. Therefore, for the purposes of this book, I will employ the term "Luddite" as my preferred method of describing those of a counter-revolutionary persuasion. Of course nobody is suggesting that all those disbelieving in the Capital Market Revolution will seek to destroy the computer apparatus at its core but such counter-revolutionaries have already been evident in actively attempting to thwart the progress of the revolution.

As I write, the most conspicuous Luddites on the horizon often occupy the exchange floors, where open outcry has flourished over the centuries. Sooner or later, if the exchanges themselves are to survive as modern institutions, then the floors of the NYSE and CBOT *et al.* must be superseded by modern technology. No other major industry has managed to keep technology away from its core operation. Nevertheless, there are many Luddites who believe that floor trading cannot be superseded, against considerable evidence to the contrary. True, they may argue that floors can exploit technology but that is to miss the primary cost-, error- and time-saving benefits inherent to this technology. Anybody who doubts this theory need only look at how in 2001/2002 the relative upstart electronic International Securities Exchange (ISE), based out of New York, was slicing market share away from existing legacy open outcry markets, most notably the CBOE where many members simply refused even to countenance the prospect of closing the exchange floor as late as mid-2002, despite ISE increasingly threatening the viability of the CBOE's core franchise.

Remarkably, despite all the progress towards online brokerage ("Schwabification" as I like to call it) and the many technological advances in financial markets, the fate of the revolution still lies mainly in the balance.

Firstly, the powers of entrenched reaction are strong where they are suddenly being challenged after generations of stability in the system. Secondly, the innate arrogance and short-sightedness of management at many of the world's leading intermediary organizations remain considerable. A sense of post-dotcom collapse *Schadenfreude* has convinced many intermediaries that their place in the food chain is no longer under threat. With regard to exchanges in particular, in this book I will refer to them as "legacy exchanges" as this precisely defines their position. The transition from club status to semi-functioning corporations is almost complete even in the most reactionary marketplaces. Next I look forward to many of them following in the footsteps of the likes of the Australian Stock Exchange, Deutsche Börse and Euronext in becoming fully fledged corporations, rather than profit-seeking entities beholden to their old members as is frequently the case in America.

As I conclude writing *The New Capital Market Revolution*, there are many deals afoot and indeed many more threats gradually becoming apparent, if only intermediaries could manage to peep through the blinds and assess what dangers lie before them. Indeed, I would argue that the reaction period to the Capital Market Revolution will have been replaced with a new wave of revolutionary fervor by late 2002 as several effects intermesh.

The "doing technology" thing largely drove the initial stages of the Capital Market Revolution ahead of the millennium. Exchanges closed floors across Europe and Asia, while US exchanges were beholden to their members, thus letting the alternative ECNs (electronic communications networks) gain a foothold. Meanwhile, everybody dreamt their intermediary could become a dotcom and launched headfirst into B2B, a market segment which has more potential than the ECNs but which was simply expected to reach maturity a lot faster than the corporate world could readily keep up with, as they themselves tried to come to terms with what the internet meant for them. While the Capital Market Revolution is mainly driven by technology, it is in fact a revolution born of a feudal state. Exchanges were clubs, brokers had cosy franchises and until deregulation began to hit home, local stock markets remained a predominantly domestic franchise. Allied to the innate power of the internet to reduce the tyranny of distance and prise open markets across the world, the world's financial markets are therefore suffering several events all at once creating the Capital Market Revolution effect.

In essence, the financial markets have been exploding with growth since Nixon let price and value determine economics rather than how much gold somebody held when he took the dollar away from the Bretton Woods standard. When deregulation began hitting Wall Street, the impact was one of helping fuel new markets and a new golden age of capital market innovation. While established industry in the US and Europe (ex-Germany) had to go through painful restructuring to maintain even a remote vestige of competitiveness, the capital markets sailed on oblivious to the crisis. Likewise, when lean mean industry was the end result of the impact of technology and a whole new set of processes for making goods, the capital markets were building capacity in all sorts of fascinating new risk transfer processes which have made life easier and overall more financially transparent for most people (although the occasional blow-ups such as Barings, Enron, LTCM and Worldcom have helped keep the media occupied as well).

Throughout a very difficult period from the late 1960s until the late 1990s, the capital markets grew so quickly and retained local franchises which appeared essentially unbreakable by outside competition, that the marketplace became habituated to observing certain shrines of capitalism (i.e. exchanges) as essentially the core of the system. Yet, ironically, as we will see in Chapter 1, exchanges themselves have actually been a poor substitute for bilateral dealing amongst the largest players for much, if not all, of the past 30 years. Nevertheless, the exchanges, the brokers and all other known intermediaries believed that there was nothing which could upset their system. It had clear cohesive roots dating back centuries in locales such as Amsterdam, London and New York. The system worked well, so why change it?

The first stages of the Capital Market Revolution from 1997 to 2001 rocked a great deal of the financial firmament but mistakenly many have seen it as merely a technological process or even more dangerously, as a red herring which will not affect the long-term viability of outmoded processes such as floor dealing. Stock and derivatives exchanges have begun to conclude that all their franchises must be worth something equivalent to the relatively giddy valuations provided to early movers such as Deutsche Börse and Euronext. Yet, as Deutsche Börse CEO Werner Seifert himself stressed in mid-2002, there are many exchanges which simply are not worth taking over due to the time required to bring together the companies. The chilling reality is that there will be predators – some might regard them as barbarians – staking a claim to every other exchange's franchise within the next two years. The technology may only be at the Ford Model T stage but it is sufficient to do everything that the New York Stock Exchange floor can manage … only more swiftly, more cheaply and with a much greater robustness in the event of an act of God or a terror attack on the headquarters building.

In the exchange world, many simple maxims have come to be regarded as truisms. The most significant one is that the first market to establish a dominant pool of liquidity will win against allcomers in maintaining primacy in that business. Yet, the near collapse of the London LIFFE derivatives exchange after 1997 was entirely due to its losing a core franchise in German Government Bond futures to its

Swiss-German rival, EUREX. Once European law permitted screens to be placed throughout the EU, the LIFFE exchange's open outcry system was instantly doomed. In the US, once the barbarians gain a foothold in the marketplace, legacy exchanges will find it difficult, if not impossible to recover.

The Capital Market Revolution almost takes intelligent exploitation of technology for granted. Clearly, it is hardly a ground-breaking revelation to state that microchips do dizzyingly fast things and can make the world a better place. All of that is already clear to most readers. If it is not, ask the ever increasing "grey army" of pensioners finding the internet a wonderful tool to enhance their lives. No, the key issues of the Capital Market Revolution relate to flexibility, strong management, risk taking and an entrepreneurial flair in exploiting the future. There are vast opportunities for traders in this new marketplace. For one thing, there are now more trading opportunities than ever before and whole new product areas are becoming available. Sports betting for one, may be viewed as something for the preserve of twitchy individuals in slightly louche betting shops but the business of trading sports is set for enormous expansion in the next few years.

Given that the internet is here to stay, it does form a sort of backbone to the Capital Market Revolution, providing communications that have never before been available to the mass of investors. In this respect, while the day trader bubble may have initially burst, this is no more a lasting phenomenon than the dotcom bubble. The ranks of skilled online trading practitioners grow daily in number. Likewise, investors can now access more and better information than has ever been their prerogative in investing history. How exchanges, other intermediaries and infomediaries deal with this vast new investor grouping is a key issue within the Capital Market Revolution. In the past, it was expensive to engage in dealing for private clients. In a digitized, commoditized world, nickels and dimes are the maximum cashflow intermediaries can expect. With internet technology, the multiple nickels and dimes of retail investors can be cost effectively integrated into significant cashflows.

Major events over the next three years within the Capital Market Revolution will, of course, include the ongoing rationalization of the exchanges landscape. An unhealthy belief remains amongst exchanges that they will all sooner or later be able to ride out the revolution with a healthy stock market valuation and a renewed/reinvigorated franchise, merely by paying public lip service to various technological mantras. Meanwhile, the B2B market appears to have come and gone if you read only so far as the headlines but then again, just as with the internet, the actual statistics for usage of B2B style mechanisms look better by the day. There is a profound revolution in purchasing taking place within the B2B field. Company valuations may be soggy but the value of business being transacted by such new model exchanges is still set to grow exponentially in years to come, despite there being rationalization (at best) for some companies once deemed the glamour stocks of the dotcom boom.

Therefore, despite drawing its origins in technology, the Capital Market Revolution is most certainly not a simple tale of markets being enveloped by a raft of computer screens which make financial markets easier for existing counterparties to transact business. It is far more radical and sweeping than that. The revolution is a genuine paradigm shift in the processes of financial markets which is completely altering not just how financiers interact but how the public at large can actually participate in financial markets with more influence than ever before in history. The core issue is not how the playing field will operate but rather what the playing field will be.

The Internet is the Gutenberg press on steroids. Gutenberg wasn't about how many Bibles were printed, but the fact that you no longer had to listen to the clerics.

Watts Wacker, consultant and resident futurist, SRI International Upside

This is a revolution in financial markets which will change the world. Since Gutenberg revolutionized the business of printing in the fifteenth century, markets and media have traditionally operated from a single standpoint disseminating via a network (covering increasing distances as distribution has been perfected). However, digital media now makes possible multiple access and dissemination from any point to any other point. This multivariable access and dissemination structure will ultimately undermine current market structures which are rooted in a handful of big cities.

There have been many times when open outcry has been written off as an anachronism, although all have proven incorrect – until now. None of the telecommunications innovations of the late nineteenth and early twentieth century hampered trading on exchanges in financial centers. Rather it expressly aided them. The invention of telegraph and later telex, telephone and fax, merely facilitated traders from further and further away being able to deal straight to the marketplace in question. The tyranny of distance to the market was reduced, if not quite removed altogether, making the trading process more accessible to all.

It has been common in tomes proclaiming the impact of technological revolution to give some space to PC chip manufacturer Intel's founder Gordon Moore's eponymous law which states that computer processing power would double every 12–18 months. That remains as true today as it was when first posited 30 years ago. Yet, Moore's law is only a technological benchmark. The changes at the heart of the Capital Market Revolution are concerned with the creation of pan-regional and perhaps ultimately global bourses, as well as vast undercurrents eating at the heart of the business of every intermediary. The Capital Market Revolution takes the bourses out of clubby city center premises and places them right back in the jungle of capitalism.

The increasing growth in computing power and the popularization of the internet means that information flow can now be sent from anywhere to anywhere, creating a whole new playing field. In the past, financial information has traditionally been freely available only to the richest and most powerful individuals and corporations on planet Earth. Now, information is widely available to all elements of society equally. Any information advantage from being rich and powerful has been eroded to the point where it now equates to a relatively negligible head start compared to the situation a mere handful of years ago. Information can be passed at little cost to every form of trader, investor and market counterparty. When the internet came along, suddenly, like Gutenberg's Bible, we all had access to ostensibly the same information as the professionals. Nowadays, even to discuss the notion of how day traders use the internet is seen as positively old fashioned. We have all become so used to real-time stock tickers on web sites, it is already difficult to recall what investing was like when you had either to call a broker, read yesterday's paper or watch a wallboard at the exchange's headquarters just in order to find a value for your shares.

The old hegemony of existing institutional investors, exchanges and brokers is doomed to collapse under what I like to call the "post-feudal marketplace" (PFM). Once upon a time, the medieval fiefdoms of exchanges were operating in a sort of holy trinity with the brokers and floor-based specialists to operate the marketplace. Now, each has to look to alternative arrangements if they are to maintain any ability to profit from their activities. When the feudal system broke down it was some years before stability reappeared in many parts of Europe. A similar era of instability, with great rewards for the entrepreneurial are now occurring as the post-feudal marketplace becomes a reality in the Capital Market Revolution.

Moreover, investment can now be undertaken from anywhere to anywhere at the click of a mouse. The PFM will affect not only market counterparties and mechanisms but also the regulators, and indeed the future wellbeing of government finances throughout the world. If any of these groupings fails to reform in line with the precepts of the PFM, they will find themselves out of business. Nevertheless, post-feudal does not suggest especially advanced. There are still bottlenecks in the system aimed at giving certain professionals a privileged position in the food chain. Likewise, some exchanges still cling fondly to their outmoded floor traders. The key is that post-feudal is still some way from modern. There is still plenty of scope for improvement in markets as the Capital Market Revolution takes hold.

Bankers must become bionic or be bypassed.

Existing financial markets are under the most concerted threat in their history. From foreign exchange markets to swaps trading, the entire marketplace is changing. The ever decreasing costs of market entry make it increasingly simple for new operators to enter marketplaces and compete with existing legacy exchanges.

Exchanges really are a rather low form of life. There is a tendency to look at exchanges as one of three things: as a utility, as an institution, or even, God forbid, as part of the social fabric. Rather, the business of the exchange is high yield, low value. The exchange is a servant of markets.

Sir Brian Williamson, Executive Chairman, LIFFE

The most frequent problem with all types of large financial institutions has been their apparent ivory tower mentality. Exchanges have become sacrosanct in the late twentieth century. Their status as revered demi-gods of financial markets is now far too perilous for them to survive without radical change. Too many high-ranking managers have spent too long trying to avoid the fray from the comfort of management offices, rather than trying to actually get into the trenches alongside their members and assess what they really require.

The more brokerage rates fall, the less able brokers are to offer a good full-service operation.

The business of technology is being driven from the US in almost every facet of business and society. Indeed, on equity markets, the National Association of Securities Dealers Automated Quotation system (NASDAQ) has become a leviathan in securities trading (even after the dotcom bubble), especially amongst high-technology stocks – although whether it can maintain this is open to question. However, when the US (and indeed the world) thinks of stocks and shares, they visualize the frenzied activity on Wall Street at the New York Stock Exchange. It is incredible, therefore, that given the clear belief shown by the US business world in new technology that, with several honorable exceptions, the overall driving force behind the post-feudal marketplace is still the derivatives markets and mainly emanates from Europe. This is all the more remarkable given the relatively statist and inflexible economics of much of Europe. Nevertheless, the fact remains that Europe is at the center of new market development. Thanks to the large concentration of foreign banks within the fabled "Square Mile," the City of London was first to encounter the dynamic processes of the Capital Market Revolution. On foreign turf, banks could afford to be more promiscuous. As we shall see in the Prologue, the revolution hit LIFFE so hard as to leave the exchange reeling and questioning the viability of its existence within months of becoming the second largest market on Earth. A similar fate awaits many more markets, especially several widely regarded as leaders in the US. Even the threat of increased promiscuity by dealers using electronic platforms means that the long-standing hegemony for many bourses the world over can never again be guaranteed.

Derivatives – defining the marketplace?

The derivatives business has been increasingly shaping the destiny of all capital markets (including commodity and any other derivation of traded products) since the early 1970s when the first foreign exchange futures revolutionized the world of finance and helped fuel a brave new vision of deregulation which has continued to bring increasing price transparency to the world ever since. Yet, despite the vast size of the derivatives business both on exchanges and OTC, it is not uncommon for observers, and even insiders, to believe that the cash markets are driving innovation. The truth, however, is that it is the derivatives business which clearly has driven all the greatest product and customer innovations of the past 30 years. Even a supposedly "cash" product such as exchange traded funds are in all reality a derivative product. The derivatives business remains a broad church ranging from simple forwards, futures and options which can help hedge all forms of trade and other risks, through to highly complicated OTC deals which can be transacted only by highly credit rated adult institutions.

One key driver of the derivatives revolution is the fact that by using derivatives (of varying complexities), institutions with a "natural" position can morph their positions to something they feel more comfortable with according to the financial market outlook. For example, a power station operator can exploit generating capacity to lock in high prices, as can a freight organization with a fleet of bulk carriers.

Likewise, a financial institution with a core business in mortgages may prefer to lower their net exposure to the property market at certain cyclical phases. From a private investor standpoint, everybody in Europe with a fixed low-rate mortgage can thank the derivatives market for the discounted rate period. All of these processes are being effected by derivatives. While there can be speculation involved in this (just like any other market) the fact remains that the core of the derivatives business exists to provide a dynamic degree of risk transfer and hedging for all sorts of enterprise, across all asset classes. This flexibility is what gives derivatives the power to drive the Capital Market Revolution.

At this stage of the revolution, while it is undoubtedly within the derivatives business that much of the creative power of the Capital Market Revolution is rooted, ironically, many of the old players within the derivatives industry themselves are faced by the perilous predicament of needing to reform and open their institutions or die … which runs against the grain of the many vested interests who can already profit significantly from existing positions. The issue of open versus closed and insiders versus outsiders will continue to polarize the players of the Capital Market Revolution. However, make no mistake, the major impetus for change has been driven by technophile derivatives traders. The aftershocks in the cash market may be the most commonly viewed symptom but the cash equity business is often merely reacting to pressures elsewhere in the system when it appears to be radicalized.

The status quo is not dead; rather, there is no longer a status quo.

The New Capital Market Revolution seeks to outline the likely future for financial markets with equanimity. Therefore, readers may find some of the possible outcomes disturbing. Like any revolution, this one is not a clean, simple and easy to master process of progressive change. Rather, it will be an ongoing chaotic process which will create haves and have nots, often stripping away centuries of financial achievement from individual dynasties, institutions and even sovereign states.

In many respects, clearing houses hold the aces. Like feudal princes in medieval times, they have the opportunity to wield power over which new model exchanges retain financial credibility. Exchanges will struggle and many will die. As I write several titans such as the Chicago Board of Trade and its related Options Exchange (CBOE) appear to be struggling to maintain their former dominance. Meanwhile, clearing houses are entering their most influential era yet. Nevertheless, not everything is golden even here. The possibility of clearing netting and better collateralization procedures on the OTC markets do pose a significant threat to the largest institutional business which may remain reluctant to come under the clearing houses' remit. Many of the bigger bulge bracket banks question why, given their titanic size, they have to post any form of margin (collateral) against their trades, least of all at the same prevailing rates that are applied uniformly by the clearing house to everybody from the largest multinational institutions to the smallest one-lot traders.

There are no more gentlemen and the players are dying. In future there will be only electronic traders.

All the revolutionary processes are gradually gaining pace in financial markets and no government or governmental body will be able to do anything but acknowledge the power of the marketplace to adjudicate how good a job they are doing. The fact that the US regulatory position is a patchwork, with the Commodity Futures Trading Commission (CFTC) and SEC representing derivatives and cash markets respectively, is an anachronism. There are dangers of protectionist regulation more to save bureaucrats than help investors emerging in many countries from Australia to the US.

Like many revolutions, it requires a little hindsight to see clearly the processes that had been in place for many years and which finally gave impetus to the revolution. The near death of LIFFE after 1997 is truly the crystallizing moment when the Capital Market Revolution can be said to have been born – although many of the individual catalysts of the revolution were apparent some time before this. Nevertheless, in almost every respect, the revolution is only now truly gaining pace. Various cosmetic baubles such as ECNs have taken center stage in the media's imaginations at one time or another but most "new" systems have really only been symptoms of the problem rather than genuinely new solutions *per se*. In reality, the ultimate solution for capital markets is probably an incredibly simple one: a vast marketplace or network of interlinked markets providing a comprehensive investing, hedging, risk management and speculation platform open to the citizens of the world, with access readily available with little, if any, intermediation. Breaking down the barriers of the current interest groups who all want to keep their piece of the existing pie, while trying to get to a much bigger pie for everybody to share is a key challenge faced by all the major proponents of the Capital Market Revolution.

Bottlenecks in the revolution

For all the benefits that new technology brings in democratizing and developing the breadth of financial markets, the Capital Market Revolution is not a simple solution to all our ills. Indeed, it comes with concomitant problems typical of rapid growth phases.

At all stages in history, man contents himself with the thought that he has created the greatest technology ever available, and he tends to be blind to the failings of the age. The Victorians had electric light but failed to develop much that would pass muster as contemporary bathroom hygiene for instance. Equally, we have barely reached the Model T Ford stage of technological development in financial markets.

The stresses on the current exchange systems (some of which are already fairly middle aged, to put it mildly, in technology terms) will be increasingly apparent as volumes grow in the next year. Equity derivatives will be an interesting case study to watch – by the middle of 2001 the LIFFE Connect system (amongst others) was already experiencing highly disproportionate quantities of data transaction in their equity derivatives compared with actual traded volume (i.e. something you get paid for!).

The old DTB nearly foundered when its growth pains became somewhat inflamed a few years back. No wonder EUREX has to date been reluctant to endorse single stock futures until the management can see a viably profitable market in the product. Then again, it is clear just how much the revolution has progressed when a bare three years ago there was a paucity of information in print to even suggest that widespread single stock futures could ever become a reality.

Management issues

In addition to the key issue of bandwidth usage, it seems fair to note here that in certain quarters a few alarming exchange management traits remain from pre-demutualised days. Moreover, as a bewildered US magazine correspondent noted in the wake of the Euronext takeover of LIFFE in late 2001, no exchange seemed to want to provide a single benchmark which could be remotely used to discuss equivalent market size – although all parties could of course demonstrate some useful benchmarks which they claimed demonstrated the virility of a very randy elephant.

In the good old days of clubbiness, we measured the success of exchanges on number of contracts traded, the quantity of press releases, size of floor space or number of new contracts introduced. None of the above ought to be regarded as measures of success by a for-profit business.

In the quest for profits, expect a crackdown on the number of committees, less office space for non-executives and indeed less influence generally for a lot of people. However, the aim is not "lean and mean" simply for the sake of it. What we're really seeking is the opportunity to build a coherent, but modestly sized nexus.

The fact is that good exchange staff with a broad range of skills will increasingly be able to demand salaries commensurate with their investment banking and trading brethren. The biggest problem in staffing for old-line exchange management teams will be finding the individuals with complete skill sets. By their very nature old-fashioned clubs often have some groups of staff who have perhaps one- or two-thirds of the required skills. This issue doesn't affect left field competitors or other new market entrants.

Above all else, remember the fact that no matter what you do, sooner or later somebody is going to emerge out of left field and endeavor to plunder your business using newer technology, fewer staff and a more dynamic management structure. This remains stunningly relevant for exchange management teams everywhere.

It has not been my habit to make apologies for the fact that my conclusions may often be unpalatable to many individuals and corporations alike. However, financial markets have always been engines of change, driving processes to create change. Now, the Capital Market Revolution is essentially reworking every single established factor about financial markets which everyday investors take for granted. To date, I am happy to stand by what has been a fairly consistent record in prophesying the expansion of digital capital markets and the retreat of outmoded methods. Having traded for myself as well as working as an analyst and broker during the course of the last 15 years, I feel happy to remain in the vanguard of the revolution having championed many of the still radical visions in the Capital Market Revolution during recent years. Given that much of my record is transparently available online via the http://www.erivatives.com web site, I hope you, the reader, will realize that this is hardly a flash in the pan doomster tome intended merely to keep exchange chairmen awake at night worrying!

My hope is that *The New Capital Market Revolution* outlines not just a sensible blueprint for future financial markets and their practitioners (both at an individual and a macro level) but also provides a helpful handbook for the future of finance in an online world. In line with my belief in openness and transparency in financial markets, all feedback is welcome using the e-mail address on p. xxiv. In the meantime, I hope you will enjoy this journey through the financial markets at this most exciting juncture and remember the key slogan:

Liquidity! Accessibility! Transparency!

Markets which operate in accordance with this maxim will find themselves in the best position to survive and prosper in the Capital Market Revolution.

The New Capital Market Revolution

Prologue
Genesis of a Revolution

Open outcry has survived every other innovation in history.
Bob Wilmouth, President NFA (National Futures Association of the USA)

It is only a matter of time before all financial instruments can be traded electronically.
Charles Sidey, broker, London

L ondon, June 4th, 1997: an almost indiscernible chill wind of
discontent had been growing for some time. Nevertheless, the
status quo still looked assured as Daniel Hodson entered the ballroom
at the Intercontinental hotel, in the heart of Mayfair. Hodson, the
CEO of the London International Financial Futures Exchange was
riding high. LIFFE was celebrating its 15th birthday with the news
that it was now the second-largest derivatives market on the planet.
The long-time stranglehold on futures and options trading held by the
Chicago exchanges had finally been broken by a European interloper
over a hundred years younger than either of the neighboring
American markets. While the derivatives business had experienced
massive growth in the previous decade, the established order had
always shown the hegemony to favor the Chicago Board of Trade and
the Chicago Mercantile Exchange, neighboring monoliths dominating
the exchange traded landscape. Now LIFFE had split the duopoly. Yet,
beneath the surface, the LIFFE board was itself split over the whole
issue of open outcry versus electronic trading. Nevertheless, Hodson
as CEO would defend open outcry with gusto, despite being acutely
aware of the reservations amongst many of his directors.

London Derivatives Week is an established event on the global
financial calendar. Leading figures from all aspects of derivatives

markets attend exhibitions, conferences and receptions scattered across the Square Mile and the West End. Syon House, the seat of the Dukes of Northumberland, would host the highlight of LIFFE's 15th anniversary celebrations. In the Tudor mansion with interiors remodeled by Robert Adam to the south-west of central London, the conclusion of Derivatives Week was a sumptuous Gala Ball for some 3,500 of the world's leading traders and financial notables.

Invitations had become hot currency in the week leading up to the event. In the multi-billion dollar global derivative business, hundreds of traders in London and further afield would be disappointed at being left without an invitation to the elite gathering. Brokers were scrambling to beg, borrow and steal tickets for key clients, while stories of journalists haranguing the LIFFE press office to secure an invitation were not unknown.

Throughout the week, Hodson was at the very epicenter of the celebrations, as the man who had helped shape the exchange in its most recent years of dynamic growth. Surpassing the Chicago Mercantile Exchange had been an achievement universally regarded as impossible only a few years earlier. Now, LIFFE had the world's number one exchange, the Chicago Board of Trade firmly in its sights. Many might have felt the future lay with electronic dealing but Hodson was in the vanguard of supporting the historic open outcry methods involving pits containing colorfully jacketed traders shouting at one another.

The centerpiece of the joint FIA/FOA conference[1] was a debate sponsored by Reuters with polling via hand-held terminals courtesy of the UK-based multinational news and information giant. Enthusiastically chairing the motion "This House Believes That Floor Trading Will Not Survive The Challenge Of New Technology" was Christopher Sharples, the Chairman of ICV Datastream, itself a major technologically oriented data vendor. An initial vote ahead of hostilities starting gave the motion a stunning 75% support level, while a mere 25% felt that floor trading held the best cards for the future.

Undaunted by this vote against the core *modus operandi* of the LIFFE exchange, Daniel Hodson rose to oppose the motion with the air of a man who knew he had everything going for him. In an impassioned speech, "dapper Dan" as one derivatives publication dubbed him, spoke as if his life depended on winning this very debate. While his first core point (always to distrust motions containing hyperbole) bore all the hallmarks of an English public-school trained attitude to debate, Hodson went on to exhort the audience "always remember that technology is far from an opponent to open outcry, rather it is a friend of open outcry." Hodson emphasized the human dimension and advantage of open outcry trading: "No electronic trading system will be able to replicate the advantages of open outcry." Indeed, the human factor was key to making floor trading more flexible, more liquid and better at "price discovery" than electronic alternatives. It was an impressive speech, more so because Hodson had stepped in at the last moment when the CBOT Chairman Pat Arbor had been unable to speak.

Moreover, the LIFFE CEO added, reliability is an omnipresent concern for derivatives markets. Unlike computers, "people don't collectively fall over or work slowly" – a barbed reference to German rival the Deutsche Terminbörse (DTB) which was suffering frequent bouts of unreliability. Concluding his rousing address with a flourish, Hodson added, "With floor trading, it is technology which will ensure its continued existence."

Despite Hodson's formidable reputation in debate, the proposition had not merely rolled over and played dead. Roz Wilton, a former Drexel Burnham Lambert supremo and now MD of transaction products at the information business's foremost name, Reuters PLC, had made some crushing points for the proposition, such as "Technology is the only way to consistently grow this business economically." Playing on the fears of hard-pressed brokers, she added: "Commissions are going down while costs are rising ... somebody must bear the costs associated with open outcry." Acknowledging the emotional nature of the debate, Wilton's final point in favor of electronic transactions was "I know it's the fairest method of trading."

Seconding the proposition, Bruce Pollock, a director of BWO Bank in Switzerland ridiculed the old-fashioned nature of face-to-face "open outcry" dealing by likening it to an outmoded period piece, such as a horse and buggy. Very pretty, very interesting but outmoded compared to contemporary alternatives. Emphasizing Roz Wilton's clarion call, he added: "I love open outcry, but it doesn't make good economic sense."

Carl Boraiko, a Chicago trader then resident in London as a trader on the LIFFE floor bolstered Daniel Hodson's arguments. Boraiko noted that, with the advancement of technology, screen trading gave more opportunity for front running.[2] The much vaunted electronic audit trails began only when a trade was entered into the computer system. If counterparties so desired, there was nothing to prevent them from pre-arranging trades before input.[3]

Cost, Boraiko agreed, was an over-riding factor in brokerage companies' considerations. However, electronic trading's cost advantage was unlikely to emerge if screen trading developed. There would be increasing customer demand for individual screens, with their own personalized traders and order teams which would inflate the overall costs involved with screen trading. The cost benefits often claimed for the move to electronic dealing would prove impossible.

On open outcry markets, he commented "we embrace technology just the same way as electronic markets embrace technology." He concluded "I could continue to expose the electronic markets for what they are – amateurs trying to compete with the pros" and cautioned the house to recall that locals (independent traders risking their personal capital to facilitate trade on exchange floors) are a source of human input and a major source of liquidity. Boraiko could not see why such locals would wish to switch to electronic markets.

When the debate was open to the floor, Bob Wilmouth was first to speak. The sexagenerian President of the NFA (National Futures Association of the USA) was firmly opposed to the motion. Business flow to the best and most liquid market was vital to him. "Open outcry has survived every other innovation in history." Thereafter, almost all aspects of the possibilities offered by new technology were covered from the floor participants. Richard Jaycobs of Computer Trading Corporation[4] raised the specter of virtual reality. He felt that open outcry would always exist, although ultimately it would be in an electronic format.

In his concluding remarks, an ebullient Daniel Hodson maintained his crushing form, noting that "Open outcry will survive and it won't just be in Managua or Bangkok." Despite the excellent speeches for the proposition, the end result hinged on Hodson's bravura performance … indeed, when the numbers appeared on the screen behind the Chairman's head, the final vote brought a collective gasp from the crowd with the votes having moved to only 57% for the motion (down from an initial 75%) and 43% against.

At the time many folk were driven to wonder was it a victory, perhaps Pyrrhic, for the battling brilliance of the excellent Daniel Hodson? Or was it, as some electronic trading officials muttered darkly, evidence of lurking open outcry supporters employing tactical voting – initially hiding their genuine feelings, only to reveal them on the second vote. Whatever the truth, the real result, it was felt, would doubtless take some years to become apparent.

In fact, the real result became apparent much much sooner. A little over 13 months later, on July 21st, 1998, Daniel Hodson resigned as LIFFE CEO. Chairman Jack Wigglesworth had already stood down. At least Wigglesworth had a job to go back to.

In a frenzied period of months, the LIFFE exchange had, as Edward Luce described it in the FT "undergone a road-to-Damascus conversion to electronic trading." In addition to seeking to dump open outcry in favor of electronic trading mechanisms, the London market launched a wholesale dumping of core principles. LIFFE demutualized its member-owned structure in favor of becoming a profit-seeking business. There were mass sackings. In the exchange's day of the long knives, at a hastily convened press conference on Monday 2nd November 1998, LIFFE announced some 600 employees from over 1000 would be made redundant, in addition to an earlier freezing in new staff recruitment.

When the first sackings took place, one bewildered former manager a few hours after being axed stated, "I thought I was okay but then I got called in on the third wave." In management terms, it all sounded akin to the trench-emptying tactics of British generals at the Battle of the Somme. Not for nothing was the new LIFFE CEO, Hugh Freedburg, described by one unnamed former colleague at Hill Samuel as "the man who put the slash into 'slash and burn.'" Throughout LIFFE's revolution, Freedburg's ruthlessness would be tinged with humanity and dignity when it came to the careers of his staff. However, with 98% of the LIFFE membership voting for electronic trading in an Extraordinary General Meeting (EGM) on May 12th 1998, the new Executive Chairman, Brian Williamson, had received the mandate he required to make sweeping changes at the very heart of the derivatives business. Open outcry may have survived every other innovation in history but time had finally caught up with it.

The Capital Market Revolution had claimed its highest profile victims to date. However, more significantly, this was much more than a "little local difficulty" for the leading UK derivatives market. LIFFE had been besieged by a foreign player in the first such direct competition in exchange history. The German DTB (later EUREX) would emerge as a significant world power within months, after barely a decade in existence. In the US, many players wrote the LIFFE collapse off as something which could never happen in the US, as open outcry was entrenched in the financial marketplace. Of course, they were proven absolutely correct, at least until 2002 when finally the Capital Market Revolution began to catch up with the American exchanges, and the intermediaries began entering their own revolutionary "reign of terror."

Notes

1. The FOA is the UK Futures and Options Association. The FIA is the Futures Industry Association of the USA. The FOA has a broad-church approach, encompassing both exchange traded and OTC derivative markets while the FIA is a more narrowly focused Washington lobbying organization for futures brokers alone. The fact that there is also a

major organization ISDA (International Swaps and Derivatives Association) entirely separate for OTC may lead readers to wonder just how such fragmentation of organizations benefits the industry.

2. "Front running" refers to counterparties entering orders ahead of large client trades, perhaps the ultimate sin a broker can commit.

3. "Pre-arranging" trades before they reach an exchange mechanism is an equally heinous crime in trading.

4. Rich Jaycobs has subsequently made some major ripples as a capital market revolutionary of note through founding OnExchange.

Chapter 1
Post-Feudal Markets
Changing the Food Chain Forever

For future historians, the salient fact of twentieth-century finance will be the sharp erosion of banker power – that is, the dwindling role of the financial intermediary. Bankers are glorified go-betweens, conduits for capital flows. During the twentieth century, they have progressively yielded power to providers of capital (both retail and institutional investors), on the one hand, and consumers of capital (notably large multinational corporations on the other, and in the process the banker's intermediary role in the financial equation has declined. A horrid term is sometimes employed to describe this phenomenon – disintermediation – …

Ron Chernow, *The Death of the Banker*

If the only danger posed to exchanges was that their historic open outcry dealing mechanisms were being superseded by computers, then many exchange personnel would sleep easier at night. Rather, there is a dreaded "D" word which has kept every senior exchange official awake at night at some point during the past few years. Those who deny it are either lying or so severely out of touch as to be prime unemployment fodder within the near future. The word in question is "disintermediation."

"Disintermediation" – the process of removing middle men from transactions.

Disintermediation threatens the firmament of every single existing marketplace. Not to mention all the other middlemen (in each and every walk of commercial life). Disintermediation is no respecter of ages, or history, or values. It is simply a bald economic fact of life. If an exchange or a broker, or any other type of intermediary cannot justify their process in adding value to a transaction, then their place in the food chain will be eliminated. In other words:

"No one person or party's place in the trading chain is now assured."

The size of any broker, counterparty or exchange before they are struck by the revolutionary fervor is irrelevant. Indeed the larger the organization and the more power it has traditionally wielded in recent times, the swifter and more dramatic will be its downfall. Until now, financial markets were effectively feudal entities. Huge power could be wielded by cabals in clubs called exchanges, frequently to the detriment of the world at large. Now, those interest groups are finding themselves being opened to genuine competition in a digital world for platform dominance. This is what I have dubbed "the post-feudal marketplace." True, financial markets will never be a genuine democracy (ironically the exchanges with the strongest individually democratic traditions are in fact by far the most reactionary), but they need to operate in a fashion where there is no discrimination against any counterparty – subject of course, to credit.

Throughout the 1980s and 1990s, volumes were soaring and there seemed to be few, if any problems with open outcry. On the surface, this was irrefutably correct. However, increasing overheads coupled to a squeeze by institutions on brokerage levels, has led to open outcry essentially shooting itself in the foot. (Indeed, it was a mixture of the cost accountants' ongoing desire to squeeze brokerage rates and the crowd of pit traders largely pricing themselves out of the market which initially undermined open outcry in Europe, rather than any particularly stunning technological innovations.) Now, only a few years later, with the power of electronic trading growing in tandem (if not ahead of Moores' law),[1] the gap between electronic and open outcry trading has narrowed significantly. Very simply, digital dealing is inexorably cheaper, faster and simpler than open outcry.

However, with open outcry apparently so successful following record global volumes in 2001, the CBOT has remained somewhat fixated with what looks suspiciously like a lose-lose situation for the senior management, apart from their stake in OneChicago, a new electronic exchange, to trade the nascent single stock futures products. If they embrace new technology and go screen trading then the floor membership will be in uproar. If CBOT fail to take account of "the post-feudal marketplace," then the fateful "D word" could quite easily see the CBOT wiped out within a handful of years.

Until the DTB/EUREX took the dominant position in volume in German Bund contracts, one law had remained faithful in derivatives markets. The exchange which got volume into a market first, won the day. It was true when the Americans launched their treasury bond and Eurodollar contracts at the CBOT and CME respectively. It was true when LIFFE launched a host of European contracts based around Italian bonds and German interest rates. The Barcelona-based MEFF (electronic) exchange had a stranglehold on Spanish government bonds which LIFFE could barely dent when it experimented with its own Bonos futures.

Then the Frankfurt-based exchange, with an immense array of incentives and enticements, not to mention a hefty marketing budget, and most significantly European deregulation permitting free distribution of screens, finally wrested control of the German Bund business away from LIFFE after almost a decade of trying. Later in this section, I will discuss how the state of play now is heading towards the most blatant turf battle with competing liquidity pools in exchange history. In every market from stocks and bonds through the panoply of derivatives, predators such as Deutsche Börse and EUREX are seeking to take business from established franchises throughout the world.

In post-feudal markets (PFM), all exchanges are now in a position to compete with each other. More significantly, the cost of entering the exchange provision market has now become a great deal cheaper. At the time of writing, the only thing halting a global free-for-all in financial markets is the regulation of financial markets. Equally, however, it is the very regulation of financial markets which is ultimately driving many facets of the disintermediation process in the first place.

New market solutions

The status quo won't do.

John Damgard, President FIA

John Damgard is absolutely right. The status quo won't do. Ironically, his own narrow interest lobbying group, the FIA (representing US futures and options brokers on exchanges) will have to reshape its ideas if it too is to prosper in the age of PFM. All exchanges must adapt if they are to have a hope of survival. However, with the increasing ubiquity of the internet all aspects of financial markets, and with it the way many areas of broader business operate, are threatened by the Capital Market Revolution. From the humblest retail stock-market punter through to vast interbank dealing operations, the future is radically different. The ongoing development of digital markets is a dynamic environment showing every sign of accelerating as new media trading opportunities explode.

Exchanges: the below-stairs classes

There is nothing more difficult to take in hand, more perilous to conduct, or more uncertain in its success than to take the lead in the introduction of a new order of things.

Niccolo Machiavelli

Exchanges are simply the most hyped, most publicized, most revered, failures in the lengthy history of financial markets throughout the world. Even those traditional titans of capitalism, the London and New York Stock Exchanges are in fact relatively minor ventures in the global nexus of commodities, money and markets. While CNBC and CNN may flock to Wall Street to be seen "right where the market is happening" the reality is that precious little business actually ever makes it to be transacted on the floor of any of the multitude of commodity, equity and financial exchanges the world over.

The powerhouses of global capitalism are all hidden behind closed doors, away from the public gaze in the tinted glass towers which house the world's largest dealing organizations. Opacity, privacy and bilateral dealing are the key facets to this marketplace. Everything is transacted in an arena euphemistically referred to as "upstairs" (i.e. above the level of the traditional exchange floors). Welcome to the over-the-counter (or OTC) market. For the average investor, OTC conjures up boiler-room stock deals in obscure (and usually dodgy) mining stocks listed on far removed, shady bourses. In fact, the OTC marketplace proper is a wonderful vista on just about every facet of life. Whatever you wish to deal in, there is a thriving OTC business trading that market. Access, however, is generally restricted only to institutions and preferably only those who boast a credit rating in the upper echelons.

True, the New York Stock Exchange may transact an average of 43 billion dollars of business per day (or 10.5 trillion for the year). This may sound staggering especially when one bears in mind that the total value of the NYSE's stocks at the end of Q2 2002 was some 11.3 trillion. However, compare this with the derivative marketplace and suddenly one sees a very different picture. Outstanding exchange traded derivatives alone (i.e. open positions being held by traders) were worth some 23.5 trillion dollars by the end of December 2001, according to the central banker's central bank, the Bank for International Settlements (BIS). That figure is only slightly lower than the total of $26.8 trillion in value of all equities listed in the world at the end of Q1 2002. However, the OTC market dwarfs the business of exchanges by a significant factor. The notional value of OTC settlements outstanding at the end of 2001 was some 111.1 trillion dollars. According to International Financial Services London, in derivatives markets alone, "worldwide the OTC derivatives market in 2001 was about five times the size of the exchanges measured by notional amounts outstanding." Even when you factor in the stock exchange volumes, the OTC market is still dominant. True, the increases in the OTC markets have been growing slower than the exchanges in recent years but the fact remains that for all the publicity given to exchanges as the titans of the capital markets, they are in fact very much the poor relations.[2]

To put the strength of OTC markets compared to exchanges into perspective, imagine your familial dinner table and consider that the

Leading stock market capitalizations, March 31st 2002 – market capitalization (trillions)

Domestic listed companies (excluding closed-end funds – official FIBV figures) all exchanges:	**$26.8**
of which:	
NYSE	**$11.3**
NASDAQ	**$2.6**
Tokyo	**$2.2**
London	**$2.1**
Germany	**$1.1**
(from http://www.nyse.com)	
Notional total outstanding for derivatives exchanges: (December 31st 2001)	**$23.5**
Notional outstanding OTC business:	**$111.1**

entire room equates to the power of the OTC marketplace. The space below the table is pretty close to the power of the exchanges.

The story so far

A system used by all financial companies could essentially become an exchange.

Michael Bloomberg on his eponymous system's potential

For all their smooth PR and massive sense of self-worth – often located behind conspicuous classical colonnades – exchanges are essentially feudal institutions. They have a long and interesting history dating back to when classical columns were in their first flush as an architectural fashion. Since exchanges were first set up they have been seen as everything from dens of iniquity to essential pillars of a civilized society. Once clubs run for members with little regard for the outside world, exchanges have suddenly found themselves undergoing industrial, technological and service orientation revolutions all in one go.

Exchanges remain little more than a playing field for capitalism and their leveling for all market practitioners is still a process which is being hotly debated in many areas. But the fact remains that despite a renewed swaggering confidence or even arrogance among many leading exchange officials, the exchange model needs to keep adapting for several years yet if it is really to achieve an acceptable level of operational transparency and profitability to keep its new shareholding owners happy. In this respect, I apply a very simple definition of an exchange – an organized, independently managed market where all players are permitted access to transactions without prejudice for any particular player. While this definition may be short, it largely covers all major issues, although the complexities of equal access to all, and trading without prejudice, can be discussed almost *ad infinitum* when we seek precise definitive answers. For instance, the process of block trading (large parcels of activity being traded only between large institutions and not as such shown to the "whole" market before transaction) may in itself appear anathema to my definition, yet as we will come to see, exchanges must embrace such activity if they are truly to dominate capitalist activity. On the other hand, providing too many incentives for market makers may ultimately be detrimental to the smooth functioning of a market, essential as liquidity is.

At present, the system of being forced to deal with a specialist or resident market maker, rather than directly from customer to customer, is a costly process for investors which brings no net gain to the investor but enriches monopolistic holders of such positions. Similarly, independence of management, while reflecting the opinions of a certain cabal or interest group, is reasonably common in all walks of life. Therefore, the old-fashioned mutualized "clubs" may have been conservative and operating in the interests of a significant group, but they were not closed to the entire world *per se*. On the other hand, the original Enron Online platform which basically operated a single market maker system becoming the counterparty to every trade, is not a true exchange, although such platforms have made a significant impact on the process of the

Capital Market Revolution and not simply on account of Enron's intriguing concept of profit "sharing."

Nevertheless, the fact remains that overall exchanges exist in a very curious vacuum. They have fundamentally failed to stop the freewheeling capitalist institutions innovating their own products in OTC markets while at the same time no "legacy" exchange (i.e. those pre-dating the beginnings of the Capital Market Revolution in 1997) has yet managed to make a really significant impact upon the public psyche by becoming a popular champion of investors' interests. True, ongoing attempts to reform capital requirements for banks are intended to try to flush out much OTC business and (risk) transfer it to the exchanges (where clearing houses help reduce systemic and other risks). Meanwhile, when it comes to gaining mass popular acclaim, investors tend to have always proven cyclically fickle. NASDAQ in America and the German "small cap" *Neuer Markt* were adored by crowds of emotional investors as they boomed in the late 1990s but they subsequently fell from grace somewhat dramatically. However, to date nobody has found that common ground where an exchange is viewed as anything other than an object of relatively intimidating activity in the public psyche.

As will be seen throughout this book, the markets which win the latter battle, for the hearts and minds of the retail investor as well as the institutional business, have the power to create a whole new era of exchange domination which may encompass the entire world. In the food world, the commoditized producers of choice such as KFC and McDonald's dominate. For coffee, Starbucks has become a global synonym. When it comes to exchanges, there is no singular exchange which captures the hearts and minds – let alone portfolios! – of the vast bulk of global investors.

Barbarians at the modems

Every strategic inflection point is characterized by a "10X" change. There's wind, and then there is a typhoon, there are waves and then there's a tsunami.

Andrew Grove, CEO, Intel

Having experienced a sudden, sharp shock treatment at the dawn of the internet age, the terrifying issue is that many intermediaries now believe they are immune to further after effects. Whether they are exhibiting a sense of denial about their impending fate or merely that their swaggering arrogance has returned to blind them to the inevitable is not clear nor is it terribly important. The simple fact remains that markets are only now emerging unblinking to see the first dawns for them of a post-feudal marketplace. America is, in the medium term at least, at the greatest danger from exchange competition. The overlapping and competing structure of regulation makes exchange trading potentially uncompetitive, regardless of the potential ramifications of transaction taxes.

The worrying thing about the above quotation is that so far as the brokers and exchanges ought to be concerned, we've so far reached only the high winds, maybe the early gale stage. The typhoon is some way down the tracks yet. Every day they dither, decision-averse entities such as exchanges will face yet more painful radical transition if they are not to find themselves being blown away by their competitors.

A gentlemen's war?

If I determine the enemy's disposition of forces while I have no perceptible form, I can concentrate my forces while the enemy is fragmented. The pinnacle of military deployment approaches the formless: If it is formless, then even the deepest spy cannot discern it nor the wise make plans against it.

Sun Tzu, *The Art of War*

Exchanges, for all their bluster, mostly harbor employees who are deeply concerned by direct competition. The simple fact of the matter is that ultimately investors, professional and retail, do not want to waste time having to shuffle across a horde of different platforms in order to achieve their desired portfolio aims. A handful of serious markets in every asset class will be reality by 2005. Indeed, a handful of major platforms worldwide across all asset classes will be reality by 2010 at the latest. The New York Stock Exchange must turn predator or become prey, whether to aggressive local opposition such as NASDAQ or overseas exchanges such as Deutsche Börse who may seek to replicate the opportunistic merger of Daimler and Chrysler in the auto industry.[3]

A century ago, the game in the US was rationalizing the local stock markets across the country which rapidly fell into key liquidity pools near the west coast and Eastern seaboard respectively. The internet has already rendered dealing distance largely meaningless. In a global marketplace, counterparties can now deal from anywhere to anywhere else. The internet allows total flexibility with an essentially infinite choice of routes for the trades themselves. While transactions may now have the luxury of infinite possibility, the reality for intermediaries is that the increasing rationalization of the exchange landscape will ultimately result in much more direct turf war, making meaningful cross-border exchange competition a reality for the first time in history. The increasing drive to see companies as cross-border investment classes in many regions (particularly North America and even further south, as well as throughout Europe and Asia), can only further drive the exchanges to greater competition.

Of course, the increasing inclination towards promiscuity among investors seriously affects every exchange. Even the prospect of increased promiscuity ought to be sufficient to keep most exchange personnel awake at nights worried about their career prospects. But somebody from outside the key players' cabal may yet manage to springboard to prominence. Equally, there ought to be a clear understanding that in what is increasingly a mix of econo-diplomatic posturing and direct competition, the exchanges with the deepest pockets have an advantage but may yet be outflanked by the most nimble.

If the exchange competition landscape must be likened to war then it is more likely to equate to the ongoing jungle warfare associated with taking small Pacific islands of tactical significance than with some form of massive all-out attack on blue riband targets. These takeovers will likely be consensual and require significant local diplomacy before government/national approval is forthcoming.

The ECN sideshow

Never interrupt your enemy when he is making a mistake.

Napoleon Bonaparte

An aspect of the Capital Market Revolution barely noted so far to date is one which has garnered many of the headlines. Electronic Communications Networks had been around for some years, led by Reuters' Instinet offshoot. The ECN is an intriguing animal in the financial markets. Essentially, it attempts to match trades on its computerized network and then sends the trade back through the clearing facilities of an existing exchange. A great many folk have found in ECNs proof that the exchanges will themselves collapse at the altar of these specialized matching engines. In reality, the truth could not be any further removed. For one thing, ECNs are not a solution to the problem but rather a symptom of the problem itself. ECNs grew up because stock exchanges became arrogant and aloof at their prospects for opening up to outside competition. The inherent monopolistic situation of specialists at the New York Stock Exchange for instance meant that all order flow essentially became "clipped" before its execution. In Europe, the successful stock exchanges have increasingly realized that only by allowing all orders equal access to the central order book will that market be seen to truly represent price discovery. Having a middleman who must process all orders with the possibility for himself to profit, is an anachronism. Specialists, and indeed ECNs are doomed – albeit for very different reasons.

The specialist needs to adjust to become a tick on the back of the rhinoceros who can exploit order imbalance rather than continue to be somebody who has a privileged position to profit by being the central conduit for every trade. Routing orders to a single person, or cabal of privileged market makers benefits nobody apart from the restrictive cartel making the market. Market makers are required in all markets but they must not have the sole right of choosing the bid or offer – this ought to be open to any order, large or small, wherever it emanates from. Likewise, the ECN business will soon enough be swept away when one of several factors starts to emerge. The ECN versus exchange issue has been a remarkably emotive one and the activities of exchanges such as Euronext, seeking to keep ECNs effectively illegal by forcing local order flow to go to its national bourse, constitute an understandable piece of protectionism but this merely propagates the concept that exchanges are arrogantly unwilling to give the customer the best deal.[4]

True, there is a rather seductive argument that all order flow ought to go to one place. Exchanges use this to try to prevent "internalization" within investment banks *et al.* – yet ironically, the real agenda is that exchanges must realize that investment banks may yet prove to be better operators of exchanges than exchanges have themselves. Nevertheless, totalitarian edicts dictating where that order flow ought to go almost invariably lead to arrogant monopolies. On the other hand, customers have a right to know where their order has actually been transacted, and in that respect some brokers' usage of ECNs has been a matter for concern, as customers may not have been gaining best execution (i.e. the best possible price for their transaction). Best execution is a process which has become somewhat secondary for many brokers to practices such as payment for order flow. The fact remains that many traders may be suffering poorer execution than they might receive on an exchange by using an ECN.

Then again, many traders are obliged to use an exchange which may not provide them with as good an order execution as alternative markets. However, really the key issue for ECNs – and the reason they will ultimately fail as an independent genre – is that they are neither one thing nor the other. ECNs are a carbuncle on the side of an existing marketplace. The ECNs who survive will all have managed to morph themselves into proper exchanges (such as Archipelago and their deal with the Pacific Coast Stock Exchange), providing a complete range of trading and transactional services rather than merely being a purveyor of narrowly focused matching services. Ironically, therefore, ECNs are merely a sideshow to the existing exchanges – until they become exchanges themselves. However, when new former ECN star performers do arrive center stage, the end results will be utterly stupefying. This is the prospect which truly ought to terrify legacy marketplaces but in most cases they largely continue to ignore the threat.

Enron and the Capital Market Revolution

Our business is not a black box. It's very simple to model. People who raise questions are people who have not gone through it in detail. We have explicit answers, but people want to throw rocks at us.

Jeff Skilling, then Enron CEO, February 2001

Why were so many people willing to believe in something that so few actually understood?

Bethany McClean, *Fortune* magazine

No book on contemporary markets would be complete without reference to the scintillating story of Enron's rise to prominence and descent to the depths in a fashion which almost challenges Icarus' attack on the laws of gravity. Ironically, in a tome which extols the merits of brand for the left-field player, perhaps the most significant achievement of Enron was to create a brand which rapidly built itself into being seen as a powerhouse of digital capitalism.

In relation to the Capital Market Revolution, there are a number of key points worth noting. The first is that transparent, genuinely deregulated energy markets (California sowed at least some seeds of its own problems by restricting generation plant production, etc.) remain the best solution for all energy users – although regulation needs to be more capable of understanding what happens and to be able to act when markets are being manipulated.

Secondly, Enron itself single-handedly helped discredit a deeply flawed electronic marketplace which grew in popularity during the dotcom bubble. Enron's markets were seen as exchanges, but in reality were a single market maker entity operating as a monopolist with clients. The lack of competitive market making means that the central counterparty is always the operating company (in this case Enron) and without a clearing house, the risk of default by the centerpiece of the marketplace (again Enron) can lead to extreme problems. In the case of those associated with Enron's marketplaces, the consequences have been deadly for some freight companies who had hedged freight with Enron as well as hedging their energy in the same way. I can honestly admit I didn't see the Enron situation as being a bubble which would burst, but I did warn counterparties to Enron deals that despite the hype, dealing with Enron left them with a significant counterparty risk that they would have diminished vastly by dealing on a regulated exchange or at least through a proper clearing house. Similarly, the issue of dealing with a single market maker (I call it a "monomarket") significantly reduces price competition for the best price of execution which may be detrimental to the client in a fashion which ought to be substantially improved in markets where access is open to many folk (I call them "polyglot markets" and they basically are the existing exchanges). OTC dealing is truly for consenting adults with significant resources only and those who fear the various counterparty risks are wise in sticking to exchanges.

Enron tried to be a commodities broker and market maker to the world, open 24 hours a day with just a BBB rating, unlike banks which have a much stronger balance sheet and the market fell for it.

Chuck Watson, former CEO Dynegy

Finally, Enron leaves us with the Andersen accounting fiasco and the issue that is in many ways the ultimate accounting oxymoron. Derivatives are also known as "off-balance sheet" thanks to their core nature. However, in a world where investors, analysts, clients and counterparties are seeking more transparency into a company's wellbeing, there truly needs to be a means of making off-balance sheet transactions somewhat more capable of being recorded on the balance sheet. An oxymoron indeed, but a somewhat compelling concept.

Know your customer, know your competitor

Glory is fleeting, but obscurity is forever.

Napoleon Bonaparte

The big problem for exchanges of all types is that they simply aren't much loved by their end users. In fact, many are viewed with some distaste by a significant proportion of their clients. Customer loyalty remains lax – at best – and indeed very few exchanges even in recent times have truly worked diligently at trying to provide customer-oriented businesses. Comparing the ability of exchanges to know, understand and even communicate with their customers compares dreadfully poorly when one looks at genuine mass-market customer champions such as US retailer Wal-Mart. The basic mentality is poles apart. And it is Wal-Mart who will continue to prosper. One of the core difficulties for exchanges nowadays is that the barriers to entry have tumbled and, regulation permitting, setting up an exchange can nowadays be a very, very rapid process indeed. So, to compound their "customer-unfriendly" mindset, many exchanges have spent a great deal of time and effort in recent years savagely cutting their own internal costs, with a net result that they're increasingly unaware of what is happening in the world beyond their executive office floors. True, the heavy overstaffing needed to be addressed (in many cases it still does) but the difficulty was that balance sheets rarely account favorably for market intelligence.

Markets have been almost perpetually agitated these past few years about what their direct competition would do. The biggest flaw in this thinking is the closed marketplace delusion. In other words, only the existing exchange players will ever compete in this space. Unfortunately for legacy players, as they continue to contemplate each other, the real threat is already sneaking up and may already be passing them. Alas, the real threat is therefore already able to sneak almost invisibly under the either closed down or wrongly aligned radar of the world's existing exchanges. The implicit threat is that left field exchanges – new players entirely, perhaps even from beyond the existing financial world – are entering the markets and may yet do a better job than the legacy intermediaries.

The left field challenge

When presented with this conclusion, exchange managements seem to have been either terrified, stupefied or in outright denial of the realities of the digital world. Their nitpicking responses to the concept of left field competition only reinforces my belief of just how likely it is that ultimately the world's biggest exchange platforms will find themselves in a head-to-head fight with at least one truly customer-oriented marketplace. After all, when it comes to the battle of the brands, who would the public feel most comfortable dealing with?

- the relatively aloof Georgian colonnades of a stock market that has invariably been fairly lukewarm towards their participation, if not downright contemptuous of it
- or the likes of Amazon, a customer-friendly and broadly trusted brand?

Indeed, eBay is already seen as the people's champion of auctioneering having neatly divided the old oligopoly of stuffy old-fashioned auction houses. Why can't it do the same thing again to the capital market business?

The answer is that there is no reason at all. It reminds me of a wonderful anecdote concerning the CIO of the Australian Stock Exchange in the 1990s when the ASX first built a website. The meeting between the dotcom casual-clad Egyptologist turned web developer and the classically tailored blue-suited CIO was as ever a clash of wills between not merely generations but arguably centuries of ingrained stock market self-belief. When faced with a suggested design which involved demonstrating the power and standing of the stock exchange and naturally that (seen from the stock exchange's standpoint) heroic capitalist figure of Olympian proportions, the stockbroker, the web developer tartly responded: "Do you think we could get rid of the blue suits and the stone columns? You are frightening the hell out of the new investor."

Of course, there are those who are swift to point out that the likes of eBay, or Wal-Mart or an existing financial brand which seeks to create an exchange probably doesn't have the technology to create that market. True, but then again most exchanges already buy from third-party vendors so what is so different here? Likewise, I have heard a most fallacious argument that there is only a finite pool of folk capable of operating a legitimate exchange. This is the equivalent linear thinking which famously led Daimler Benz in the early years of the twentieth century to predict a cap on the global automobile market barely into five figures because this was how many carriage drivers would realistically have the skills to be transformed into chauffeurs.

The day a consumer-oriented corporate like Amazon, eBay, easyJet, Wal-Mart or Virgin adds its brand to an exchange established for it by outside consultants and a core team of industry insiders, is the day when even the strongest tranquilizers will fail to prevent sleeplessness for the Chairmen of the world's legacy exchanges. Exchanges spend too much time fretting about what their existing competition is up to without giving much thought to where new competition could emerge that poses an even greater threat to their franchise.

But then it can't happen here ...

The legacy exchanges are quick to suggest that a new brand entering the financial markets and establishing a completely new venture in an existing space is simply impossible. This argument would have greater weight if it remotely reflected what has been happening in the world of late. Jeff Sprecher's brainchild, The Intercontinental Exchange sprang from humble start-up to predator eating the opposition alive within a matter of months. Before it took over Europe's leading energy marketplace, the London International Petroleum Exchange, it had been rebuffed by the New York Mercantile Exchange, NYMEX, when ICE sought an alliance. In the wake of 09/11, NYMEX was reported to be seeking an alliance with ICE.

In the equity options field, the New York based International Securities Exchange was created as a direct electronic competitor to the existing oligopoly of floor-traded options markets in Chicago, New York, Philadelphia and San Francisco. ISE, the new entry stock options marketplace based in New York, was also in the vanguard of American exchange demutualization in early 2002. The bravery of taking on the establishment demonstrated by founders such as David Krell, looked increasingly justified as the scalable cost benefits of the electronic ISE started to really kick into their balance sheet, while the opposition largely agonized about walking the diplomatic tightrope with members over maintaining their floors. Meanwhile, ISE's volumes kept racing ever higher at the expense of their legacy exchange competition.

Microexchanges – the miniature marvel of microcommerce

When there may be no more than 500 real players in a world market, then you have to aim your product at a community, not at the World.

Colin Howard, Chairman, COMDAQ

While the world of B2B (see Chapter 3) was being much hyped and its short-lived titans enjoyed fleeting multi-billion dollar stock valuations, the real revolution in commerce was occurring in many of the most opaque and relatively smaller commodity markets on Earth. Indeed, the prospects for the very, very small centralized marketplace – which I have christened microexchanges – are some of the most exciting around. Market fragmentation assures us of more rather than fewer exchanges in the next few years, even if the largest securities markets set about rationalizing themselves on a grand scale.

Cost is perhaps one of the bigger driving forces in the creation of microexchanges. In the days before deregulation, government-appointed boards commonly managed many commodity markets – they still do in many parts. Yet the merits of exchanges are considerable. In South Africa, the now defunct government Maize Board had a frictional cost of up to 150 Rand for every ton of maize it handled as the central counterparty to that market. The SAFEX agricultural derivatives market has reduced that frictional cost to ten cents (i.e. 0.1 Rand). How much is a Rand worth? Who cares, it's the percentage reduction that truly counts. However, anybody retaining a degree of skepticism about the merits of deregulation ought to consider tattooing that last statistic to their forehead.

Of course, the market in South African maize may not remotely appear on the radar screens to be plausibly profitable for many of the existing leviathans and legacy exchanges. That's where specialist microexchange providers enter the fray to create truly tiny marketplaces. Leading the pack is COMDAQ, a London and Rotterdam based company whose technology is developed in India. COMDAQ has markets in many different raw commodities and manages with a handful of staff in each market. One intriguing issue with COMDAQ is that "These are markets that often look at technology with suspicion," according to Development Director Clive Furness. Therefore, the COMDAQ structure even allows for what they refer to as "broker assisted markets" where there is some degree of intermediating brokerage provided on behalf of the central exchange to advance deals towards completion. Given that COMDAQ traded about $1 billion worth of commodity products in 2001, the model seems to be working.

Chairman Colin Howard is more forthright in his view of revolutionizing some traditionally highly opaque marketplaces:

> The "expert", who an employer dare not challenge and cannot audit, will inevitably be called to account as compliance receives more manageable information. Gone will be the days of sharing fat margins at the expense of producer, company and customer alike.

COMDAQ is not in the business of multiple transactions per second like Rolls-Royce execution systems such as LIFFE Connect. Rather, it often entails a significant quantity of flexible user inputs allowing buyers and sellers to negotiate online. There is however, one vital issue, according to Howard:

> The critical component is the electronic capture of a party to counterparty contract, in a form that exactly records the transaction. This requires detailed and specifically targeted input, not a global ERP approach.

In the future, microexchanges may well rationalize into larger entities but in the interim, the prospects for tiny markets with perhaps six or fewer staff operating a local, national, regional or even global market niche are truly enormous. Many markets won't be the usual freewheeling open trading systems as equity and futures traders have become used to but rather will often be more simple auction platforms operating regular sales, maybe daily, weekly or monthly, as opposed to continuous daily trading sessions. Potential markets range from those markets still regulated by governments through to specialist commodities and other markets which may be multibillion dollar markets world wide but simply do not reach the radar of the relative leviathans, the legacy exchanges.

New markets, new capital

Victory or Death.

Rudolf Ferscha, CEO, EUREX, at Burgenstock Meeting 2002

One key Luddite argument is that the revolution is simply doomed to fail on account of a lack of liquidity. Throughout history, the core ease of dealing in substantial size, i.e. the "liquidity" of financial markets, has been largely provided by varying forms of independent capital. On the New York Stock Exchange, specialists (i.e. market makers "specializing" in particular stocks) were traditionally family-run businesses, although many equity markets have increasingly benefited from corporate capital providing liquidity in more recent years as the equity bull market developed. On the derivatives markets throughout the world, the markets are reliant on the independent "local" traders to provide liquidity to facilitate smooth transactions between large institutions. But the business, as floor locals have been used to transacting it, is doomed and however inevitable this is, there continue to be Luddites out there who will try everything they can to turn back the tide and, in their view, preserve their livelihoods. This attitude is both irresponsible and ironic.

Nevertheless, that won't stop those who see a very handy livelihood being threatened behaving like the Luddites of the early nineteenth century who sought to destroy the looms and the factories that they felt threatened their livelihood. Ironically, it was the Industrial Revolution which propelled the earnings of the average worker to highs previously undreamed of during the previous centuries. Likewise, as the revolution takes hold, the opportunities for capital, and especially independent capital, are greater than they have ever been in history. Ironically, part of this is fuelled by the increasing nervousness of stock market investors at the difficulty of predicting earnings of proprietary trading investment banks, leading them to cut back on their market-making functions. The space remains enormous for the right kind of capital. Naturally, it will not be the same job as the floor traders' but then again it has more upside than any pit trader could ever imagine.

Very simply, there is a massive new realm of opportunity for independent capital within the post-feudal marketplace. Already there are new legions of capitalists seeking to exploit these opportunities.

Survival of the fittest

I can't understand why people are frightened by new ideas. I'm frightened of old ones.

John Cage

While many traders have already adapted to the wonders of electronic trading, there are those who don't want the relatively solitary trading experience. Having enjoyed the camaraderie of the floor, they are seeking out opportunities to trade in some form of dealing community. In response to this demand, there are increasing numbers of dealing rooms where freelance traders can rent a desk space. Such "trading arcades" have existed in one format or another for a century. Wall Street histories of the roaring twenties positively bulge with anecdotes of men watching the ticker tape pass on price information.

In the 21st century, the "trading arcade," like its amusement arcade cousin, is a much more high-tech version of the original idea. Rather than having to write down orders and hand them across a counter to a broker for execution, the traders are given direct access to the market through interactive terminals which stop dealers overstepping agreed trading limits and prevent them trading if their cash reserves are too low. Despite the ongoing talk of locals being increasingly unwilling to adapt to electronic trading methods – new dealing positions at trading arcades even within the confines of exchanges themselves, such as the Chicago Board of Trade's historic art deco building, rent out within days (even in the wake of the supposed "death" of the day trader following the dotcom bust). At the CBOT building in West Jackson Boulevard, even the lure of a trading floor only yards away, is insufficient to dissuade the new breed of independent traders that they are better off learning how to exploit screen dealing systems.

The old-style local trader worked on a floor and traded a lot of contracts for a small turn in every trade, often just one tick.[5] The locals were favored in the floor-dealing environment as they could buy and sell without there being a priority on when an order entered a pit. In other words, if the market was 25 bid and 26 offered, the locals, sensing a "paper" (i.e. client/end user) buyer, could quickly jump in and "lift the offer" to get in ahead of the end users. With electronic trading, the methodology of "first in first out" can be employed with ease thanks to the in-built computer technology. This can be both good and bad. In many open outcry markets, the concept of proportional allocations meant that clients often got parts of their orders filled even if they had only recently joined the bid or the offer. Equally, with the new "FIFO" agenda, much of the advantage previously accorded to locals is eliminated. Their old style of "jobbing" is effectively stunted, if not eliminated entirely.

For those locals who are skilled only in the art of jobbing (buying and selling frequently for a very small "turn"), then oblivion looms in the post-feudal marketplace. Locals must be able to survive in whatever market environments they can find. The new reality of post-feudal markets may frighten many with its social-Darwinist overtones. However, at no previous time in history has Napoleon's concept of "la carriere ouverte aux talents" been a more realistic proposition.

Meanwhile, spare a thought for the trader who has long known his levels of trading for the day and often found himself squeezed out in the crush of the pit. Nowadays, he can enter his orders before an electronic market opens and when the market reaches his prices, the FIFO (first in, first out) algorithm automatically gives him time/price priority of execution. End result? A great many folk once viewed as journeymen locals with some strange ideas have found themselves transformed into vastly more profitable traders, thanks to the democratization of digital trading.

The new "faceless" environment

Customers are losing their old-fashioned loyalty to the exchange and are looking more and more at the bottom line. They don't care where they execute deals, as long as it is quick and easy.

Brian Kaye, Managing Director, Fimat (brokerage arm of Société Générale)

Screen-traded markets can do many things very well. However, the screen revolution – while providing cost advantages – does remove the important element of face-to-face "bravado" which helped to make floor trading so efficient. Online markets run the risk of becoming a pale facsimile of their previous floor traded incarnations. During the late 1980s and early 1990s, the sudden disappearance of firm quotations at the first sign of volatility on the Italian screen-traded MIF, was the very reason why the pit-traded LIFFE BTP future held a sizeable advantage over its Milanese screen-based rival throughout the volatile period from the late 1980s on.

So, while screen trading may today be dramatically in the ascendant as of now, many markets will have to pay a great deal more attention to just how successful their exchanges are in actually facilitating the trading process. Cheaper and more certain technology doesn't necessarily mean better. And given that the major screen-based systems have not been proven "under fire," i.e., in a serious outbreak of volatility, pit traders may yet demonstrate a second wind in the event of a crisis – such as the ERM débâcle of 1992 or the Stock Market crash of 1987. True, there have been no massive crashes like 1987 in recent years but given that daily volatility and market ranges are significantly greater than they were even a decade ago, it seems fair to presume that really the arguments in favor of open outcry are becoming less relevant by the day. The shocks of LTCM, Enron and WorldCom *et al.* during 2001–2002 have been smoothly dealt with by electronic markets. There is simply no reason to believe that while electronic market technology may not be 100% reliable, it is certainly strong enough to cope with major shocks to the system.

Equally, the mutterings amongst some market practitioners of late that they have finally routed their local traders, are so asinine as to be dangerous. Exchanges need liquidity and it will be the new breed of independent traders who will facilitate trading, be it individuals in tax havens such as the Caribbean or Monaco, or from large dealing rooms within financial centers, or on the cusp of large conurbations. New technology can be utilized by "old" locals – provided they are willing to adapt. Moreover, in the post-feudal marketplace, the screen-based locals can now pay more attention to trading markets traditionally beyond the horizons of their pits, across other futures exchanges, in equity markets and beyond. Locals need exchanges and exchanges need locals. The sooner both parties recognize the merits of change and the ongoing requirement for each party to be involved in the trading process, the sooner the world will be a happier, more liquid place for traders of all shapes and sizes! For locals, it won't be the same as the golden era of open outcry but nevertheless it will be a place of great opportunity for the correctly oriented trader.

Who is your customer anyway?

Opportunities multiply as they are seized.

Sun Tzu

One issue that has become clear to all keen observers of markets is that in many ways, exchanges were blindsided to just who their clients were in the first place. End users needed brokers and only brokers knew who they were. Exchanges often deluded themselves by thinking that knowing the exchanges well meant they knew the clients too. The reality in an era where the margins for both traders and exchanges are under fire, is that exchanges have sought to leverage their information margin while some exchanges have set up their own marketing teams to seek out the end users and build the knowledge base they didn't need when they were truly clubs run for the benefit of the commission merchants.

In many respects, brokers and exchanges may yet be locked on a collision course, as in the long term it is difficult to see customers wanting to pay for the services of both. Exchanges have often deluded themselves that they have genuine processor power in the digital age. Bourses are merely the end matching and clearing engine for the genuine processors – the brokers who to some extent physically generate and then bring together order inputs from all around the world. In the latter respect, the killer brokerages of the post-feudal marketplace era will be those with a massive footprint across many markets, with a large client base. By giving smaller markets access to their networks, the Chicago Mercantile Exchange is one market trying to replicate this processor advantage which tends to lie more naturally with brokerages.

Meanwhile, stockbrokers are often parochial and localized, derivatives brokers are slightly more cosmopolitan. Likewise, the derivatives brokers already have the advantage that going from futures to mere cash transactions is a lot easier to engineer than the considerable scaling up required to turn a cash brokerage into a margin-friendly derivatives brokerage. In an era when broking a range of products in a derivatives world will become increasingly vital, the prospects for some sleepy local brokerages are simply bleak. On the other hand, new powerhouses in brokerage have already been carving out their territory in the past few years. Refco employed the softly spoken New Yorker Joe Murphy with a brief to revolutionize its business. Refco nowadays holds over 200,000 client accounts for dealing in futures – more than some folk believed was the total potential marketplace for derivatives traders only a handful of years ago. Naturally, the bulge bracket brokers such as Refco must wonder just why they have to bother with exchanges who still over value their services when the likes of Refco can provide a healthy marketplace of its own away from the restrictive practices of the floor traders and specialists.

The phases of exchange development – a brief overview

In an attempt to crystallize the many different reforms and processes being undertaken in the dynamically changing environment of the Capital Market Revolution, I have categorized a series of phases through which the exchange world has passed or will pass through on their path to profitable enlightenment. These begin with the origins of the revolution in 1997 and are as follows:[6]

1. Retreat
2. Phony war
3. The ecstasy of value
4. Merger *Blitzkrieg*
5. The reign of terror

Dating such phases precisely is difficult, although I have tried to include a catalyst point for each. Equally, such phases don't necessarily end simultaneously in all regions. Despite a certain degree of overlap throughout the phasing, overall it is clear that each phase has already applied, or will apply, to all the world's markets.

1   Retreat

For derivatives exchanges, this phase was crystallized as LIFFE lost the Bund contract to EUREX (then the DTB) during 1998 which we will discuss in greater length presently. In the equity business, this was the point when electronic communications networks (ECNs) suddenly looked like a threat to the equity exchange business, although it was really only ever a symptom of the bourses' maladies. Luddites the world over started protesting as more trading moved online and the world became "Schwabified." (I use "Schwabification" as shorthand for the relentless overall growth of online brokerage over voice systems.)

The retreat period quite simply saw exchanges and intermediaries head for their bunkers and put up the shutters. The innate conservatism of the exchange clubs was evident as they all became simply terrified that theirs was now a redundant business model.

2   Phony war

In many ways the opening signal of the phony war took place in the midst of the retreat stage. The DTB produced its now infamous advertisement in the *Financial Times* newspaper offering to install its system for free at LIFFE. Ironically, this move was against a LIFFE embattled and down but far from out of the picture. This was the period when everybody was warmongering but without actually setting foot on their opponent's turf in any meaningful way. Crosslisting (i.e. copycatting products on different markets or dual listing of shares in the same time zone) was being mooted by lots of exchanges in cash and futures markets while little or nothing was actually happening. It was an exciting time for journalists but highly unproductive for the trader. The fact that exchanges were still benchmarking themselves through column inches of publicity or product launches and not revenues (or, God forbid, customer service) was in itself a sign that they did not yet understand the need to serve the customer rather than their own often Machiavellian ends.

3 The ecstasy of value

This phase undoubtedly overlaps with phase four and is really only a miniphase but it has garnered much publicity as the exchange clubs have corporatized and sought to list their own shares. Gradually, the exchanges emerged from the long dismal onslaught on their patches and came to realize that in fact they had something going for them. When the sun rose, liquidity still went to their platforms and indeed, with a few judicious changes in the housekeeping, suddenly they could become plausible profit-seeking corporations.

Once upon a time nobody could venture to suggest what an exchange was worth. Then the Australian Stock Exchange (ASX) listed in Sydney (Sweden's OM listed first, but I would argue it has always really been seen as a technology group which happened to have an income stream from exchanges), and after a while it became clear that listed exchanges had some merits.

Recent additions to the club are numerous, with the real biggies being the Deutsche Börse and Euronext during 2001 while the LSE listed its shares for trading on its own platform but avoided actually undertaking a (cash raising) IPO. Some exchanges, such as LIFFE experimented with a judicious mix of venture capital and private equity provided via Battery Ventures and Blackstone respectively in 2000. In the twilight of his lengthy spell at the Sydney Futures Exchange (SFE), CEO Les Hosking quite cleverly mounted an exercise in price transparency by garnering expressions of interest from various parties including Computershare and then the ASX. The fact that the ASX was subsequently forbidden from taking over the SFE was an issue of local politics rooted in a competition Tsar whose answers are invariably quite impeccable, although sadly his remit led to him being asked entirely the wrong (parochial) questions about Australian capital markets without reference to the outside world.

With most players "cashed up" or able to obtain it through tapping the stock market, we arrived at the point (by late 2002) where all exchanges have their claim to being pre-eminent ... which leads us neatly to the next phase.

4   Merger *Blitzkrieg*

The man with the finest credentials to become the first Emperor of the cross-border merger in the modern era is undoubtedly that rather Napoleonic figure, Jean-François Theodore, who steered ParisBourse into the historic tripartite venture Euronext, initially with Amsterdam and Brussels and more recently Lisbon/Oporto and the LIFFE derivatives market after an audacious takeover bid. Elsewhere the most fascinating deal of all so far was the summer 2001 takeover of the UK's International Petroleum Exchange (IPE) by left field player, the Atlanta-based online exchange the Intercontinental Exchange (ICE), which is backed by a number of multinational oil companies.

All the major players will tend increasingly to behave like the great powers at some Hapsburgian dinner party during the mid-nineteenth century. Each is eyeing the opposition and looking for the chinks that will allow them to forge brave new alliances, or potential weaknesses which may offer a chance of hostile invasion if necessary. The danger is that a fringe prize may seem worthwhile but may, in fact, leave a "Great Power" exchange struggling to digest its prey just when a real jewel becomes available. Not for nothing was DB's Werner Seifert dismissive of taking over the smaller European bourses in early 2002. In some cases, with only one or two major stocks of any note, the directly competitive approach could be a much simpler and cheaper avenue to taking over the second- and third-tier stock markets in many regions. Even then as the dust begins to settle, the real challenges will only just be starting. After all, what could be sillier than a vast grouping of incumbent players who just two years ago were exhibiting palpable signs of fear that their goose was cooked and yet now are largely convinced they are even greater masters of the universe than they were originally!

The stock-market dinner-party game

Virtually everybody with a degree of financial literacy has a viewpoint on the future independence or merger intentions of the world's leading stock exchanges yet there is always a great deal of difficulty in truly measuring exchanges. Volume figures can be highly distorted according to the underlying stock's price (traditionally higher – per unit – in the rest of Europe and the US than in the UK for instance). Total market capitalization is a good idea but this can be cyclically distorted according to local economic factors. Similarly, when it comes to measuring hybrid markets with derivatives and cash exposure, the volume issue becomes a real challenge and often a source of some controversy. In futuresland, EUREX was bigger in 2001 by volume of contracts traded but LIFFE would be keen to point out that its own underlying contract value was higher overall. This meant it nominally transacted more in Euro or Dollar terms, if not so many contracts, because its biggest contract was worth more Euros than EUREX's.[7] Anyway, in an attempt to resolve this game, I have become accustomed to practicing the stock-market dinner-party game which can be played by any number of adults and is perhaps the simplest way to appreciate the world's stock markets.

Step one: A player picks a stock market and states how many stocks he wants you to name (maximum five).
Step two: The assembled guests then try to name this number of stocks from that bourse.

The ensuing play is usually a good indication of the relative importance of a stock market. For the NYSE, for instance, it is easy to name five listed shares even for most non-investors; just pick some major global brands such as Ford, McDonald's, KFC, Chrysler, Goldman Sachs, etc. Likewise, London isn't too difficult and Deutsche Börse ends up a simple repetition of all the efficient white goods you have in your kitchen or the cars several of your neighbors drove to the dinner party.

So far so good, but when you have exhausted the big bourses and been through the argument on whether Microsoft is on NASDAQ or NYSE (it's on NASDAQ), we start to get to the interesting and educational part. Start on Asia: Hong Kong, Singapore, or Sydney? Can you name three stocks on each? What about Finland, how many can you name there?[8]

The object of the exercise is not quite as flippant as its ensuing play although, like financial markets, the play is somewhat self-regulated. If half the guests have never heard of a company they will tend to admit it and this can then be discarded from the list or perhaps counted, depending on how raucous you want the game to be! Quite simply, nothing demonstrates better the strength of a stock exchange than the strength of its big stocks. True, all exchanges usually have at least 10 or 20 times as many middle cap and small cap stocks, so their strength can be in depth as well as in the Blue Chips. However, in the big game of global domination for the big investor dollars, what the world's major stock exchanges want to achieve is a method by which they can garner as much liquidity as possible and that is to be found in the big stocks, not the traditionally illiquid penny stocks that can occasionally produce staggering gains. Likewise, on the exchanges where you can easily name a handful of stocks (London, Euronext, Germany, Switzerland, NASDAQ and NYSE), it is not difficult to see they are the markets that other exchange operators covet. Indeed, Deutsche Börse CEO Werner Seifert noted in an aside early in 2002 that he wasn't interested in taking over smaller stock exchanges for the sake of it. For the Chairmen of the second/third tier "prey" exchanges out there, it was a chilling warning that their single or handful of liquid stocks would be a prime target for the business to be dragged from the marketplace. Given that a stock like Nokia dominates its local bourse, it was already apparent from his public utterings that Werner Seifert was eyeing the prospect for directly taking liquidity from the Finnish stock market without worrying about having to actually take that exchange over. After all, the biggest center for trading options in Nokia is already within Seifert's empire, as EUREX have stealthily advanced into cross-border options trading for several years.

5   The reign of terror

Coming soon to a market near you … everything is up for grabs.

This is the time when product cross listing starts in earnest. This has become increasingly commonplace in derivatives markets during 2002, with relentless cross-border listing of equity options by the likes of EUREX (perhaps most notably taking significant liquidity in Nokia options away from Helsinki and with a strong attack on the core Euronext LIFFE equity options markets in London, Paris and Amsterdam). However, while looking inside the industry for competition is wonderful for linear analysis, it is unlikely to lead to a sound vision of how play for bourse domination will conclude. The real catalyst to provoke the reign of terror will be the arrival of the "left field" competitors.

The problem with exchanges thus far has been that until ICE (the Intercontinental Exchange based in Atlanta, Georgia) came along and shook up the energy business, nobody except the traditional players was truly involved (although LIFFE as I mentioned above did pioneer "left field" shareholders within an existing exchange infrastructure in 2000). When ICE first started, the New York Mercantile (NYMEX) somewhat haughtily decried the initiative and saw no sound reason for any alliance with the upstart market. When ICE bought the IPE after NYMEX had spent years wooing the London petroleum exchange, there was somewhat of a sea change in NYMEX's views. Rumors – ultimately unfounded – circulated in the *Financial Times* in early 2002 that a NYMEX-ICE merger was being discussed. The argument against such a move was simply why on earth would Jeff Sprecher's nimble ICE seek to tie itself up with the relatively bureaucratic old line NYMEX, where individual members still held massive sway over management?

There is no doubt, therefore, that left field players will shape much of the future development in the exchange business – the opportunities in the business of small, niche marketplaces are enormous. From the current smugness borne of surviving, and receiving share options, the exchange business is very likely soon to see a renewed wave of guerrilla action. This will be a reign of terror, as a whirlwind of cross listings and new competitors create a very, very exciting marketplace for investors. Hopefully it will result in a better deal for the trader too. But even before exchanges begin to get to grips with this next phase of their strategic development, they have some rather more pressing problems which have been rapidly bearing down on them for several years, and on which they will now have to act.

Notes

1. Moore's Law: "The processing power of a computer will double every 12–18 months." First posited by the founder of chip manufacturer Intel, Gordon Moore, in the 1960s and still valid today.
2. Interest rate contracts accounted for 80.1% of the total amount outstanding in OTC contracts, foreign exchange made up 17.3%, equities were 1.9% and commodities made up 0.6%.
3. For a highly readable analysis of this takeover, I would strongly recommend *Taken For A Ride* by Bill Vlasic and Bradley A. Stertz.

4. The European Union published a directive on open competition in European bourses in September 2002.
5. A tick is the smallest quantity open to dealing on a futures floor, usually 0.01 of a basis point for financial contracts, sometimes less. The fact that locals can manage to keep bid-offer spreads for dealing so narrow is a big boon for derivatives markets compared to the stock market. In equities, corporate capital such as market makers have invariably made spreads much wider compared to the derivatives locals.
6. My thanks to erivatives.com for permitting me to reproduce these exchange phases which first appeared in my management report on the prospects for intermediaries in 2002, *The Promiscuous Investor*, published by erivatives.com
7. The full year 2001 figures for LIFFE (without any Euronext component) and EUREX compare as follows:

LIFFE volume: 215,748,027
LIFFE value of volume: 156,713,207,104,682 Euros (156,713,207 Euro millions)

EUREX volume: 674,157,863
EUREX value of volume: 50,937,159 Euro millions

Having said that underlying financial value is not necessarily as clearly cut as it seems on a volatility basis, one could argue that Bonds (EUREX's biggest contract is the Bund) are more volatile than the bigger (in cash terms) but less volatile Euribor short-term interest rates.
8. For those game players who are always eager to win, I would suggest you try to recall the mantra of "airlines, banks, brands, telecom." This ought to give you a head start – although it can also trip you up where certain brands are subsidiaries of quoted companies and not necessarily quoted themselves. In the case of Singapore, the cheat is just to append Singapore to any business-like noun you can think of – Singapore Airlines and Singapore Telecom (SingTel to be precise) spring to mind as obvious candidates.

Chapter 2

The LIFFE and Death Struggle
Open Outcry Runs Out of Room

Worldwide, once confident, even arrogant, futures exchanges face a fast-mounting challenge to their primacy.

Robert Clow, *Institutional Investor Magazine*

The last days of open outcry – or the twilight of open outcry

While the first outright battles of the Capital Market Revolution date back to the late 1990s, the seeds of the revolution were sown many years previously. In the beginning, dealing was in small localized markets. With the birth of telecommunications, exchanges migrated to larger centers. With the growth of the internet and the explosion in computer technology during the late 1990s, the world's financial markets were poised for their greatest upheaval in history. A landmark event similar to the storming of the Bastille, which demonstrated that the Capital Market Revolution was under way, took place in early 1999 when the world's oldest modern futures exchange, the Chicago Board of Trade, saw its position as largest in the world overtaken by the entirely computerized Germano-Swiss EUREX Exchange, a digital upstart headquartered in Frankfurt and founded in 1991 (as DTB). The CBOT, on the other hand, was founded during mainland Europe's last major wave of continental food blight as long ago as 1848.

Electronic trading first swung to global prominence in October 1997, when the German DTB market (founded as an exclusively electronic market, and soon to be merged with Switzerland's SOFFEX to create EUREX) first broke through a 50% volume share on the key German Bund futures contracts, which had previously been held at the open outcry LIFFE. The winds of change blew through London first, largely because it is the most cosmopolitan of all the world's financial centers. Foreign banks can afford to be more promiscuous than local banks, as the latter will always have greater customer and political problems if they are seen to be removing their business from the local economy. In contrast, foreign banks can largely act with impunity away from their home markets. In London, much of the deal making and trading capacity is created by these foreign banks thanks to the open history of the "square mile." Thus it was that the battle of the Bund was resolved by foreign banks moving their business to Frankfurt in a mark of approval for cheaper electronic systems over the existing floor trading system of London.

In many ways, in fact, the EUREX exchange has been a key catalyst of the Capital Market Revolution. Nevertheless, given the ferocity of the revolutionary process still threatening intermediaries, it is by no means certain that even a market leader such as EUREX will survive the ongoing radical upheaval which ultimately questions the very need for an exchange, the role of the broker and brings traders into an entirely new dealing marketplace where their skills are often redundant in the face of the demands of new technology. Note that one vastly over-hyped myth of the 1990s is also exploded by the simplest tenets of flexible digital dealing. The notion that Frankfurt could become Europe's financial capital had been largely debunked (despite being a serious concern for many bystanders) when EUREX came to prominence and the European Central Bank was headquartered in Frankfurt. Rather, the business of financial centers continues to be situated in those key hubs such as London and New York where there is an abundance of skill sets for all facets of financial markets. Frankfurt, for its part, has profited through exploiting investors' promiscuity to trade where they get the best deal, utilizing flexible digital architecture which removes the constriction of dealing locally or only on fixed telegraphic relationships.

Before the revolution, an open outcry process had been the established basis of market transactions since ancient times. Modern stock markets dating from the seventeenth century in London and

Amsterdam initially met in coffee houses to discuss trading in conglomerates of sailing ships searching for exciting new import products to be brought from the nascent colonies of their respective empires. Gradually, these meetings became more organized and an exchange structure developed commoditising the process of trading in joint stock companies. Indeed, many of the vivid character portraits brought to life by the pen of Joseph de La Vega in *Confusion de Confusiones* could easily be mistaken for traders on any of the various US Boards of Trade still mated to open outcry, despite the fact that De La Vega was writing about the Amsterdam Stock Exchange in 1688. In the twentieth century, exchanges have become an established way of life, delivering a ready marketplace for shares, bonds, and commodities. Hybrids such as futures, options and other derivative[1] products have also become widely available on exchanges throughout the world.

Open outcry is making its last stand in the US as I write. The year 2002 saw staggering volumes in most futures markets, although anemic equity prices meant that stock market volumes were relatively weak. However, commodities and interest rate products, as well as equity indices, boomed, leading many to believe that their future in the pits was assured. Nobody would seek to dispute that the open outcry system provides perhaps the purest face-to-face "price discovery" available. However, the difficulty is whether this commoditized world really values the hand-made service provided in the pits. In Chicago, the futures markets are huge business and the city fathers are rightly concerned at the prospects for the closure of the floors.

Another significant problem for Chicago (or indeed New York) is that it tends to see only its side of the business. Important as the core exchange floors may be now, the truth is that for various reasons they are essentially redundant. The fact that many floor traders will cling on to the bitter end will not make their prospects any better. Similarly, calls to have market makers rewarded for their price provision are simply ludicrous. Nobody indulges in capitalism for altruistic reasons and if floor traders couldn't make any money in the pits, they simply wouldn't be there. Likewise, while independent capital has been very beneficial in the pits of Chicago and New York (and indeed the rest of the world before it predominantly went electronic) nobody can provide a veto on liquidity. However, what really concerns the floor traders is that their method of trading is going to have to change and that is why they are fighting their final stand in the two American cities with potentially the most to lose from electronic trading. But it is a battle they cannot win.

Open outcry is expensive

One has to question whether we need exchanges in their current form. Why maintain a floor for what is essentially an electronic business?

former SEC Commission Member, Steven M.H. Wallman

Open outcry may be a perfect means of "price discovery" but it is equally true that there are inflationary tendencies built into its very make-up which continually increase the cost of the system itself. Open outcry also creates a cut-throat marketplace with heavy tendencies towards discounting brokerage services. These contrary forces combined to literally tear the open outcry system apart. Once a technological alternative was available, even if not a match for existing methods, there was a stampede to embrace electronic dealing. Quite simply, open outcry priced itself out of the market. In the remaining American open outcry arenas, public letters from users during exchange board election campaigns[2] have commonly tended to complain about access charges to end users. A certain antagonism remains between independent capital (locals) who believe themselves to have a certain divine right to be the counterparty to most futures floor transactions and institutional capital which tends to believe that the locals "scalp"[3] excessively, hurting the institutions' trade profitability. The whole situation has tended to become somewhat animated over the years, especially in the US where independent traders have a one-member-one-vote democracy which in practice tends to be somewhat unwieldy and discriminates against the large institutions who control the serious capital.

Floor exchanges are staff intensive. It is a simple fact. A client speaks to a broker, who rings the floor where a booth clerk takes the order and hand signals or shouts the order to the pit trader who executes the order prior to handing a trading card to a runner who takes the order and processes the paperwork. This process is essentially the same on all futures floors. In some larger pits for instance, the broker may require two pit traders, one to show prices to the phone booth staff. Often one person is assigned the job of just commentating on activity in the pit to give clients an insight into market action while others take orders directly from clients and from the brokers' offices. Whatever the precise differences between one floor and the next, the point is that floor trading is people intensive and such staff are invariably not cheap to hire. The problem of paying pit traders is further exacerbated by the fact that in such a highly visible environment as pit trading, any dealers (or booth staff) showing anything much beyond a remote semblance of competence are invariably prone to offers of employment from rival firms at higher wages, thanks to the transparency of their talent. This process has resulted in even the most junior staff barely qualified to trade in the pits being sought after in a business where volume has expanded rapidly throughout the past two decades.

Such escalation in costs would have made little difference to the prospects for open outcry had the cost increases been matched by commensurate revenue growth. However, despite the massive explosion in volumes, revenues for brokers have been to all intents and purposes stagnating since the late 1980s. In many ways, the floors were victims of their own success in this regard. Access to the futures and options exchanges was relatively easy. Anybody sufficiently capitalized could join an exchange and once through the examination procedures, establish themselves as a broker. This made competition intense in the brokerage business and institutions exploited the competition to reduce their costs.

For instance, in the mid-1980s wholesale commissions per contract, for a large institution, on an exchange such as LIFFE could have been as high as US$25 per round turn. By the late 1990s the same organization would have paid barely US$5. Indeed, discount retail brokers offering no frills to private clients are now offering execution services for US$25 – or perhaps even less – to complete novice traders, only trading in a single contract at a time. In years gone by, retail clients had paid $100 or perhaps $200 or even more.

While technological innovations in the back office have helped reduce some costs through increased use of computers and decreased paperwork, the costs of being a broker have increased due to the ever spiralling wage demands of floor traders. And although in the 1990s increased volumes meant the companies made profits, margins were under attack. Accountants, ever eager to adopt the mantra of cost cutting at the expense of actually improving the capabilities of their banks as a means to increase profitability, were blinded by headline figures showing the payment of six-figure checks for brokerage services rendered. They were oblivious to the fact that many brokers were now working for little more than a standard transaction fee charged to customers for buying or selling travelers checks.

By the late 1990s, it was too late to save the bean counters from causing the brokers to bleed. When accountants garner the faintest whiff of a multi-million dollar saving there is little to stop them going for the kill. The irony was that while cutting brokerage rates by 50 cents per trade really made a big difference to returns for brokers, any trader who needs an extra 50 cents off his brokerage to stabilize his trading profitability ought not to be allowed to trade for profit according to even the simplest tenets of risk management. Indeed, in the modern age, brokerage charges per transaction may themselves become redundant, as users pay some form of bandwidth subscription or perhaps a share of their profits instead of a direct execution charge. The online betting exchange Betfair for instance encourages traders to make various transactions within a single event by charging only a net percentage of profits. Likewise, various software vendors and even exchanges are looking at their routing networks being charged on some sort of volume usage rather than volume transacted basis. Note, this is distinctly not the same thing. After all, it costs as much in processing time to enter an order and then cancel it, currently at no fiscal benefit to the exchange, as to actually execute an order earning revenue for the marketplace.

Meanwhile, as the brokers increasingly suffered, desperate moves have abounded to keep open outcry going in New York and Chicago. The image consultants had obviously been at work behind the scenes at the CBOT where there was a new spirit of referring to open outcry as "open auction" amongst some senior management, as if this would somehow save the pits from their inevitable closure. Admittedly, protectionist measures such as increases in brokerage for electronic trading and cuts for pit traded contracts were also being employed. Short of actually barring access to the screens altogether, however, there is nothing which will stop the juggernaut of electronic trading closing the old floors.

Essentially, open outcry has had its day. Many Luddites still cling to "flat earth" arguments about the reasons why open outcry has never been superseded to date. Alas, their arguments are hollow. Open outcry is simply too expensive and too labor intensive. Fascinating as it may have been to watch in years gone by, the idea of trading being routed electronically only to end with a comparatively slow, less efficient human interaction is not going to be a long-term proposition. Ultimately, open outcry has run its logical course.

Protectionism and open outcry

These machines, they're, they're pure evil – we've gotta stop them somehow, goddamnit, before they take over the earth and I think I have a plan. This may be crazy but it might just work ...

from the movie, *Satan's Satellites*

Neither the European Union nor the US trading bloc have anything to particularly pride themselves on when it comes to protectionist attitudes at the macro level, despite their claims of trying to spread open markets in the developing world. Open outcry itself has, alas, come to be seen as a protectionist activity – rightly or wrongly – during the past decade. This is caused in part by regulators and also by the floor traders themselves. End users simply want fast, cheap, and error-free execution. Floors have been a great boon to the development of deregulated capital markets during the past 30 years but computers can process orders faster and more cheaply (with less downtime) from anywhere in the world than any individual could ever manage. And now even open outcry's price discovery claim is under threat.

Price discovery in electronic markets has improved markedly in recent years and, indeed, an electronic market with more players than an open outcry market must, evidently, be providing the better price discovery process. Floor traders, whether locals in Chicago or the specialists of the New York Stock Exchange, have essentially lived a charmed existence. They paid for a license (a seat on the exchange or a permit to trade) and they were then given access to all the order flow of the world's leading end users of that product. Essentially, specialists are an anachronistic monopoly – all business must be funneled through them before anything can be transacted. End users have grown frustrated at this extra mouth in the food chain and they increasingly wish to trade directly with each other for the least frictional cost. In this respect, market makers on electronic platforms have evolved. The protectionist tendencies built into maintaining local/specialist monopolies had many merits when they were established. Unfortunately for them, nowadays many end users instead view them as protectionist cabals.

The move against protectionist pricing and order monopolizing behavior in the pits has also been dealt a blow by the computer algorithms on electronic markets which are helping to democratize order execution in favor of end user clients. In the pit, anybody can make a price and trades are distributed proportionately amongst those in the market (100 lots would be divided 10 lots each amongst 10 locals for instance). In electronic trading, time price priority is increasingly the norm – the so called FIFO ("first in first out") algorithm. FIFO is fair, democratic and reasonable in the vast majority of market situations. When exchanges need to encourage order making or allow for different types of matching priority, other algorithms can be employed. A proportional matching process is common in less volatile markets for instance while hybrid models are being increasingly employed where more complex inter-month or other spread trades are required. Where necessary, electronic markets can match proportionately more efficiently and faster than open outcry. Where a different algorithm is required, it can be inserted overnight. Changing the lifetime habits of individual local traders and specialists takes significantly longer. Protectionism may be an emotive word in that context but the locals and specialists need to understand that even if they are merely sandbagging to keep open outcry going, it intensifies the frustration of the institutional traders who ultimately control the vast majority who do view it as protectionism – or at best an impediment to their trading as efficiently as possible. Alas, even by late 2002 it was increasingly evident that many traders neither foresaw the impending death of open outcry nor would they do anything except fight to the last man to place roadblocks in front of innovation.

Crunch time for brokers

Never before in the history of the financial markets has it been so easy, convenient, and inexpensive for individual investors to participate in the financial markets on their own terms.

Charles Carlson, *The Individual Investor Revolution*

The Capital Market Revolution has in many ways been all about retrenchment by stealth. Few overall brokers have pulled out of key business areas but they have all used natural wastage and any turndown in business to trim and keep trimming their staffing levels. However, on the remaining exchange floors, by late 2002, the pace of redundancy was rapidly growing, with almost a flood of brokerages trimming floor staffs, as they sought to add the trading capacity to their electronic brokerage desks (but with commensurately fewer staff). The more the locals and specialists seek to maintain their privileges and keep their floors open, the more they dig themselves into an untenable position. During the CBOT board election campaign of 2002 some members were demanding an extra payment for the "service" they provided the market as locals. Few people really believed that liquidity-providing altruism was behind their reasons for being on the floor in the first place. If the floor traders militancy becomes too great, the markets will simply trade the same product on digital alternatives – and that may involve entirely bypassing the existing "legacy" exchanges. Brokers aren't dead – yet – but having a man in an office acting as salesman with another floor trader executing orders (and a host of other staff processing the trade in between) is a horrendously cumbersome operation in the modern age.

For those being swept up in the rip tides of the Capital Market Revolution, the core problem remains quite simple:

The more brokerage rates fall, the less able brokers are to offer a good full service operation.

Ironically, therefore, while brokers have found electronic markets can still enjoy "broker assistance" to maintain smoothly organized markets and liaise with clients, the difficulty is finding an efficient means to pay salaries and maintain networks while receiving only modest commoditized cashflows.

Renewed hope for the floor?

Always remember that technology is far from an opponent to open outcry, rather it is a friend of open outcry.

Daniel Hodson, former CEO, LIFFE

While the bald cost factors favored electronic trading as long ago as late 1997, the fact remained that exchange floors could still embrace new technology in an effort to remain competitive. Hand-held order terminals are increasingly popular for order entry to adjoining pits on the floors of Chicago and New York futures exchanges. Indeed, such terminals allowed better audit trail analysis (a key feature to computerized systems), as well as potentially allowing hard-pressed brokers to trim some staff. There were also potential synergies allowing traders to execute simultaneous orders in cash markets and other exchange or OTC products while standing in a pit.

Simultaneously, there have been increasing moves towards electronic order routing and back office systems removing the need for so many booth staff runners. Electronic devices such as headsets were available in some futures markets to further automate the process. However, as Sydney Futures Exchange (SFE) CEO Les Hosking noted back in 1998: "Every investment bank is developing an electronic order-delivery system. Ultimately they are going to say, 'Why the hell do we do it to the edge of the pit and no further?' " Indeed, a quick visit to the floor of the likes of the Chicago Board Options Exchange in recent months would have revealed some remarkable anachronisms. A broker standing in the corner of a crowd, using a digital stylus to match orders which were being shown on a tablet in the corner of the pit. Even a hand-held computer could have "matched" the order faster than the individual on the floor – but of course that risked annoying the independent floor traders who, sadly, increasingly represented the forces of reaction in financial markets. Likewise, what is the point of having a hand-held terminal offering a better audit trail to the point of execution in the pit? Too many folk in Chicago were watching the chicken while the egg hatched. An electronic terminal can be used for the entire order entry process in an electronic marketplace without all those cumbersome floor processes to actually "match" the order.

Alas, for the floor, technology is a false friend as ultimately it seeks to replace the pits rather than enhance them. The short-term interest markets looked impregnable to computerization due to the human brain being more versatile when it came to swapping around different spread orders between months (for instance in short-term interest rate futures). However, as LIFFE Connect originally demonstrated and the CME's new module released in 2002 confirmed, even in the Model T Ford stage of exchange technology, electronic markets are always improving their ability to be a cheaper, faster, simpler alternative to human trading interaction.

Perhaps floor trading is more reliable than electronic markets but then again the electronic markets have a great deal less down time than they had five years – even one year ago. Moreover, as floods in

Chicago and the atrocities of 09/11 have shown, nothing is at greater risk of terrorism than a floor-based marketplace reliant on having several thousand traders reach its portals each day to transact business.

The innovative dynamic

Another big problem for floor trading was that it had become prohibitive to introduce new products. Incredibly, this is refuted in some quarters by those who believe that open outcry can always provide a price for a new product. New product launches on derivatives exchanges are a painstaking process. After months, or even years of research, exchange officials solicit commitments from different companies to be respectively market makers or brokers to the new products. The market makers agree to make prices at all times during a trading session while the brokers agree to commit staff to being in the pit throughout the day to transact new business. In return, the designated brokers and market makers receive incentives such as exchange fee "holidays" or rebates during the formative months of a new contract. However, as salaries grew and demand for experienced personnel remained high, institutions were increasingly reluctant to invest the huge amount of staff costs required to deal in new products when the returns might not be seen for several years. Indeed, the LIFFE German Bund futures struggled along for a couple of years with barely significant turnover (compared to the cash market) until the catalyst of the Berlin Wall falling suddenly propelled the market into an upward spiral resulting in Bund futures being the biggest in the world at one point in 1998, challenging the massive CBOT 30 year US Treasury Bond market. Ironically, by the time Bunds were challenging American Treasury futures, volume had already migrated from LIFFE to the electronic Deutsche Terminbörse or DTB.

Nowadays, the innovative dynamic favors electronic markets. Introducing a new contract on computer screens is much simpler and cheaper for all parties. Market makers can make a price in several markets from an office environment, while brokers can access markets directly from their terminals without requiring extra staff to process orders. During recent years, even in Chicago, there have been electronic-only launches but frequently members have demanded that these products be traded on the floor. Once again such protectionism is more likely to endanger the franchises of the exchanges than actually make a difference to the marketplace. Ultimately, cheaper, more liquid electronic markets will win the day.

The meaning of LIFFE

In other to place the Capital Market Revolution in context, one needs to understand that it has already been taking place at a different pace across different continents throughout the world. Going back in capital markets history even five years may seem like a relative lifetime. Nevertheless, since 1997, there have been a series of events which have created the copy-book case studies that have already gone down in history. By studying the near-death experience of LIFFE, the remarkable rise of EUREX to global leadership, as well as various travails and woes of the US exchanges and the French MATIF, we are much better placed to understand the power of the revolution to humble once mighty institutions and realize just how well deployed technology can create huge value for new and existing intermediaries.

As I have previously mentioned, the LIFFE U-turn was unparalleled in capital markets history. The exchange changed just about every facet of its organization and operation in a matter of months. The motivation was the inroads made into the London market's volumes by the electronic DTB exchange operated out of Frankfurt.

The primary battleground between DTB and LIFFE was in German ten year Government Bonds (Bunds). For years LIFFE had dominated the market. By March 1997, the DTB had managed to capture only a very paltry share of 35% of Bund futures trading. In April, this creaked up to 37.5% but after six years of head-to-head contest, progress was hardly significant. Then as 1997 progressed, volume began to drift upwards on the DTB. It wasn't a passive situation, the Frankfurt management had made a no-holds-barred attempt to coax the business away from the London market. Turnover reached 43% in July 1997 when trading hours were extended by 90 minutes. Conveniently this matched the opening hours of the LIFFE contracts, although DTB officials claimed the move was purely to make the market more accessible to American users. The major catalyst, however was the Maastricht Agreement which guaranteed free trade throughout the European Union. Amongst the treaty's many provisions, one permitted any European market-place's terminals to be sited anywhere within the other European nations. Once Maastricht was implemented during the mid-1990s, the DTB's quantity of terminals in London (and elsewhere outside Germany) began to creep up. Market share in Bunds followed soon afterwards.

By September 1997, the gloves were off and the knuckle dusters on in the fight for market share in Bund and Bobl contracts (futures and options). Exchange or clearing fees for trading were waived at both the DTB and LIFFE. At one stage fees looked like going into reverse with exchanges paying members to trade their Bunds there. On September 4th, the Deutsche Börse (the stockmarket parent of DTB) upped the stakes further by announcing that they would operate as a common market with the Swiss Exchange (including the SOFFEX derivatives market) under the EUREX banner.

By October, LIFFE's share of the Bund business was down to 52%. However, the DTB's policy of disseminating their screens far and wide (by now they had members operating direct to Frankfurt from a network including London, Paris, Chicago and New York often on very advantageous terms) was beginning to pay off in terms of volume growth – and more significantly market share. The 10 US DTB members alone were contributing some 18% of Bund volume. It was a technological warning which LIFFE failed to heed until it was too late for their Bund business. Alas, in Chicago and New York, there are already many signs that those markets may not have realized that once electronic platforms are gouging your market share, it is already too late to save your market. The London exchange appeared to be paying too much attention to its sudden elevation to second biggest exchange in the world status. The full frontal assault on LIFFE's Bund business went ballistic on January 1st, 1998. The DTB dropped up-front admission and annual membership fees for full members and market makers, and slashed those for clearing members. Telecommunication line fees were also dropped, replaced by a minimum transaction fee of DEM 4,500 per month.

On Wednesday October 22nd 1997, the turning point had been reached. The DTB surpassed LIFFE's Bund market share with 52% of that day's volume. From then on, the Germans never looked back. Monday October 19th, 1987 may be remembered by investors the world over as the day of the "Black Monday" crash. However, in exchange terms it was October 22nd, a "Black Wednesday", that is arguably more significant. This was the day the death sentence was passed on open outcry (although as ever the appeals procedure has kept it merely on death row in America).

LIFFE feels the heat

Even before this shift in power was mathematically proven, it seemed as if LIFFE had already blinked when looking into the headlights of the DTB juggernaut threatening the core Bund business. Within weeks of its spectacular June 1997 anniversary celebrations, the LIFFE board announced a "strategic awayday" on July 8th. The result largely reaffirmed LIFFE's faith in the status quo, even when their business was threatening to crumble away in front of their eyes. Open outcry would continue and the expensive property developments at Spitalfields (a whole new floor) and on the old Stock Exchange floor (an overflow facility for LIFFE's stretched existing pit capacity) were still going ahead. Overall, it looked like LIFFE had lost the plot in the face of a very determined opponent.

After a few months of relative silence, however, big league exchange politicking broke out with a vengeance during March

1998. First up was LIFFE. The London exchange now opted to develop a world-beating screen-based system in an attempt to wrestle back Bund volume from Frankfurt's (or rather "virtual" Frankfurt's) DTB exchange. From publicly supporting open outcry a mere eight months earlier, LIFFE had reversed its decision and had climbed into bed with what it had previously regarded as the devil. In addition, LIFFE was also attempting to rebalance the economics of brokerage operations – which it wouldn't even recognize as a problem a mere six months earlier.

The previous July's away-day jolly had done little to assuage the growing concerns amongst many LIFFE members and users. On March 9th, the exchange unexpectedly announced the results of a more comprehensive "strategic review" which would be put to members at an EGM on May 12th. The depth and scope of the change evidenced an organization which was beginning to reconsider every aspect of its ethos:

- The exchange will develop, by Q4 of 1999, a world leading automated trading system to enable the intraday listing of all major contracts, notwithstanding that such products will also continue to be made available on the floor.
- Proposals should be adopted which will have the effect of maximizing the commercial attractiveness and effectiveness of access to the new trading system, which the Board expects will include a different relationship between Exchange share ownership and trading rights. The Board recognizes that these are likely to lead to a revision of the corporate structure of the market and will publish recommendations – including products to be listed on the new system, on April 17th and submit them to an EGM of the market on May 12th.
- Transaction fees will be cut from April 1st, to be funded by a reduction in budgeted expenditure of GBP 30–40 million.
- Investment in the efficiency of open outcry trading and the renewal of core systems will continue. The Board will review the premises requirements.

- There will be a review of the rules, procedures, and other activities and processes of the Exchange with the object of maximizing the flow of international wholesale market business to the Exchange.

The apparent shift in emphasis towards screen trading naturally caused annoyance amongst the locals. To some it came as no great surprise but to many it looked like a vile plot to put them out of business. The vested interests of exchanges are frequently the market's worst enemies.

There was much consternation at the time. Given the extent of the bombshell to hit the membership, this was hardly surprising. For a start, many members wondered why there had to be a wait of almost 18 months before the new trading system could be introduced. Admittedly, if it did handle STIR contracts effectively in the spreading department then the floor would be deserted within days. Equally, some members wondered why the existing after-hours APT system couldn't be used by all contracts in the interim. As APT was the closest thing the first-generation screen trading systems had ever managed to replicating pit trading on a computer terminal, there was some justification in this query. The worrying factor on everybody's minds was that by the last quarter of 1999 it could be too late to save any of LIFFE's business.

EUREX comes up trumps?

On March 18th, at the exclusive Boca Raton Resort during the FIA's annual conference, CBOT and EUREX stunned many of the 2000 delegates. With a letter of intent to create a far-reaching alliance, "the basis for a global derivatives market" as it was intended the plan "eventually will be rounded out with a strategic partner from the Asia-Pacific region."[4] After making little impact on even the domestic derivatives environment for a decade, the German-led EUREX alliance was suddenly in bed with the leading global market. For LIFFE, the effect was even more marked as only months earlier the

London exchange had suspended their joint open outcry linkage with CBOT for German Bunds and US Treasury Bonds on each other's exchanges. At the time, it had looked as if the CBOT was merely seeking to expand their after-hours "Project A" system. Now, it transpired, they were actually looking at a radical deal which appeared to put LIFFE on the backburner and EUREX in pole position in the run-up to EMU. The fact that the CBOT and EUREX were confident that their global communications network would be in operation by Q4 of 1998, a full year ahead of LIFFE's radical new Automated Trading Platform (ATP would therefore replace APT) was a further irritant for LIFFE. That the CBOT and EUREX would have dual market access from a single screen (for daytime EUREX and after hours CBOT Project A) by Q2 1999, only rubbed salt into LIFFE's wounds.

The immediate reaction was that the entire affair boded ill for LIFFE. However, while it appeared bleak on the surface, there were some possible straws for LIFFE to clutch at. Nevertheless, the big problem was that LIFFE had delayed any discussion, let alone a move, to electronic trading for at least a year too long. Ironically, there were many heavy investors on the board buying new technology for their brokerages (often on DTB) while keeping LIFFE on the open outcry track. Meanwhile, despite reigning supreme in the Bunds, the DTB had made nothing more than a minuscule dent in the LIFFE Euromark volumes.

Meanwhile, the impending arrival of the Euro between 1999 and 2002 was sitting on the horizon clouding the long view *in extremis*. Finally, there was the fact that having promised much, almost all derivatives exchange linkages to date had achieved little and ultimately been dissolved, often amidst some rancor. For every good, successful link-up the anterooms and plush hotel suites of international financial conference venues are scattered with the wreckage of numerous agreements. The CME/SIMEX Eurodollar Mutual Offset (MOS) link in the 1980s was a rare gem. It launched the Singapore market onto the forefront of the world stage and secured vast swathes of business for the CME in Asia.

Equally, electronic trading platform agreements had been almost universally unsuccessful to date. The Reuters-developed Globex had been inconspicuously unsuccessful until the French MATIF joined it, and even then it failed to reach its true potential. "If Globex was a dog then Project A was a dog with fleas," to paraphrase Gordon Gecko. The fact remained that the members of the CBOT weren't interested in trading Bund contracts on their beloved floor, (any more than they were interested in trading their own contracts on their Project A system) which made it difficult to see them finding EUREX products more attractive once they were on the screens encompassed by the alliance. The fact remained that Middle America was not overly fussed about what happened in the rest of the world. Chicago had built its reputation on Mid-Western grains and other commodities. Its successful financial products had all contained a US dollar component.

Schadenfreude makes its mark

On March 23rd, the Deutsche Börse (DTB's parent company) took out full-page "open letter to LIFFE" ads in the *Financial Times, The Times* and *Wall Street Journal* offering to implement the DTB system at LIFFE – for free. "Why don't we work together and strengthen the new pan-European trading grid?" it asked. LIFFE promptly issued a testy reply, pointing out that not only did the DTB system have several deficiencies, but also following intensive evaluation of all available electronic systems, it did not score as highly as several alternatives.

Ironically, in what looked like a short-term victory, the end result for DTB was that it indirectly created a fiercer competitor. If DTB had wanted to put LIFFE in its place, it ought to have killed it outright. In a very rare tactical miscalculation, Jorg Franke humiliated LIFFE as it hemorrhaged and actually reanimated the LIFFE machine. A clear sense of anger pulsed through many practitioners and exchange officials alike. LIFFE might have been on its knees but it was about to fight back from its near death experience. Nevertheless, the largest and most irritating flaw in the exchanges' increasing tendency to try to score points off one another was the fact that both markets were still too remote from their end users in terms of finding out what they actually wanted.

The big players in the financial business are big, very big. In fact they're huge. Each and every one of the world's major exchanges was being "supported" by a monstrous bureaucracy which appeared to be getting ever larger – although many traders can't see any difference in the ultimate service to the end user. As exchange bureaucracies were spiralling out of control, there was a great danger of complacency overwhelming the premier exchanges.

Technology can undoubtedly facilitate more flexible exchanges. The SFE – amongst many others – quoted this as one of the reasons for switching to computerized trading. It could also permit new entrants to the exchange business. The Swedish OM organization is a good example of a niche exchange, operating on a "for profit" basis and, therefore, largely bereft of the vast overheads and bureaucracy so beloved by its weightier brethren. In the FX market, the Reuters 2000–2 dealing system wreaked havoc with the profitability of this sector of the money broking industry in no time at all. Originally launched in 1992, junior traders (nicknamed "Gameboys" after the Nintendo product) were assigned to the system while the "grown-ups" continued to shout at each other over telephone lines.

For the biggest foreign currency pairings (e.g. Dollar/Yen, or Dollar/Mark) the "grown-ups" "matched" orders in enclosed rooms filled with brokers, each of whom had barked prices through a telephone desk to dozens of clients for 10 or 12 hours a day. The rooms themselves were somewhat surreal, being closed to outsiders, with windows which merely emphasized the feeling that one was in fact at a zoo and not in the heart of financial market dealing in London, New York or Tokyo. However, Reuters 2000–2 and similar electronic systems simply blew the old-fashioned voicebroker market away. Transaction and market entry costs plummeted (electronic systems were also better at watching credit lines)[5] and suddenly liquidity was on Reuters in a way that had never truly been seen since the collapse of the Bretton Woods agreement had led to free floating foreign exchange markets in the first place. The FX voicebroker has today all but vanished from the banker's bestiary of potential vocations. They remain in a few isolated locations, or dealing in the more exotic currencies for a few specialist brokerages. Overall, however, foreign exchange broking has become a screen traded enterprise.

The foreign exchange market was openly contemptuous of the prospects for electronic foreign exchange trading. Alas, the majority of brokers, exchanges and other intermediaries remain largely unaware of the ramifications of the Capital Market Revolution for their long-term survival prospects. After the good volumes of 2000 and especially 2001 in derivatives markets, many brokers and exchanges have regained their customary arrogant swagger – and evidently remain as incapable as ever of understanding just why their position is being challenged in the food chain. As cash equity volumes continued to sag during 2002 many lay-offs were occurring from brokerages in Wall Street and the other major financial centers. However, most firms appeared to be merely cutting capacity rather than strategically reshaping their businesses to be more electronically commoditized for the next upswing.

The sheer size of exchanges and their importance in the food chain (whether realistic or perceived in their own ivory towers) has continued to create a distance. It is not merely technology which can be a way forward to bridge the divide, it is embracing a whole new flexible means of thinking which currently eludes many exchanges and the key liquidity providers manning their floors. Their reluctance to embrace technology coupled with the all-important shift in perceptions will prove fatal. Above all else, exchanges need to spend their time interfacing with traders and actually trying to improve the dealer's lot. The current, endless power conferencing around the world portrays an image of an industry that is increasingly out of touch with its clients. There is a third way to create mega exchanges, and the sooner the existing players realize it, the better it will be for them. I will look at the challenge from left field in due course.

The perils of transition

Meanwhile, in Paris, a previously somewhat obscure French career bureaucrat, Jean-François Theodore, had taken the helm of the French Stock Exchange and merged it with the MATIF, France's domestic derivatives exchange, founded during the Mitterrand Socialist Presidency in 1986. The MATIF had quickly carved out a successful niche for itself trading French government bonds, interest rates and stock futures. There were forays into commodity products and strong volumes in options. Briefly, during the late 1980s MATIF even edged ahead of LIFFE in overall volumes. However, LIFFE successfully diversified beyond the UK marketplace while MATIF remained a healthy but French domestic exchange (although with the globalization of trading, naturally it had end users throughout the world).

Theodore's exchange "merger" (really a takeover by the stock market of the futures exchange) was one of many such "cross asset" mergers which were in vogue during the late 1990s. Deutsche Börse also took over the DTB futures market, for instance. In the US such mergers have not been popular due to clashing regulatory structures between the SEC (stocks) and CFTC (futures). Fundamentally, there can be considerable value for end users in bringing cash and derivatives markets together although one must always be wary of the maxim that "marrying your cousins does not necessarily improve the quality of the gene pool."

There were two key threads to the strategy devised by MATIF CEO Pascal Samaran and Jean-François Theodore. MATIF was the first European exchange to launch a big push towards being a core player in the EMU derivatives born after January 1st 1999. Sensing the move to cost effective screen trading measures and keenly aware that the Globex system would have been an unmitigated disaster without MATIF's participation in the after-hours market mechanism developed by Reuters, Globex 2 was to be housed on a platform developed by the SBF (Société de Bourse Français – the Paris Stock Exchange, MATIF's parent). Sensing an opportunity to carve itself a reputation in history as the first market to switch from open outcry to electronic trading as its primary means of dealing, the MATIF lunged headlong into a whirlwind period of six months which almost spelt disaster for the Paris market. Indeed, Paris' initial legacy to electronic trading was to provide the textbook case study of the perils and pitfalls affecting electronic trading errors.

We are the "big swinging elbows"

On July 23rd, 1998 a frenzy of selling rocked MATIF. After a relatively quiet session, suddenly orders flooded into the French Government Bond futures contract (known as the "Notionnel"). Official MATIF correspondence outlined the incident as follows:

> At 4.12 p.m. on Thursday, July 23, the NSC trading system received over 100 fill-or-kill sell orders at market price for the September 1998 delivery month of the Notional contract from the order-management server (SLE) of a member based in London. On this occasion, over 230 transactions representing a total of some 12,500 contracts were executed in the space of two minutes. As a result, the price fell by some 150 basis points to 103.61 before the market recovered to set the price back at 105.10, the level prevailing prior to the incident.

When the selling abated, the market bounced back rapidly to the earlier levels. Rumors of hacking abounded. This remains a dreadful dilemma for exchanges and software providers as there remains no clear delineation of where hacking begins or ends. If it occurs to a software vendor linking to the exchange, just where does exchange's liability arise for instance?

A letter to MATIF members from the exchange CEO Pascal Samaran began:

> The incident which occurred on July 23 has caused considerable concern among market participants who understandably want to know the reasons for the abrupt fall in the

Notional future that day and how it could have happened. This has given rise to much comment, not all of it well-informed.

Confidence in MATIF and its management slumped. The counterparty who had initiated the trades attempted to deny all knowledge of the orders being anything to do with them. An enquiry was immediately instituted with Cap Gemini and Kroll O'Gara jointly placed in charge of making a report to the market on behalf of both the counterparty and the exchange. The results were little short of astounding. Or rather, terrifying.

The keyboard mystery?

If you can't get rid of the skeleton in your closet, you'd best teach it to dance.

George Bernard Shaw

The smart money was on "human error" being to blame. Nevertheless, with the counterparty denying any error on their part, the MATIF went through several months of severe media scrutiny. This error had been the latest (and largest) of several which had severely dented market confidence. In the end, the affair created a series of simple blueprints which management ought to consider as being a good way to avoid such foibles in future. Ultimately, when the report was issued, the egg ended up squarely on the counterparty's face.

It transpired that Salomon Smith Barney, one of the biggest and supposedly most brilliant of American investment banks, had in fact sold over 10,000 Notionnel Bond futures thanks to the sort of elementary error which, if it were the centerpiece of a plot in a thriller, everybody would discard as being too ridiculous to be true. In the 1980s, Salomons had been portrayed by former employee Michael Lewis in a rather unflattering light. Lewis' book *Liar's Poker* was famous for bringing the Sallies mantra "we are the big swinging dicks" to public prominence. Remarkably, this time around it was "the big swinging elbow" which brought Salomons back into the limelight.

The independent report included a gem of an excuse from the hapless "trader" who had sold the 10,000 lots …

We've done all these because we were on another screen and leaning against the keyboard and I guess we were trading.
The voice of the SBIL trader on the Salomons' tapes

As the investigators were gathering their information regarding that fateful Notionnel trading session in late July, that most famous of ex-Sallies trading supremos John Merriwether was occupying the limelight with news that his Long-Term Capital Management Hedge Fund had essentially achieved the fiscal equivalent of biodegrading. It was not a classic month for a bank widely regarded as being a generally crack outfit amongst the world's derivatives elite. Even with the benefit of significant hindsight, it remains difficult to really say anything without adding to Salomon's already considerable embarrassment. Substantial forensic examination of Workstation 201 showed there had been nothing wrong with the terminal except the inadvertent human input which had begun the wild trading swing.

Many folk felt the revolutionary process might stall. True, Jean-François Theodore had made a tactical error in going for 100% electronic trading instead of a staged introduction. It was a salutary lesson which has made exchanges more conservative about introducing technology ever since. Open outcry advocates like to note that errors in pits are more transparent because they can be seen by everybody on the floor, while electronic errors occur in the vacuum of cyberspace. Nevertheless, while conspiracy theorists may enjoy such instances, traders would be forgiven certain errors and the trades cancelled. However, when it comes to screen trading, the conspiracy theorists can have a field day as they claim there is little transparency as to what has actually happened on most occasions. If the bank claims to have not inputted the trades, as was the case with Salomons Brothers, then it is difficult to do anything other than undergo a lengthy and detailed forensic inquiry. However, the resulting weeks of wait only serve to harm confidence in the market in the first place.

Transparency of trade, facility to move mountains – or at least blocks

A key lesson from the MATIF error that holds true today is that the actions of wrongdoers need to be transparent and they must be named in their actions and named where they have endeavored to evade any possible degree of responsibility, no matter how unjust this charge may be. Without such market transparency, exchange derivatives trading disclosures could become as murky as many stock exchanges (which are notoriously lacking in transparency and liquidity compared to their derivatives cousins). Keeping transparency to a minimum with disclosure of "block trades *et al.*" often being permitted many hours or perhaps days in arrears of the trade, may be frustrating for smaller traders trying to analyze volume and market action – only to find out that retrospectively the price history can be altered by a later block trade declaration.

Overall, the lesson whether related to errors or block trades is that the more information is withheld from a trader, the more an information elite is allowed to be created. The purpose of information-dense resources such as computers is to permit all parties to trade with equal access to price. To restrict access to information and trading is to miss the very crux of the information change driving the Capital Market Revolution. Nevertheless, exchanges must develop a fine balancing trick between keeping their big block trading clients happy (who will otherwise migrate to the OTC market) while letting smaller traders feel they are not being overly excluded. Meanwhile, those who seek to ban block trading outright must remember that they are diluting the benefit of the exchange as transparent price arbiter and handing business to the dominant "upstairs" OTC marketplace. With capital adequacy requirements (as defined in agreements such as the Basle accords) trying to push business from OTC back to exchanges, it will be the flexible exchanges providing services to all levels of practitioner that will win out against competition from markets seeking to cater only for, say, specific retail or institutional clients.

F12 – Somebody's least favorite function key

Meanwhile, back with the MATIF's textbook error in 1998, the factor culpable on the MATIF NSC-VF terminal was the F12 key, which permitted a lean to become somewhat of a new-fangled lien in financial markets. If double clicked, this key would instantly enter an order, regardless of magnitude. Admittedly, Salomons could clutch at one straw which was that an upgrade to the NSC software had not been implemented on their system (which was at the Salomon Brothers International Limited offices in London). This upgrade from version 4.10 to 4.10a would have eliminated the dangers of the "double F12" functionality and had been available since July 1st.

To tie up the loose ends of the recalcitrant elbow, interestingly, the MATIF allowed (in compliance with the existing exchange rules) the opportunity for trades in this error to be cancelled if both counterparties agreed. Rumors abounded of rather panicked calls from Salomons staff seeking to cancel as many orders as possible. However, from an executed error total of some 10,607 contracts Sallies ended up having to "wear" (i.e. keep) some 10,488. Presumably, the rumors were as erroneous as the claim that a hacker did the trades in the first place.

Dealing with electronic errors

Meanwhile in the development of screen trading, EUREX has not been immune to errors and there have been several large instances in recent years which have invariably been due to shoddy risk management on the part of a member firm. While many of the reactions to these errors were somewhat hysterical, nevertheless the issue consistently raised has been whether it is in an exchange's interests to keep a counterparty's name anonymous when surely naming and shaming would be a significant deterrent to future lapses of such gross negligence. There is another possible solution: the exchange ought to create its own risk-management module which is obligatory to all counterparties. However, this would unfairly penalize those many institutions who have been sensible enough to protect themselves in the first place with state-of-the-art risk-management systems and suitable bells and whistles to remind them when something is going pear shaped. The fact remains however, that canceling trades often adversely affects innocent traders and arbitrageurs (who may be left with legacy positions they had used to hedge). Uncertainty as to whether a trade will be honored in such a volatile situation may yet result in less liquidity during uncertain times which is to nobody's benefit. Markets need to be much clearer about where and when they will cancel trades and endeavor to make people wear their obligations in essentially all circumstances.

After all, in the case of many, if not most, of the errors outlined above, a simple filter on orders would prevent them. In the latter case, it would seem that the house that entered the trades had not thought through the ramifications of such electronic trading activity – a failure on the part of both dealing and systems management. Increasingly, institutions will favor intelligent front-end systems integrated with their middle and back offices which provide a strong preventative risk control system. Nevertheless, the safety catch on a pistol is only any use if it has been properly configured. In that respect, some hapless soul at LIFFE deserves a mention for inadvertently turning off the "live" CONNECT market system believing they were switching off the test session during the early days of LIFFE's otherwise very successful electronic market transition, which I will return to shortly.

The very earliest electronic trading error of note which itself bore a key lesson for the future was at the screen-based Tokyo International Financial Futures Exchange (TIFFE) when it opened in 1989. A trader dealt in the wrong month, placing an order out of line with the market. It was instantly executed and the TIFFE management made the bank wear the instant loss (of *circa* 100,000 dollars) in order to encourage an orderly market. At the time, many brokers (schooled in open outcry) thought this sheer madness. Nowadays, with screen traded markets prone to being manipulated by large dealers who can cry "wolf" if their position goes against them, the likelihood is that brokers and dealers will have to be very careful what orders they enter as the market will want to see them making good on all entered orders.

Meanwhile, brokers who have simply looked at the up-front cost savings of the move to screen trading may be terrified to find that suddenly they are wearing a lot more error positions than previously could be easily canceled, or removed on the "kerb" in an open outcry market. Once again, simply implementing technology without radically rethinking your business may not leave you appreciably better off than sticking with the legacy open outcry system and other established practices.

(MATIF's) brave new world

Electronic trading is not the end of human intervention in the trading process and I believe some good sense doesn't hurt anybody.

Pascal Samaran

MATIF had been slightly to blame for their groundbreaking error, through Jean-François Theodore's insistence on a very rapid establishment of 100% trading capacity. Parallel trading (i.e. a floor and electronic systems replicating the same functions) came in with the market having a full complement of several hundred terminals available immediately, in a number of different locations including London as well as Paris.

MATIF officials and members alike were stunned by the migration of business from floor to screen within a staggeringly short period of time. The first parallel session was in early April. By the end of May 1998, MATIF announced a move to exclusively electronic trading. The cost pressures to use screens was just too great. Somewhere between 600 and 700 floor staff lost their jobs to the new technology.

Market practitioners in Paris universally liked the new NSC system with VF for futures and VO for options. The whole transition looked like a stunning success. But as ever, there were some hiccoughs to be sorted out. Overall, the NSC hardware has proven tough, reliable and user friendly. However, subsequently the

Euronext market would opt for LIFFE CONNECT's superior electronic technology for futures and options markets – but we will deal with that story at the appropriate time. The last words of Pascal Samaran, the MATIF CEO on the whole Salomons error are as true today for technology innovators as it was in 1998:

Everyone understands that when you move from an open outcry system to an electronic one, there is a learning curve. We've been climbing that curve quite steeply.

Pascal Samaran, CEO MATIF

Meanwhile, Jean-François Theodore learnt from his errors and set about crafting his ParisBourse into the organization which would become a power base of European bourse rationalization with his tenacity to do deals marking him out as a key figure in the Capital Market Revolution. And Pascal Samaran was ultimately proved correct when he claimed: "MATIF is the first derivative exchange in the world to move successfully from open outcry to electronic trading." But it had taken collateral damage and created a blueprint of tips for other exchanges to bear in mind. The process was certainly not as smooth as it could have been but then again, navigating entirely new terrain rarely goes as smoothly as a walk in the park.

Those who were too hasty in writing to write off Jean-François Theodore's overambitious, headlong move to electronic trading were, however, deprived of having the last laugh. Indeed, Theodore demonstrated a remarkable capacity to learn from his mistakes – not necessarily the classic hallmarks of an ENA-trained bureaucrat. Theodore saw and understood the errors made during this process and was ruthless in ensuring they would never happen again. It is his ability to learn in adversity, and indeed come back from being constantly written off as a nearly man of global bourse politics, that makes Theodore such an impressive figure in the battle to unify Europe's bourses. When ParisBourse looked like a Euro-zone rationalization also-ran, he created Euronext with Amsterdam and Brussels. At the Burgenstock conference in 2001, the momentum appeared to have run out for Theodore once more. Within weeks he had audaciously snatched the LIFFE derivatives market from the jaws of the London Stock Exchange. Theodore's ability to fight back in adversity has become a hallmark of his reign at ParisBourse and subsequently Euronext. He could yet achieve the sort of continental unification that eluded even Charlemagne and Napoleon.

A matter of LIFFE and death

But what of LIFFE? As we saw in the Prologue, the fall from grace of LIFFE CEO Daniel Hodson was swift and merciless. In the most aggressive portals of capitalism it was always thus. Nevertheless, it would be unfair to point all the blame, or even a significant quantity, directly at the LIFFE CEO's door. Certainly, Hodson made errors but he also fell victim to significant lack of foresight by his exchange board; errors which many mortals could have missed and, indeed, Chairman Jack Wigglesworth and CEO Hodson both failed to see coming. Or did they? Shortly after standing down as Chairman, Jack Wigglesworth noted that "Our members would not even let us talk about electronic trading for the last two years."[6] This was a remarkable statement, as other board members laid the blame for not discussing open outcry squarely at Wigglesworth's door.[7]

The LIFFE board had included several discontented members for some months. Indeed, in the global business of derivatives trading the LIFFE board found itself becoming somewhat of a political football. The board is elected by the members – each corporation has one vote. Exchange boards are often over-representative of brokers compared to traders, as the former category are not only more actively involved in all aspects of the derivatives business (many institutional traders have a relatively narrow focus) but equally brokers, by their very *raison d'être* of selling services to lots of traders, tend to be better known. The Chicago Mercantile Exchange during mid-2002 began a move towards an IPO yet with little outside representation on the company's board or its key management committees. Other exchanges also hoped they could maintain their internal strangleholds on management even when they were no longer member clubs but shareholder-driven organizations.

At LIFFE, the problem seems to have been that some LIFFE directors appeared to be maintaining faith in LIFFE's espousal of open outcry providing "steady as she goes" encouragement at board meetings. Yet at the same time, there was significant evidence of these self-same board members actually joining the DTB and buying in electronic trading capacity for their companies simultaneously. Board acrimony reached a peak on March 26th 1998 when LIFFE announced its details of exchange fee reductions. By all accounts, the decision process was far from smooth. Reportedly, up to 40% of the board stormed out before the end of the meeting. Talk of resignations abounded. The LIFFE Exchange looked on the verge of tearing itself apart. Something had to give.

The meaning of LIFFE?

In a blizzard of announcements in the wake of the acrimonious board meeting, LIFFE adopted a new management structure. The Exchange moved from being a mutual organization owned by membership without a profit motive, to being a fully for-profit corporation permitting third-party (i.e. non-market) shareholders, and revised trading rights.

In July, the Board announced the first full-time salaried Executive Chairman (previous appointees had been elected board members, and representatives of member firms) on a three-year term. The appointee was Brian Williamson CBE. The City of London cheered. At 53, Williamson was already a legendary figure in financial markets. One of the original directors, a driving force behind the establishment of LIFFE (and Chairman from 1985 to 1988), Williamson retained icon status amongst the LIFFE community. Of his few detractors, one retiring LIFFE board member referred to him as "a bloody control freak." "It's about time LIFFE had one!" was the retort of another senior City figure. As a founder (along with Mark Davies and Christopher Sharples) of Gerard and National Intercommodities, a leading global brokerage, Williamson was sufficiently wealthy not to require the Executive Chairman's salary.

For Williamson, it was a case of returning to LIFFE to bring it into the new millennium from a position of renewed strength. It was a challenge he would relish.

On Tuesday July 21st 1998, Daniel Hodson resigned as LIFFE CEO. Hodson stated that Brian Williamson "is exactly the right person for the task ahead and, in common with the entire LIFFE community, I wish him great success." Williamson returned to the reins at LIFFE determined to shape the market to his new vision. It was a vision to which only Williamson was privy but it was soon clear that radical surgery was required for LIFFE to meet his new model. The CEO had already left the field clear for him almost two weeks before Williamson officially assumed office on August 3rd.

Meanwhile, even after the difficult period culminating in his resignation, Daniel Hodson retained his usual self-effacing charm. Prior to a spot of gardening at his English country house, Hodson departed for his Greek holiday villa after placing the following note in *The Times* diary column: "To hire: energetic and experienced chief executive with a proven thick skin and a sense of humor. Will travel."

In a matter of months, the LIFFE organization appeared to have been left reeling from both the loss of market share and internal dissension. But, incredibly, the truth was far more positive than that. The painful and necessary process of adjusting to the realities of the Capital Market Revolution had at least begun. There were promising signs that at last the market had got on top of the short- and medium-term problems facing it. Nevertheless, nobody was left in any doubt that LIFFE was in intensive care and there was every possibility the patient would not pull through despite extensive surgery.

The LIFFE revolution

The dynamism of Williamson on saving the LIFFE exchange was instantly evident for all to see. Anything which anybody within LIFFE had ever held sacred now came under direct fire. In a whirlwind process, Williamson set about not so much reshaping the exchange as entirely demolishing everything and starting again.

Previously sacred cows were being slaughtered left, right and center without a second thought. Williamson wasted no time in making clear his intention to get his "hands dirty."

> The Exchange's customers are my number one priority and I will be embarking on an extensive consultation programme with them as soon as my appointment begins. But I want them to know that I am resolved to act with speed and determination.
>
> The Exchange must continue to play a full part in maintaining and growing international business in the City of London to ensure that it remains the pre-eminent international financial centre.

The last bombshell of a hectic 1998, LIFFE reserved for November when the exchange announced that it was:

> ... to take decisive action to restructure its business to meet the needs of its customers in the future. It will make access to the exchange cheaper and easier for users and achieve efficiencies by internal restructuring and cost-cutting.

With South African Hugh Freedburg now employed as CEO, (the man, remember, who from his time at Hill Samuel was described as "the man who put the slash in slash and burn"), the LIFFE exchange was ready finally to put the nails into the coffin of the *ancien régime*. As Williamson put it:

> We have to deliver an efficient trading platform together with the products that our customers want, at a price they are prepared to pay. It is clear that nothing remotely like our current cost base is sustainable and that we shall have to cut jobs to remain competitive. We will also achieve cost savings by overhauling our regulatory structure so that it suits today's market. In addition, there is the potential for us to win new business by forging new links with other business partners, in London and internationally.

These new links could include network and technology providers, exchanges, clearing houses and related businesses. Williamson had already appointed a council of wise men – leading City of London figures, to advise the exchange on its future strategy.

Freedburg was no less forthright: "We will be driven by the marketplace and our focus must be on meeting the needs of customers. Customers expect efficiency, ease of access, flexibility and speed. We will deliver the right technology and the right products at the right price."

At last a leading exchange had actually grasped the nettle and were seeking to adopt a new model environment with which to secure the continuation of the exchange. Nevertheless, there was a long and difficult journey ahead. And for all to see – although not all to appreciate – open outcry was not a part of that journey.

The view from America

1998 marked the 150th anniversary of the CBOT. On February 18th, 1997, the venerable exchange had moved to a new home. Chicago Mayor Richard Daley inaugurated the largest trading floor in the world, occupying some 60,000 square feet at a cost of US$182 million. It was large enough to house a Boeing 747, the CBOT website trumpeted breathlessly. As Chairman Pat Arbor looked out upon the floor during early 1998, he could have had no idea that the next twelve months could be so tumultuous both for him and the world's oldest and largest futures exchange. There had been trading on the CBOT in agricultural products since the last widespread mainland European food blight. As Lafayette witnessed the last of three French revolutions in his remarkable lifetime, the CBOT was already trading cash grains. Forward trading had begun on March 13th, 1851 while 3000 bushels of corn for June delivery marked the first futures transaction as long ago as 1865.

Arbor, even during the first six months of 1998, had endured a bumpy ride. In March, members vetoed a proposal to raise Arbor's salary from $240,000 to $400,000 per annum. Ironically, even if it had been agreed, this raise would still have left the CBOT Chairman trailing the best local trader incomes by many millions per annum. Arbor himself seemed to have cut a deal with CBOT CEO Tom Donovan. Donovan would keep a close hand on the reins while Arbor would get the opportunity to create his dream floor. In 1998 in Chicago, nobody really had conceived that open outcry could ever even be remotely threatened by upstart electronic markets. The internecine factionalism of Chicago exchange politics was dominated more by local issues than any concern for a broad vision of the trading world. With what realistic end in sight? Well, with open outcry in so perilous a state when Boeing decided to move their corporate headquarters from Seattle to Chicago in 2001, it was clear in my mind that one key advantage was the potential to have a purpose-built marble showroom facility for Jumbo jets in the heart of the Chicago "loop." Indeed, they could probably hang a prototype sonic cruiser from the roof for good measure too.

Meanwhile at the CBOT, the LIFFE open outcry link had been gently discarded. Even a few years later it seems almost incredible that in the late 1990s, exchanges still believed that open outcry links were the future for traded markets when evidently liquidity on screens was by definition global. However, when you're in a business that had compounded double digit growth for almost 20 years, there wasn't much need for analysis, just people to pile up the business. Back in Chicago, the groundbreaking alliance with EUREX announced at the Boca Raton conference in Florida, shook the derivatives firmament. Nevertheless, the volumes piled up and the CBOT remained top dog. Even merger talks with longstanding Chicago rival the CME were ongoing. However, first up was the common clearing issue.

With OTC business, where there is no common clearing, institutions must deal with each other using credit lines – a series of credit relationships where different sized banks all have different quantities of "lines" (ability to deal) related to their creditworthiness. While the system tends to work well overall, the danger remains of a counterparty default causing a bank to lose a profitable position.

Therefore a clearing house has several advantages. For one it permits institutions and individuals to meet and transact business on an exchange without having to be concerned about the other parties' creditworthiness. Equally, even when the likes of Drexel Burnham Lambert collapsed after the demise of Michael Milken's financial career in the 1980s, independent local traders and institutions alike were not blighted by losses suffered from dealing with the ill-fated kings of junk bonds.

The problem in Chicago was that the two big exchanges, the CBOT and the CME, both operated separate clearing houses. This was bureaucratically cumbersome for members of both markets. With the CME having the biggest short-term interest rate contract in the world (the three-month Eurodollar deposits) and the CBOT holding the Treasury Note/Bond complex on their floor, there was also the fact that trading spreads between these and other contracts across different markets became relatively expensive for traders interested in both markets. Margins tend to be offset to some degree by certain combinations of trades. In the case of traders wishing to trade the American yield curve, they had to pay margins to both markets. The same applied if they were spreading commodities listed on the two different exchanges.

This inefficiency was not something which could be tolerated in the new financial climate. The Chicago exchanges needed to merge their clearing quickly in order to be seen to be healing their history of enmity between the neighboring markets.

Despite strong CBOT volume in the first half of 1998, Arbor's fate would be surprisingly sealed in the second half of 1998. Indeed, Arbor would be the last Chairman of the CBOT to hold office while the exchange was unequivocally the strongest derivatives exchange in the world. Within four years the CBOT would be besieged by its own members' Luddite views and the failure of management to take the exchange forward to meet the key challenges of the revolution.

The burdens of individual membership

The two Chicago exchanges are on a path towards mutually assured self-destruction, and it's working.

Verne Sedlacek, COO John Henry and Company

In the US, as opposed to more corporatised Europe, membership of exchanges tends to be organized on an individual level. While this means a greater degree of democracy in so far as every single pit trader (including hundreds of independent "locals") can each vote, it can also hamper an exchange's attempts to progress. The Chicago exchanges have over the years suffered a number of difficulties with their members when members have tended to put their (short-term) self-interest ahead of the needs of the market for development.

In early September 1998, this militancy on the part of the membership resulted in a petition to the CBOT board complaining about the terms of the deal to create common clearing. At a stormy board meeting, the CBOT board "voted to rescind its support for creating a common clearing house with the CME." This was despite the CME apparently agreeing to a last minute request by the CBOT that their clearing house be used as the corporate structure for the joint entity. CME Chairman Scott Gordon immediately expressed "disappointment and frustration" at the CBOT's withdrawal. FIA Chairman Ronald M. Hersch was equally upset: "We are extremely disappointed by the CBOT's retreat from their commitment and the failure of the two Chicago exchanges to come together on a customer-driven initiative. It is obvious that exchange politics continue to prevent these institutions from supporting the type of cost-driven initiatives needed to grow our markets."

At the Burgenstock conference only days later, the FIA's President John Damgard was little short of incandescent. Damgard, a tall and somewhat dashing figure, a classic example of the laconic but sharp mid-western American, could barely contain his anger, "it's a very sad day in Chicago," he noted, bristling with indignation. The Burgenstock meeting itself was somewhat of a curious affair. The leading European conference for derivatives markets was marked by a large amount of jostling for position and claiming of territory without any particular announcements of note. Nevertheless, the stress was showing for many leading exchange executives.

A press conference called by the CBOT and EUREX to announce the cementing of their co-operation agreement after the lawyers and regulators had had their say, left many onlookers wondering quite what the CBOT had let themselves in for. The event itself was a sort of corporate love-in and it served only to underline concerns amongst many industry onlookers that the dynamics of the derivatives industry were beginning to pass the grandees of the CBOT by. They looked increasingly out of place when sitting alongside the smooth technocrats of EUREX led by Jorg Franke. When CBOT CEO Tom Donovan stated categorically that "EUREX has the best electronic system in the world ... it doesn't go down," many onlookers had to stifle a laugh. Whether Donovan had merely suffered a momentary lapse on account of jetlag or the Alpine air in the Swiss resort, his comment was never adequately explained. Quite simply there was no serious basis in fact for such a statement. There was much documentary evidence of the DTB's system continually slowing down in mid-session and leaving orders within the system, much to the horror of traders who were powerless to do anything about it or make any amendments to their orders. Nevertheless, the EUREX management worked hard to overcome their growing pains and within months the EUREX system was a much stronger vehicle better able to cope with volume levels significantly higher than had ever been expected. Unfortunately, the CBOT vacillated and failed to grasp the nettle in their move towards electronic trading.

Meanwhile, LIFFE had held a meet-and-greet cocktail party with its new executive Chairman Brian Williamson who, unlike his equivalents from other markets, spared the assembled multitude any comments about his grand designs for the future. Sipping his whiskey[8] and oozing charisma, Williamson proved the most enigmatic draw of the conference.

Pat Arbor had, like Tom Donovan, looked out of his depth at the Burgenstock meeting. This was a remarkable turn around for Arbor who had a deserved reputation as a survivor both in trading and trading politics. A sleek bald figure with a reputation as somewhat of a Lothario, Arbor had long been a smooth operator but nonetheless a somewhat colorful figure in the Chicago trading community. Arbor famously lost a paternity suit in the 1970s to a famous black *Playboy* centerfold. Their daughter Kelley Arbor later posed for *Playboy* herself while at Harvard. Colorful trading character Victor Niederhoffer subsequently reported that the February 1996 issue sold twice its usual volume at kiosks in the immediate surrounding area of the CBOT.

The very act of inking the deal with EUREX did Arbor immeasurable damage in the eyes of the membership. In a vote on December 9th, 1998, Arbor was unexpectedly voted out by members increasingly vexed at the prospect of open outcry being usurped by what was seen as Mr Arbor's advocacy for screen trading. Members were uncertain what, if anything, was likely to benefit them from the EUREX-CBOT deal. The CBOT had already spent several million dollars on the deal and yet members could see no tangible value aside from conspicuous quantities of glossy direct mail assuring them this was a move for the future benefit of the market. The consultants may have been handsomely rewarded but the membership of the market was on the verge of revolt. Meanwhile, a vast number of pit traders didn't want the existing food chain involving the floor threatened, regardless of the fundamental merits of any exchange technology/linkage deal. A relative unknown beyond the walls of the CBOT, local trader David Brennan was elected Chairman in a move which startled the world's markets. Brennan had been a classic "protest" candidate intended to frighten Arbor. The softly spoken Brennan was reputedly amongst those most surprised when he emerged victorious. Already the first reaction to the revolution was under way.

Notes

1. Derivatives are so called as they are products "derived" from cash markets.
2. The American FIA produced two such letters ahead of CBOT and CME elections in March/April 2002.

3. "Scalping" is the act of locals profiting from buying and selling in between the "paper" (i.e. client orders). Locals live by taking ticks off the back of the financial rhinoceri. Although in this case, "ticks" are the smallest incremental movement in markets. Some end users tend to complain that locals move markets to the detriment of the execution of institutional business.

4. The Boca Raton resort in Florida is a regular haunt for many US industry groups throughout the year for their annual retreats. It is an originally pretty art deco resort which nowadays looks and feels as bloated as the bills delegates usually receive at the end of a conference. Boca Raton conferences often resemble an extra holiday for many delegates who spend most of their time on the golf course. In the case of the CBOT-DTB deal, it was seen as so groundbreaking that some senior derivatives industry figures apparently delayed their tee-off times until they had more insight into the deal.

5. In traditional OTC markets, credit rating is of vital importance. The deals are bilateral and therefore each bank/institution tends to have a pre-agreed credit line with every other bank with which it wants to deal. The HQ of a major bulge bracket bank would have large limits, and a representative office in some far-flung place might have only a tiny limit. In the OTC markets which are still voicebroked, one can still hear the brokers telephone speaker boxes crackle with the words "can't do the name!" when they are told details of a deal. In other words, they have insufficient limits to complete the transaction. This leaves the broker having to shuffle deals around until everybody is happy. Obviously, an electronic system can surmount most of these problems. The system can be pre-programmed with the counterparty limits of all banks and then simply preclude any bank dealing with another when it is not able to. In this respect alone, computers far exceed the capabilities of humans for dealing in many markets.

6. Jack Wigglesworth, quoted in *Institutional Investor*, June 1998.

7. I am happy to note that in *The New Capital Market Revolution* I am repeating an accusation made originally in *Capital Market Revolution*. I think it only fair to note that Jack Wigglesworth has very strongly disagreed with this assertion. Therefore, it is only fair to note his disagreement, although other board members at the time also vehemently disagree with Jack's recollection of events. I would also like to thank Jack for other input on *CMR* about which he was quite correct and which I hope has been amended to his satisfaction.

8. For the record, at Burgenstock there seemed to be a dearth of "whiskey"

and Brian Williamson apparently had to settle for Scotch. However, at the risk of annoying my Scottish editor, I am using the Irish spelling as Sir Brian Williamson and the author both have some element of Irish roots and therefore prefer sipping Irish "whiskey" wherever possible.

Chapter 3

Inaction, Reaction and Revolution
Legacy Exchanges and the Struggle for Flexibility

The reaction began in Chicago while LIFFE was feverishly battling for its survival. The Capital Market Revolution was operating on entirely different transatlantic wavelengths by late 1999. In the US, there was a certain fear laced with ongoing arrogance about the power of legacy exchanges to be destroyed by the forces of the revolution. While the online brokerage boom was helping to fuel volume in the ECNs, few people were willing realistically to consider that the open outcry exchanges were under threat. On the other hand in Europe and Asia, the lessons of LIFFE's near decimation at the hands of the electronic EUREX was leading to a headlong rush to electronic trading. The story of LIFFE's decline and ultimate resurrection remains the most fascinating tale of the revolution to date. The story of Chicago and New York's relative indifference to the fact that their franchises would come under fire next equally reveals the ongoing swaggering arrogance ingrained in many established marketplaces. Ironically, those markets which have done least to prepare for the next wave of revolutionary fervor as markets increasingly cross list their products will find themselves having much less scope to reverse their business models in the way which LIFFE was doing during 1999 and thereafter.

LIFFE on the rack

LIFFE was buffeted by the full power of the Capital Market Revolution first and in early 1999 it was still fighting for its life. The cynics had long since written it off and the media was largely hostile to any prospect that the market could pull itself together. Yet, by holding firmly onto the bootstraps, Chairman Brian Williamson[1] was hauling LIFFE back onto a firm ledge while all the time trying to rebuild its foundations. At this time, there was almost a siege mentality pervading the exchange – and with good reason. Its friends were few on the ground. Many journalists were referring to the exchange as "troubled" if not "embattled" and "beleaguered." Indeed Williamson would subsequently, with his typically raffish charm, offer an award at the Boca Raton futures conference in March 2000 to the last journalist who had referred to LIFFE using these phrases.

It was clear, however, that those journalists and market insiders who were quick to damn LIFFE evidently hadn't paid a lot of attention to the revolution going on beneath the surface at the London exchange. When he arrived Williamson described his job as placing the exchange in "intensive care" and hoping to nurture it out of the recovery wards. And as he went about his life-saving responsibilities he approached the business with a refreshing honesty towards other markets in both cash and derivatives products: "Nobody is the enemy," he opined sagely shortly after re-entering the Chairman's office.

Williamson made a series of issues key areas of focus. The most notable was impossible for any visitor on the LIFFE management floor to miss. In early 1999, the exchange erected a massive whiteboard upon which was written every day the traded volumes and market shares in LIFFE and rival exchanges' three-month Euro interest rate contracts. With the introduction of the single European currency, this became a key focus in the exchange's battle for survival. Williamson wasn't joking when he added frankly that if LIFFE failed to dominate the Euro interest rate market it was dead (EUREX had of course stolen the Benchmark (German) Eurozone Bond futures precipitating LIFFE's crisis).

While LIFFE had a very focused start, it still wasn't all plain sailing. Industry cynics were quick to point out that the exchange's choice of Eurolibor (London rate) had been flawed when the market preferred Euribor set in Frankfurt where the European Central Bank (ECB) is based. With a stroke of genius, marked by great bravery and not a little tenacity, CEO Freedburg set about changing the contract specification as it traded. The Euromark future had been converted into Eurolibor by January 19th 1999 but within days it was clear LIFFE had the wrong benchmark. The exchange then managed by February 17th once more to convert all open positions from a Eurolibor to Euribor basis. By the end of this process, it ought to have been clear that if LIFFE could change a contract in mid-trade, there was a remarkably high chance that it was not merely going to recover but indeed it was likely to return to some element of prominence. Nevertheless, widespread market and media doubt remained that LIFFE would be able to become even a modest subset of the London Stock Exchange, if not disappear entirely. In fact, LIFFE would go on to steamroller competitors in three-month Euro futures. Meanwhile, focus was maintained through the daily updates on the percentage market shares on the Euro whiteboard in the management offices.

While the closure of the floor was a painful experience for all concerned, Williamson made a habit from his first day back in the Chairman's office of holding a weekly open "surgery" in the "Pit Stop" café beside the floor where he would listen to disgruntled traders' grievances or hear the suggestions of others. While the management of LIFFE tried to ascertain as much about the problems and issues facing their own traders, the focus towards customer-centricity was moving at an equally rapid pace. A team of specialists was quickly established to maintain customer liaison functions and LIFFE quite simply somersaulted from its previous "club" status to a very fine for-profit corporation within a matter of months. Williamson, described the radical task simply. "We're riding the tiger here," he noted.

A new deal

LIFFE astounded many when they announced a radical new departure on Monday November 20th, 2000. The Massachusetts venture capitalists Battery Ventures, in concert with investment bankers and private equity group Blackstone, would invest £60 million in the exchange. The deal was significantly driven by Battery's belief that new technology would be the key issue in the financial markets and that LIFFE's Connect system provided a magnificent platform for developing electronic markets. By 31st December 2001, the Battery/Blackstone shareholding in LIFFE amounted to some 29% of the total exchange. The Battery Blackstone deal, masterminded from Chicago by Brian Williamson's longstanding friend (known as "the father of financial futures") Doctor Richard Sandor marked the first occasion that venture capitalists and private equity specialists had stepped into a foreign exchange. Evidently, Battery and Blackstone saw a remarkable upside which to date had eluded many of the cynics still writing off LIFFE's chances of survival. Once again it was soon to be proven that the smart money would win the day.

LIFFE continued their aggressive reconstruction strategy with the launch of the world's first international single stock futures early in 2001 alongside a continued development of their Connect software platform both for internal usage and external sales. By late 2001, customers for the platform, increasingly seen as one of the best in the exchange marketplace, included the Tokyo International Financial Futures Exchange, and Old Mutual who wished to create a London-based ECN.

Meanwhile, in Chicago the election of David Brennan as the CBOT Chairman, had occasion to arouse the tempers of many market participants when it was discovered that he had somewhat hamfistedly tried to oust Tom Donovan, an astute political operator and the veteran CEO of CBOT. Donovan was incensed and demanded a public retraction from Brennan. On Monday April 19th, 1999, a CBOT Press Release headlined "CBOT Board of Directors Takes Action" included a rather humiliating apology by Chairman Brennan:

> President Thomas Donovan has my complete support and confidence, as well as that of the Board of Directors, through the term of his contract (December 2002). I sincerely regret and accept responsibility for the events of the past week. I intend to demonstrate that Tom and I can work together and

I will enthusiastically work with and support President Donovan and his staff at the Chicago Board of Trade for the balance of my tenure as Chairman.

In fact, Donovan's tenure was not remotely assured and in early April 2000 rumors began circulating that Donovan was in talks to bring his contract to an early halt. In the end, Donovan resigned and exited stage left on April 14th with reputedly as much as $10 million in his pocket. Donovan had been President and CEO of the CBOT since August 18th, 1982 having first joined the exchange as Secretary in May 1979. His departure marked the end of an era at the CBOT – although it didn't mark an end to the exchange's endless politicking nor did it materially improve the CBOT's chances of surviving the revolution in the short term, despite Donovan having long been seen by many observers as somewhat out of touch with the digital world now beginning to shape capital markets.

Brennan himself exited the Chairman's office on December 6th, 2000 when Nick Neubauer deposed him by the narrow margin of 7 5/6th votes. Then again Brennan had edged out Pat Arbor by only 18 5/6th votes. Brennan was in many ways the reluctant Chairman and his general lack of gregariousness probably hindered his impact in that office. One Chicago derivatives personality subsequently noted that as far as he was concerned "Of course, BooBoo the chimp would have been a better Chairman than Brennan." The most significant issue once the interminable politicking was stripped away was that the CBOT was hugely divided amongst its membership and no Chairman appeared capable of uniting the disparate factions. In an effort to demonstrate his desire to be seen only as an interim figure in the CBOT's transition, Neubauer committed himself to serving only one term as Chairman.

About his role of Chairman, in March 2000, Neubauer said

People asked me, "Why did you want this job?" Their assumption was that the Board of Trade was in trouble. Well, I wanted this job because I believed that the exchange could turn itself around and be highly successful by following simple business practices. As a businessman who owns memberships at the exchange, I believed our problems were those of just about any other membership organization, whether it is another exchange or any organization which was run in a not-for-profit manner. The Board of Trade was just not running things as efficiently as we should have been. And by taking a business approach, I knew we could capture the sound business potential that we have at the exchange, and that we could turn it into a successful, for-profit institution.

The CEO of the Board of Trade Clearing Corporation, the central counterparty settlement agency affiliated with the CBOT (but operating independently even nowadays on behalf of competitors to the CBOT such as Brokertec) Dennis Dutterer, became acting CEO of the CBOT between April 19th 2000 and January 15th 2001. Perhaps his most significant achievement as acting CBOT CEO was to launch the a/c/e electronic system (part of the final EUREX/CBOT agreement of October 1999) using EUREX technology on time, within budget and without any headline-grabbing problems on August 27th 2000.

With the arrival on February 20th 2001 of a new CEO, David Vitale a former Vice-Chairman and director of Bank One, the CBOT's top management became transformed although the truly radical overhaul the exchange needs if it is to survive credibly still eludes it at the time of writing.

Alas, the retrograde forces were making greater inroads at CBOT than anywhere else. The CBOT's restructuring plan was starting to look less feasible as members of the old guard within the pits disliked losing the power to control their destinies. By late 2002, rumors abounded of friction between the pragmatic CEO Vitale and Chairman Neubauer who appeared to be moving towards the reactionary camp. Self-interest to keep making money the old-fashioned pit-trading way was becoming more of an issue than the overall prospects for the CBOT institution. Tragically, there is a sense amongst too many traders in Chicago's and New York's floor trading communities that they are the only game in town, or perhaps in the world.

Part of the swaggering arrogance of many CBOT members had been built up over its apparent initial victories against recent competition. The world's largest cash Bond brokerage, New York based Cantor Fitzgerald had established Cantor Exchange and tried direct competition with the CBOT during 2000 and 2001. However, the Cantor Exchange lacked volume in futures and when the parent company suffered vast staff losses when its headquarters in the World Trade Center were destroyed, the Cantor Exchange was suspended and has not reopened at the time of writing. Meanwhile, the Brokertec consortium consisting of ten leading US-based investment banks had created an electronic cash bond platform and subsequently a futures platform which launched in late 2001. The CBOT traders remained dismissive of its potential, although the flexibility and caliber of the Brokertec management, not beholden to any of the legacy issues at the CBOT, and armed with a state-of-the-art OM-based trading system made Brokertec a formidable foe. The fact that the CBOT locals felt they were increasingly invincible was a frightening indictment of just how much they had begun to believe in their own invincibility and were reluctant to see the game in a holistic fashion. Whether they ever do or not, their destiny will increasingly be shaped by forces they can have no hope of controlling. As a hardened observer of the Chicago pits noted:

> One of these days, the pit traders could wake up and find themselves trading baseball cards with each other, while true price discovery and risk-management is conducted electronically elsewhere by people who don't have to be members of the club to play.

The situation at the CME across Chicago was somewhat more subtle. There, the movement towards reform was moving ahead at greater speed under Chairman Scott Gordon and the experienced investment banking CEO Jim McNulty. Nevertheless, there remained simmering discontent from some quarters. Meanwhile, at the CBOE options exchange, the sudden slide in the value of the stock market had left volumes somewhat depressed. Overall, the predominantly open outcry Chicago exchanges seemed as far removed from each other as ever when suddenly a bombshell was dropped by the resurgent LIFFE.

LIFFE-NASDAQ – a moldbreaking joint venture?

The exchange world has long held that alliances are beneficial when, with a couple of possible exceptions, they have barely been worth the frequent flyer miles earned during their creation. This was especially true of the likes of the "Global Equity Market" (GEM) alliance which was created by NYSE exhibiting a sort of imperial viewpoint of the world and which was essentially joined by various overseas exchanges which had grown tired of being "two-timed" in their negotiations with NASDAQ. NASDAQ had long been held to be promiscuous in its dealings with alliances, having a multiplicity of bilateral ties which seemed to be shuffled as and when the NASDAQ empire believed it had a better prospect looming from another (perhaps competing) bourse. The end result was a gem which was rough and uncut.

The NASDAQ exchange, having long sought a means to create a foothold in the derivatives business, finally found a groundbreaking deal by announcing a joint venture in early 2001 with LIFFE to create an American-based platform for the nascent Single Stock Futures product, gradually emerging from regulatory purdah after reforms at the tail end of the Clinton regime in late 2000. The new market was a 50/50 joint venture and LIFFE would provide the Connect technology to build the world's first single stock futures exchange. For LIFFE, this meant they now had a strong bridgehead directly into the world's largest equity market with a universally recognized brand and the killer Rolodex of American cash equity contacts to add to LIFFE's compendium of names from the derivatives business world-wide.

Suddenly with the gauntlet thrown down, Chicago rallied and in an unprecedented move, the CBOE, CBOT and CME came together to create the first United Chicago venture, later christened OneChicago. As befitted its somewhat lesser status in the equity derivatives arena, CBOT would have a 10% share and the

CBOE/CME were dominant with 45% each. Perhaps most significantly of all, the new venture agreed that it would trade only electronically. The former reformist Chairman of the US regulators CFTC, William Rainer, was appointed as CEO, helping to calm outside fears of the potential independence of the board. As always in Chicago, many onlookers were concerned that the organization may yet be riven by political infighting between the board members representing the self-interest of their shareholder exchanges.

The creation of OneChicago was a watershed in Chicago exchange history and the deal had been driven primarily by Chairman Gordon and CEO McNulty of the CME. It demonstrated several issues. For example, the newly commercializing exchanges (US markets were mostly moving towards demutualization at different paces in 2001/2002 with CME largely ahead of all the others) would do deals for the best interest of the body corporate and not necessarily the local traders and seat holders. The creation of a separate company which was all-electronic served as notice that floor trading would not have an indefinite lifetime, while at the same time nobody wanted a disorderly transition from floor to screen as it was invariably detrimental to both individual traders and the exchanges as a whole. Equally, the joint venture route emphasized the independence of management from traders' narrower issues. Finally, the idea that the Chicago exchanges could at last get their act together to create a single venture (albeit on new turf where each market had a certain potential synergy but no business *per se*) was a very dramatic turning point in the Chicago exchange landscape.

The biggest question still overhanging the single stock futures marketplace was just when they would finally get the green light from regulators. The politically charged relations between the SEC (equities) and CFTC (exchange traded derivatives) over this hybrid product continued to ensure delays to the product launch. These delays were compounded by 09/11 after which the two main exchanges sought a delay in trading until March 2002. But by that date, the regulators still hadn't managed to complete their required tasks and the launch of single stock futures continued to delay. The regulators finally agreed the necessary rules in late summer 2002 and OneChicago expect to begin trading in November 2002.

With a very powerful duopoly already established, it looked as if single stock futures would be fought out exclusively between LIFFE NASDAQ and OneChicago. However, in February 2002, a third player entered the ring. The Bourse de Montreal had been the first to trade single stock futures in North America during January 2001. However, the relatively small Canadian market had failed to attract much business, at least in part due to the regulatory ban south of the border. Nevertheless, CEO Luc Bertrand saw a clear opportunity to press his business into the US and they announced the creation of a venture with leading global online company Interactive Brokers LLC (based in Greenwich, Connecticut) and the Boston Stock Exchange to develop BOX, the Boston Options Exchange Group LLC, a for-profit company to deal in options on US equities, equity indices, ETFs and single stock futures. While initially an options market, BOX evidently had intentions to offer the broad range of equity derivative products.

The single stock futures agreement of LIFFE NASDAQ undoubtedly proved a catalyst in moving the Chicago exchanges towards co-operation culminating in OneChicago. Nevertheless, each Chicago exchange faced internal political issues which left them fighting differing amounts of rearguard action when they needed to move forward rapidly with their own businesses. Sharp volume increases during 2001 in many products in some ways masked the problems the exchanges faced while there was still the possibility that exchanges were spending too much time evaluating the threat of existing markets attacking their franchise rather than concerning themselves with new market entrants.

Meanwhile, in left field ...

Of course as all these maneuverings were going on, relatively little attention was being paid to the more interesting movements from left field. On March 21st, 2000 the upstart Intercontinental Exchange (ICE) was launched. Founded by exchange outsider Jeff Sprecher and based in Atlanta, Georgia, it has become a leading global player in the precious metals and energy product arenas, since its commencement of trading in late August 2000. Sprecher's charismatic ability to build a shareholder base comprising key investment banks and major energy companies has been a significant factor in the rise to prominence of ICE as a significant player in the energy and precious metals marketplace.

Within a year of beginning trading, the IPE made a significant strategic move in June 2001, acquiring the London International Petroleum Exchange in a deal valued at £90 million. The strategic purchase of Europe's leading energy exchange, was all the more remarkable given that the world's biggest energy and precious metals exchange, the New York Mercantile Exchange had been pursuing the IPE for several years and found itself being squeezed out by an upstart newcomer. This was the first instance of a significant left field player coming from absolutely nowhere to make a significant impact on the legacy exchanges.

Of course, to the members of the New York Stock Exchange or the various American Boards of Trade, such a takeover maneuver in the energy markets may have seemed far removed from their own markets but the fact remains that left field players can emerge much faster than many established exchanges can coherently deal with that threat. There are multiple product areas which could be copied by a newcomer like ICE and the notion that the world's exchange playing field will remain the sole preserve of the legacy providers of exchange services has already been disproved by ICE.

The B2B revolution

It was Bob Metcalfe, inventor of the Ethernet networking standard, who in many ways demonstrated the innate power of what has become the B2B ("business to business") revolution, when he first noticed that the value of a network increases by the square of the number of people or things connected to the network. With the rise to power of the internet, many people have sought to harness the power of that network to bring together customers and businesses in various fashions (e.g. consumer to consumer (C2C) such as eBay's online auction platform, B2C like Amazon.com or indeed C2B as in Priceline.

The B2B revolution may be over according to some misinformed folk. In reality, it is only in its very earliest stages. What one needs to differentiate between is the price bubble in dotcom stocks, including many B2B shares, and the actual activity of the B2B marketplace. True, many venture capitalists got their fingers burnt but then again a lot of people got caught up in failing to spot the key essential to the Capital Market Revolution – technology is merely a tool. Giddy values were ascribed to the technology itself when in reality it could be readily replicated. The cost of building and selling an exchange system for the vast majority of B2B applications ought to be low. Yet by AD 2000, the market was flooded by multi-million dollar solutions. By mid-2002 the market was readjusting with much more reasonably priced offerings from the likes of COMDAQ to create tailor-made online market solutions at a fraction of the top of bull-market prices.

Likewise, many early B2B entrepreneurs failed to readily gauge the needs of their marketplace and also the many likely impediments to technological innovation placed by folk in the supply and pricing chain who felt their jobs to be at risk. Thirdly, a key foible of the B2B exchange revolution was to fail to differentiate between the one to many market and the many to many market. In this respect, Enron was never a genuine exchange as it was merely a monopoly supplier of prices to its customers. On the other hand, one key lesson of Enron was the lack of central counterparty clearing infrastructure during the birth period of electronic B2B market. In this respect it was more the difficulty in finding clearing arrangements due to the lack of speed of clearing houses in responding to the B2B explosion which arguably exacerbated the problem of CCP in new markets. Admittedly the clearing houses could reasonably claim to have had other issues taking up much of their attention – such as the race for Eurozone clearing domination. Likewise, many initial B2B markets sought to replicate the large derivatives and cash exchanges with continuous hours of trading which really was a few steps further than the sort of auction-based and/or tender processes that the fledgling B2B market actually required – and indeed was ready to cope with. Nevertheless, the prospects for the B2B exchange remain enormous as their core business model harnesses the concept of increasing returns from scale as opposed to the diminishing returns of the industrial age.

The initial overemphasis of the B2B community on fully automated exchanges was a problem but subsequently more marketplaces have been built on the other models, namely, auction markets, post-and-browse markets (essentially sophisticated bulletin boards) and trading hubs ("virtual storefronts" creating almost a sort of "virtual mall" with both buyers and sellers). While some organizations have already made a vast impact on the B2B community, such as ICE in precious metals and especially energy products, the B2B business remains in its infancy with vast possibilities throughout the world. True, raw commodity markets may be difficult to trade because of government subsidies *et al*. However, for those markets which can manage to operate below the current scale required by the large legacy exchanges, there are many great niche opportunities. The author for example was a founder of the world's first essential oil exchange COMDAQ EOE in 2001. Essential oils such as Tea Tree and Lavender are used throughout the world in massage therapies and other health treatments but increasingly find their way into everyday cosmetics such as toothpaste, bath oils and so forth. This is a multi-billion dollar market but still too small for the large legacy exchanges to justify their attempting to add it to their portfolios which are more directed at ubiquitous mass-market commodities such as precious metals like gold and general foodstuffs like wheat as well as energy products such as oil and gas.

The trumpeting that B2B was a killer internet application may have become almost inaudible in the wake of the dotcom bubble bursting but the fact remains that B2B has enormous potential and is actually quietly continuing to reshape supply chains, the transportation process and remove or reorder intermediaries in the supply chain in industries from automobiles to travel. The "rainforest effect" (i.e. the intense competition required in the dense ecosystem under a thick canopy of trees to reach the sunlight – which when achieved they can spread out and grow vast lush green leaves) has been much discussed in the B2B exchange world. The dotcom bubble merely increased the difficulty of planting the seedlings. There is no reason to disbelieve that sound B2B projects will not continue to be created which can ultimately help reshape the dynamics of business supply and inter-business commerce. The dotcom burst was a reaction which corrected the initial over-enthusiasm of some revolutionaries. Nevertheless, the revolution remains intact *per se*. Expect to see greater B2B breakthrough and potential morphing into the legacy exchange business as already practiced by ICE during 2002.

September 11th, 2001

It is difficult for any financial markets professional to remotely express the depth of their feelings as to the events of 09/11. It was a truly abominable event and we all felt for those we knew who were killed, as well as the many thousands in our industry who were affected by the deaths of their friends, colleagues or loved ones. Looking at that dark day some months hence, there are several issues apparent from the simple rationale of the Capital Market Revolution which ought to be addressed, without seeking to discuss Al Qaeda or the atrocity wrought by their barbarism.

From the standpoint of the Capital Market Revolution, several issues became apparent following the events of 09/11. For one thing, despite the fact that the New York Board of Trade's floor at the World Trade Center was destroyed, that exchange has continued to seek a replacement floor. Yet, if anything was apparent from 09/11, it was that target buildings remain a massive terrorist risk. This has been equally true of the London Stock Exchange and many other floors (e.g. the Colombo Stock Exchange in Sri Lanka, often evacuated for fear of attack by Tamil Tiger separatists). In a digital world, it is notable that the whole ability to wreak havoc is much reduced, if the exchange has no true physical core. Already, the NYSE has reduced its plans to build a 90-story tower for its new headquarters. I remain doubtful that there actually will ever be a new floor for the NYSE. Given the unhealthy economics of floor trading and the need to reform the specialist system of market making privilege, sooner or later it seems plausible the NYSE will look at building their marketplace as an electronic exchange, or face oblivion through the fierce competition of electronic markets.

One other issue which was readily apparent from 09/11 was the lack of true thinking behind disaster-recovery procedures. Many telephone lines ran through the WTC and surrounding area or were dependent on satellite towers on its roof. The nature of redundancy, if not many of the basic tenets of disaster recovery, have already been rethought and with justification. After 09/11 many banks moved to their disaster-recovery sites in nearby New Jersey across the Hudson River, but found themselves still unable to operate as their telephone lines ran through the WTC and immediate surrounding area. Similar situations with core hub phone networks exist in other centers – for example just outside the Bank of England in the heart of the City of London. Meanwhile, one key issue for all banks (and indeed other organizations) should be to follow the example of several London organizations (such as LIFFE) who, while acknowledging that their back-up locations exist, refuse to inform the public domain where they are located. Such secrecy seems eminently sensible.

There is already an increasing movement of many staff out of central business district (CBD) areas. While I expect many banks to retain their headquarters downtown in the CBDs, there is no reason to keep support staff within expensive downtown real estate. 09/11 only accelerated this already growing trend. Similarly, the sheer number of people in the food chain will continue to be reduced. Nobody really wishes to note that many of those tragically killed on 09/11 are now being replaced by automated systems. Certainly, the brokerage market has become increasingly digitized in recent months. Once faced with the choice of restaffing or reworking procedures, on account of this tragedy, brokerage bosses have moved to reduce as many people from the food chain as possible. City authorities face a difficult task in stabilizing their CBD's economics but it remains a goal they can achieve, even if it may mean some pain in the medium term.

Paper overhangs

Perhaps the least discussed and yet potentially the most systematically dangerous issue of the 09/11 attacks (from a purely operational viewpoint) was the danger posed by some of the US's relatively antiquated clearing systems. At 55 Waters Street, a few blocks from ground zero, stands the fairly nondescript headquarters of the Government Securities Clearing Corporation (GSCC) which clears government bond transactions. In the vaults are literally millions of certificates relating to redeemed and still active issues of Bonds. The GSCC is a very clear example of how the front end of markets may seem to be in the vanguard of digital markets but, in reality, sooner or later the paper trail emerges from the bits and bytes, creating something falling short of the digital market ideal. Quite simply, too many transactions end up being validated by possession of a sheet of paper. The buzzword of clearing by 2005 will ultimately be "dematerialization" – the ability to remove the paper chain and take certificates out of circulation. Until then, the prospects of a massive event (whether man-made or natural disaster) destroying a major depository such as the GSCC or the DTCC (equity clearing house) could simply render a market such as the powerhouse US stock or Bond markets closed until further notice. Such an action could cause a truly cataclysmic economic response as a result of a rather justified collapse in confidence in the system. In the medium term, I expect to see ultimately a US government response to aid the clearing process, as dematerialization will probably take some five years in the US. This will be a major project but it remains a vital one if markets are to be made impregnable from cataclysmic events, and indeed if markets are to be able to truly profit from digital straight-through processing (STP).

The reaction

Nevertheless, while the obvious conclusion to the 09/11 disaster was to see many reasons why technology is needed to shore up the system and remove potential problems in the future, the Luddites have continued to work hard to stymie progress. The fact that the NYSE and NYBOT, to name but two, have hardened their view that new floors must be built is simply remarkable. Ironically, the New York exchanges themselves have been at loggerheads in some instances. The NYSE's "hospitality" towards its cross-town rival AMEX (whose floor was closed for some weeks) seemed to be at best a bear hug suffocating the AMEX's exchange traded fund (ETF) marketplace to the benefit of the NYSE's nascent ETF market. The NYSE was accused of – amongst other things – restricting local trader access to the NYSE room where AMEX was temporarily housed, creating what *The Economist* termed "bitter sweet charity." Ironically, while NYSE's fledgling ETF market boomed at AMEX's expense, the biggest winner was the Island ECN whose electronic order matching became the biggest single transaction platform for ETFs in the world. Ironically, the latter fact seemed to go unnoticed in the wake of AMEX's parent NASD placing the exchange up for sale early in 2002.

Theodore turns up the heat

In the weekend after Labor Day and just days before the events of 09/11, the Swiss Futures and Options Association in the scenic Burgenstock resort above Lake Lucerne, hosted its annual meeting for the world's leading derivatives exchanges. One especially troubled-looking figure was Jean-François Theodore, CEO of Euronext. Having taken ParisBourse from the periphery of the European stock market dominance game when Deutsche Börse and the London Stock Exchange were regarded as the likely final duopolists, Theodore had managed the first significant cross-border European merger bringing Amsterdam and Brussels together to create Euronext on September 22nd, 2000. However, by September 2001, Theodore's impetus was running out of steam. In fact, it was beginning to look like he would occupy a mere footnote in history thanks to his creating the first pan-European merger. Nevertheless, he had managed an IPO in a fairly poor market on July 5th, 2001 which had raised some 400 million Euros, a handy war chest if a suitable deal should arise. Fate was to deal Theodore a wonderful opportunity within days.

The LSE makes the pace, loses the race

When she was appointed as the first female CEO of the London Stock Exchange, the BBC tartly noted "The stock exchange is in dire need of a strategy to beat off the competition." The appointment of the Canadian born to Dutch parents, Furse, a 43-year-old derivatives veteran was greeted with some surprise in late January, 2001. Furse had been on the LIFFE Board from 1990 until 1999 and Deputy Chairman during the later stages of this tenure. The LSE itself had fought off an audacious bid from the Swedish OM group in late 2000 and had also failed to cement a merger with the Deutsche Börse some months earlier. The LSE's Chairman Don Cruickshank, a former telephone regulator, was under fire for his handling of affairs at the exchange and the previous CEO, Gavin Casey had been pushed out following members' unease at the failure of the Deutsche Börse merger. Indeed, the CEO position at the Stock Exchange had been a poisoned chalice for some years. Casey's predecessor as CEO, Michael Lawrence, had left office in 1996 under a certain storm of criticism while Peter Rawlins left office after the débâcle concerning the failure to create a workable Taurus back office system in 1993. One leading LSE figure, Brian Winterflood, greeted Clara Furse's appointment with the words: "The boys have made a mess of it, so why not let the girls have a go?"

During 2001, the London Stock Exchange spent months courting LIFFE with a view to a merger. Ironically, it had shown no desire to take LIFFE on when it was in difficulties during the dark days of 1998/99. However, with the appointment of Furse as CEO, the LSE had suddenly become enamoured of the many benefits to be had from a merger of the two organizations. However, as I have noted before, while cross-asset-class exchanges can be beneficial, merely "marrying your cousins does not necessarily improve the quality of the gene pool."

The smoothly oiled wheels of the LSE press machine spent the summer assuring the public via many fairly complacent media outlets that the future of LIFFE was assuredly in the LSE's hands. Yet in the event, the LSE would fail to acquire LIFFE, having made various rather significant errors in the process.

LIFFE was officially recorded as being "in play" on Friday September 28th, when LIFFE issued a press release noting that they had received approaches about a takeover. The release had been precipitated by a story in the British *Daily Mirror* newspaper headlined "LIFFE Saver – Treasury and Bank [of England] Yes to Stock Exchange Deal." In the background, the Euronext team and a group at EUREX pressed themselves into action to try to wrest control of LIFFE from the jaws of the LSE. In the event, the LSE opened proceedings by somewhat shooting themselves in the foot by making an opening offer then attempting to withdraw it when the LSE claimed it wasn't aware of the extent of LIFFE's executive options scheme. This seemed an interesting gambit given the fact that all the details were publicly available in the LIFFE annual report. In the interim, LIFFE essentially put itself up for auction. For LIFFE, the decision was precipitated by several issues, not least of which was the fairly substantial sums of money being readily offered. Equally, the exchange's management knew that a major shareholder, Battery Ventures, had suffered enormous losses in the dotcom collapse and the possibility of a cash injection through selling LIFFE shares would be a welcome relief. The LIFFE Board invited presentations from interested parties on Tuesday October 16th. Throughout, much of the media were convinced that the LSE was simply about to walk the process. In reality, behind the scenes, it appeared that the LSE's negotiating approach must have become somewhat disconnected from the *realpolitik* of the situation.

On Thursday 25th October, the recently appointed CEO of EUREX, former Goldman Sachs banker Rudolf Ferscha, made a brilliant pitch. A year earlier it would have been almost inconceivable that EUREX would have even come close to making a bid for LIFFE. In truth, the bidding war was probably just too soon into Ferscha's tenure (DTB/EUREX founding CEO Jorg Franke had himself pragmatically retired earlier in 2001 having steered the exchange from nowhere to global leadership). Some reports later suggested that Ferscha's pitch had even managed to ease the LSE into third place in the overall bidding. Certainly whatever the LSE said during that meeting, it was insufficient to win the day. However, LIFFE made all the bidders wait just a little while longer before announcing the result of their deliberations. On Friday 26th October, LIFFE noted it would continue to consider its options over the weekend and announce a result on Monday 29th.

The end result of this auction process was fascinating. Despite tabling the highest bid of £19 per share, the LSE lost the day. Instead, it was the all-cash offer by Euronext which was recommended by the board to shareholders of £18.25 per share. When it came to the crunch, the LSE had made an offer of £19 part in cash (£12) and part in shares (£7). There was surely some irony in Europe's supposedly leading capital market being unable to tap its members for enough cash to buy the LIFFE exchange. After all, if the LSE which was listed on its own market could not manage to raise a few hundred million pounds using its own apparatus, who could? Certainly, LIFFE's board was unimpressed and voted for the better operating synergies and all-cash offer as presented by Euronext. Remarkably, despite a great deal of fury in the City of London at the LSE's apparently rather inept bidding tactics, both CEO Furse and Chairman Cruickshank kept their jobs. Euronext, led by Jean-François Theodore, had outpointed the LSE not merely through their all-cash offer but also thanks to a very strong degree of management flexibility afforded to LIFFE to run not merely their existing business but also to integrate the existing Euronext derivatives business in Paris, Amsterdam and Brussels.

The London Stock Exchange had according to some sources appeared the weakest of the three presentations. It wasn't clear what synergies they offered. After all, LSE Chairman Don Cruickshank, a former UK telecom regulator, had publicly rubbished the LIFFE Connect software only months earlier. Intriguingly, despite offering a very close rival system called NSC VF, Jean-François Theodore had bravely praised LIFFE Connect in public at around the same time. Ultimately, LIFFE Connect became the derivative system for all Euronext products. However, the LSE not only appeared to have a slightly schizophrenic approach to their bid, they also spent an inordinate amount of time briefing the press about how favorably it was going. The end result was somewhat embarrassing not merely for LSE but also for many reputable financial journalists who had lapped up the LSE message. One leading London newspaper correspondent reportedly walked out of a briefing simply incandescent with rage that the LIFFE management could have done a deal which the media had largely failed to see coming.

The future of LIFFE, once written off by the very same journalists who had championed the LSE's unsuccessful bid left several key winners. Jean-François Theodore retained his mantle as the Charlemagne of the European bourses (with not a little of Napoleon's strategic brilliance and sheer opportunism). From a

British perspective, however Brian Williamson was the hero of the hour. He would soon be deservedly knighted for his services to Britain's financial markets for being the only man in history to nurse an exchange from intensive care, against all odds back to a profitable position with remarkable prospects ahead of it. Perhaps more significantly for Williamson personally, he took a handy slice of about £6 million in profits from his shares – many of which he had bought when nobody else gave LIFFE a remote chance of survival. Some in the UK media, as is their wont, felt Williamson's profits were somewhat over the top for his input. Yet, had Williamson taken LIFFE via an LBO, he would have undoubtedly pocketed a vast percentage of the profits. In the result, his share was not merely entirely deserved, it was arguably small fry for the man who had single-handedly engineered the resurrection of LIFFE back from the dead to become a stunning example of the potential for markets in the Capital Market Revolution.

> For the want of a nail, the shoe was lost;
> For the want of a shoe, the horse was lost;
> For the want of a horse, the rider was lost;
> For the want of a rider, the battle was lost;
> For the want of a battle, the kingdom was lost!
>   George Herbert.

The Capital Market Revolution is continuing to occur against a background of what is truly a "winner takes all" scenario (although competition regulation may retain competitive duopolies rather than permit monopolies in exchanges). In this respect, the winners and losers in these processes can be seen to be very marked. The London Stock Exchange, having failed to merge with Deutsche Börse and then repelling the OM merger, had set acquiring LIFFE as its key target. Unfortunately, in failing to go that little extra distance in guaranteeing management flexibility and providing an all-cash offer, the LSE suddenly found itself for the first time effectively lagging a DB/Euronext duopoly for domination of Europe's exchanges. The LSE's whole future strategy was in doubt.

Meanwhile, Jean-François Theodore had once again come back from being written off. In the late 1990s he seemed to have done a sound job in bringing the ParisBourse closer to the mainstream of digital capitalism but had little chance of getting his charge into the winner's enclosure. By creating the first substantial pan-European exchange merger in Euronext he suddenly catapulted himself back to prominence. Having sat by while the DB/LSE merger talks foundered, Theodore had demonstrated the utmost tenacity in snatching LIFFE out of the jaws of what had been seen as a foregone conclusion in favor of the LSE. Euronext still had a long way to go but by bringing all its derivatives operations together under LIFFE's auspices, suddenly Euronext was close to being the world's biggest exchange by volume alongside the Swiss-German EUREX powerhouse. EUREX itself was unlucky that the LIFFE auction occurred earlier than it would have liked but it retained a significant powerhouse potential in the derivatives markets which, with the strength of its Deutsche Börse parent, made the organization still look like a winner. Indeed, Deutsche Börse itself would begin 2002 with a striking victory, taking over the 50% of the Clearstream clearing settlement organization it did not already own. Some market participants were unhappy at what they regarded as a virtual annexation of Clearstream when DB used their exclusive negotiation option to secure a takeover deal. Werner Seifert looked every inch a winner as he neatly added a great deal of bulk to his "vertical silo" (i.e. "one-stop shop" encompassing everything from trade processing to clearing and settlement.

Having built a strong though by no means monopolistic franchise in German stocks at Deutsche Börse, Seifert would find himself faced with a new challenge in June 2002 when the NASDAQ exchange made another foray into Europe. Having purchased EASDAQ, a NASDAQ-style growth market as a sort of bridgehead into Europe in 2001, NASDAQ agreed in mid-2002 to partner with various German banks and brokers seeking to compete with DB. In some respects, it looked like a nightmare scenario for the pipe-smoking Seifert. A pair of major banks (Commerzbank and Dresdner) combining with a major US exchange and the tiny Berlin and Bremen stock markets in his own backyard seemed formidable on paper. On the other hand, NASDAQ had not made any great progress with its various overseas developments previously such as the NASDAQ Japan venture. Whether Deutsche NASDAQ would be any different remained to be seen. However, somewhat luckily for Seifert, the arrival of a local competitor now made it easier for him to press on with his empire building under less threat of coming under pressure for being a monopolist in his market sector. In one respect at least, NASDAQ may have played right into Seifert's hands.

Amex – unloved?

Meanwhile NASDAQ had been trying to sell off its open outcry Amex stock exchange bought in the late 1990s. Despite being a sound pool of liquidity in several arenas, such as ETFs and options, buyers were thin on the ground. With the US International Securities Exchange demonstrating great advantages in its electronic trading platform over the established open outcry markets and following a difficult period for Amex after the closure of its floor in the wake of 09/11, buyers were relatively scarce. As DB's Seifert noted in mid-2002, the issue of taking over exchanges was all a question of how much one wished to digest an exchange rather than merely seeking to suck it dry of its content through outright competition. Increasingly, the leaders in the revolution were seeking to embrace the reign-of-terror phase of the revolution in exchange terms, rather than just buy every pool of liquidity they could find. Few smaller exchanges would take notice of this fact until it was too late. However, the fact is that with big being better for exchange profitability, unless smaller markets could occupy a sound niche, they faced extinction when the big players sought to lay siege to their products.

So, the American Stock Exchange, originally the kerb exchange around the corner from Wall Street, remained unsold. Of course, the fact that the only proven predators in the global exchange business were still fixated with European domination probably didn't help.

Nevertheless, as summer went on, the rumors continued that the London Stock Exchange was looking across the Atlantic for its next move.

With EUREX seeking to make its silo dominant, the Brussels/Paris-based mutual organization Euroclear announced a merger on July 4th 2002, with London's CrestCo, the settlement company set up when the LSE abandoned the Taurus project in the early 1990s. With more than half of Europe's domestic bond business and some 60% of Europe's top 300 shares, the new institution was a strong rival to DB. Euroclear and CrestCo had settled some 120 million transactions during 2001 with a total value of some $213.6 trillion. They held more than £6.6 trillion of assets in custody at the end of the year. Market users were eagerly anticipating the proposed cost cuts for cross-border settlement costs in Belgian, Dutch, French, Irish and British securities by more than 90%, although most of these savings would not emerge until the delivery of a new single settlement engine due in 2005 while full consolidation was not expected until 2008. Market cynics were wont to note that on this timeframe, it was a case of tomorrow's jam being forward discounted somewhere into the midst of the yield curve.

US reactions and reverberations

While the Europeans were still jostling for position in a sort of sophisticated land grab rather akin to the actions of the great powers in the nineteenth century, in the US exchange politics continued to be dominated largely by the position of individual members keen to maintain the status quo. The CBOT seemed to be somewhat stagnant under Chairman Neubauer while the CBOE options market was losing market share at giddying rates to the pioneering electronic ISE which had begun trading only on May 26th 2000, yet was already the overall market leader in all the options it listed just over two years later. On May 1st 2002, the ISE announced its demutualization while the CBOE was beginning a round of bloodletting. The problem for CBOE was that the members regarded the floor as a sacred cow and in the Capital Market Revolution nobody could afford to have any sacred cows, especially not those which occupied tens of thousands of square feet of prime CBD floor.

In late April 2002 the CME underwent what some might call a sort of perverse velvet revolution. Chairman Scott Gordon had assumed office when the CME felt very much pressurized by the potential pressures of the revolution. In close co-operation with new CEO Jim McNulty (who had a strong investment banking pedigree) they set about radically revising the entire make-up of the CME. Previously dominated by committees, by early 2002 the committee structure had been slimmed down by some 85%. Nevertheless, as a result of various initiatives, such as seeking to cut out the annual six-figure US dollar retainers paid to former Chairmen Leo Melamed and Jack Sandner, ultimately Scott Gordon himself was gently eased out of the Chairman's office in favor of Hog trader Terry Duffy. The CME was moving forward but even in the most advanced revolutionary organization in the US, there was the possibility of reaction. The CME's biggest problem seemed to be that the members were unwilling to give up their influence in return for a proper corporate governance structure.

Gordon had achieved a remarkable amount during his office from January 1998 until April 2002. His legacy would remain as perhaps one of the most successful CME Chairmen of all time. When he entered office the exchange had been bitterly divided on so many grounds it seemed almost to his credit that he had been edged out of office on such relatively trivial issues! When Gordon had entered office, his members were wondering how he could save the exchange from extinction. By the time he left, the exchange was *en route* to an IPO, with a viable electronic trading system often being used for daytime trading as well as a range of after-hours markets. The floor was gradually being phased out and the CME had become a for-profit demutualized corporation in 2000. Given that exchange Chairmen have often left office with some form of petulant behavior, Gordon's mature approach to leaving office only added to his reputation. In his resignation letter of April 25th, 2002, Gordon added sapiently:

We have much to be proud of, but we cannot let our recent success lull us into complacency. The fact remains that the competitive landscape is no less treacherous than it was four years ago. The bottom line is simple. We must continue to embrace the change that surrounds us and turn every challenge into opportunity.

Every exchange ought to have this statement at least on their desk if not tattooed somewhere highly visible.

No rest for the wicked

For Sir Brian Williamson and his team under Hugh Freedburg in London, having nursed LIFFE back to life, there was no rest to be had. Integrating the Amsterdam, Brussels and Paris markets (as well as Lisbon, a recent arrival in the Euronext organization) onto LIFFE Connect (including closing the successful Amsterdam options floor) was now a priority for the LIFFE team. More job cuts were undertaken within months, as the organization sought to rationalize itself to fighting weight. If anything was apparent to Chairman Williamson and CEO Hugh Freedburg, the revolution made breathing space for no man. However, the challenge of becoming the derivatives powerhouse of Euronext was a task which both men would relish.

Lest LIFFE Euronext or other markets might feel inclined to rest on their laurels for even a nanosecond, there was a breakthrough announcement from Chicago on July 11th, 2002 that the CBOT had downgraded their partnership agreement with EUREX to become effectively a customer for the Swiss-German exchange's software platform. The dropping of most of the restrictive covenants on listing US dollar contracts (aside from in each party's core markets) placed EUREX back into a position to start garnering business directly in the US dollar marketplace. For EUREX it was a green light for growth, for CBOT it was an opportunity to try to reduce costs (despite claims to the contrary from the CBOT management). The reign-of-terror phase of exchange competition was under way with a vengeance.

Note

1. It is an interesting issue for chroniclers of history just where to refer to somebody by their title. In this instance, while I will attribute quotations to Sir Brian Williamson whether they occurred before or after his well-deserved Knighthood, where he is discussed in meetings or other events, he will remain "merely" Brian Williamson in the narrative until his Knighthood occurs in late 2001.

Chapter 4

Teaching Old Dogs New Tricks
Why Exchanges Need to Rethink their Relationship with the Outside World

In the future, the stock market will not revolve around brokers, or dealers, or specialists. It will not be limited to the physical location, to a trading floor, even to a central database. The stock market of the future will take place wherever individuals access each other to trade securities. A seat in the stock exchange of tomorrow will be any chair in front of a computer with a modem.

Andrew Klein, founder Wit Capital Corporation (issuer of the Internet's first IPO)

A death in the club

It is no wonder that so much of the market is resistant to the acceptance of electronic trading. Once information is available on line then the power of the middleman evaporates.

Colin Howard, Chairman, COMDAQ

The status quo in stock markets is not dead. There is simply no more status quo.

The world's major stock markets have undergone considerable transformation during the past twenty years. Unless they wish to face oblivion, they have a lot longer to go yet. In the 1970s and 1980s, the stock market "club" broke down. Fixed commissions and other anti-competitive practices were gradually abolished, although many exchanges are still reluctant to permit new practices. Hong Kong for instance, refused to bite the bullet in 2001 and once again drew back from removing the fixed commissions which cushion an incompetent cartel of brokers from economic reality and harm clients' best interests. When new technology was first mooted, the innate reactionary forces at stock markets across the world meant they balked at change. Such forces remain strong in markets such as New York, where the NYSE holds a tentative grip on the largest stocks but is under increasing fire from the electronic NASDAQ market which has garnered the cream of new technology stocks. Nevertheless, even NASDAQ, despite an image built on a technological theme reminiscent of futurist films such as BladeRunner, still more closely resembles a legacy marketplace than the titan of new technology it likes to proclaim. Nevertheless, in trading terms, the introduction of Supermontage moved it back towards the forefront of digital dealing systems. Moreover, even before Supermontage had appeared, its relatively flexible fully electronic dealing interface was already helping to pressure many ECNs into finding a more tractable revenue model, as mergers in the ECN arena, along with greater diversification into becoming cash and futures exchanges, as well as exploring joint ventures with legacy exchanges, gathered pace.

The Reuters-owned Instinet bought Island in early 2002 not only to bring in new management but also to garner an advantage with the Island exchange projects which were being built up to give the ECN the opportunity to make the key morph of being a proper market as opposed to merely a carbuncle on other exchanges. Likewise, Archipelago had tied itself up with the San Francisco Pacific Coast Exchange in a similar effort to become a proper market as opposed to merely a "bolt-on appendage."

Despite their reputation in many ways as being in the vanguard of innovation, it ought to be clear by now that many exchanges are in fact in the almost oxymoronic vanguard of reaction! A former senior exchange official relates a classic story about an Asian exchange which amply demonstrates the distaste for modern open practices felt not just in this region but throughout the world during recent decades. When a fledgling electronic stock trading system was being demonstrated, the official noted that "the great thing about electronic trading is that it levels the playing field and permits total transparency for all market participants." "Oh well, we certainly don't want that!" replied the Exchange Chairman somewhat indignant at such an irksome notion as providing every trader with the same information.

With the breakdown of fixed commissions came the breakdown (to a large extent anyway) in the old cartels or other rather unsavory practices which marred some areas of stock market trading. Nevertheless, for all the mutterings about the likes of the "Big Bang" in London's securities trading during 1986, the fact remained that stock trading for those outside the large institutions was essentially a difficult business to enter on even remotely equal terms with the other players.

For those who expect the forces of revolution to muster first in one of the very top financial centers such as London, New York and Tokyo, ironically, it was in a country somewhat removed from the financial mainstream where the biggest upheaval would take place before the revolution was even directly under way. In Sydney, the Australian Stock Exchange was created from the disparate regional markets in the major cities of the Antipodean continent during the 1980s and within a short period of time began a nuts-and-bolts reform of the entire dealing process which involved making stock trading electronic in the mid-1980s and ultimately led to the exchange dropping its membership status and metamorphosing into a "for profit" corporation listed on its own marketplace on October 4th, 1999. The process of going electronic was a harrowing one. Former Information Services Director Rory Collins describes it as being akin to "changing the engines on a Boeing 747 while climbing to 35,000 feet across the mid-Atlantic!" Then again, ASX chose a remarkable date to begin their electronic stock trading: Monday October 19th 1987. For the record, after a somewhat stressful session, the system survived the crash unscathed, which was more than could be said for many investors!

But even with such upstart renegades causing waves, everything continued to look fairly rosy for the club to at least continue under slightly more competitive pressures through the mid-1980s and early 1990s. The status quo appeared assured.

The lawyer, the brewer and the case of the very public offering

True originality consists not in a new manner but in a new vision.

Edith Wharton

Lawyer Andrew Klein probably never expected to become a capital market revolutionary. However, following his much publicized offering for the Spring Street microbrewery which was issued directly to the public via the Internet, Klein opted to create the first virtual investment bank in cyberspace. Wit Capital Corporation now issues shares on exchanges direct to the public.

At the height of the dotcom boom, individual investors were embracing the online culture faster than many existing stock exchange members could comprehend. For individual traders, news that Wit were adding considerable free research to their website for all clients to read was only a final confirmation that the old system of broker research being withheld only for the wealthiest private clients and the institutions was dead. Information and price transparency are at the core of the Capital Market Revolution. The fact that even such leviathans of the securities market as Merrill Lynch began giving away their research (for a "trial period") only served to emphasize that the markets were becoming more accessible to retail investors throughout the world. Ironically, like all such events, when given free access, gluttony broke out. The retail investors bought to excess, the venture capitalists helped feed the boom and recriminations would abound in the aftermath with analysts accused of not being objective. It was a classic post-bubble environment. An angry investing public fails to identify its own failings and seeks scapegoats. Genuine issues of fraud and other misleading activity were discovered in many cases. It was little different from the initial railway boom. Nor did the aftermath appreciably differ from the events following the explosion in other new technology situations, for example, railway stock during the initial railway booms of the 1840s in the UK and subsequently in the US. As legendary fund manager John Templeton had noted: "Technology may have changed the world, but it has not changed human nature."

The dotcom bubble was an over-reaction. Retail investors found themselves for the first time with a gilt-edged invitation to the trading buffet and they ate more than they could digest. Ironically, while the recriminations abounded and the analysts cowered under regulatory attack, the fact was that the online marketplace was actually becoming more efficient and cheaper than ever for those who hadn't already blown their investment funds in the bubble. However, the technology was hardly to blame, nor was the revolution itself. Rather, many investors had realized the potential benefits of the digital world but they had simply allowed that basic greed instinct to overwhelm them and they bought stock without thinking that ultimately there needed to be profits to underpin the growth in the share prices. Parameters might shift but ultimately a great many economic realities remain regardless of what some folk may proclaim during such bubbles. Of course in the wake of the dotcom explosion, the fact remained that the infrastructure was still intact for investors to do their own research and create their own portfolios without any human broker input, if they so desired. The online investor retains an unprecedented ability to be master of his own destiny, for richer or poorer, for better or worse.

If an online investment bank can offer to sell equity online and a trader can deal in this stock using the internet, then this begs once again that hoary question of just how much such investment banks are willing to pay for executing business through a particular exchange. With electronic marketplaces such as the Anglo-Swiss Virt-X in the UK able to offer all the facilities of its older and less flexible rival, the London Stock Exchange, it is only a matter of time before the current large exchanges find themselves taking enormous collateral damage from smaller, cheaper, faster markets dependent upon new technology with minuscule staffs. Ironically, those new, smaller hybrid markets will probably be able to undermine even relatively new players such as Virt-X, unless it can demonstrate an ongoing appetite for change.

It is clear, however, that regardless of the shifting landscape of the marketplace the core process of actually buying and selling has remained largely the same. Some markets have experimented with more novel approaches such as Optimark which matched securities trades in a series of "fixes" during the course of each session. Nevertheless, with the exception of some auction features for opening and closing prices at certain markets, the core operation, buying and selling by bidding and offering on a continuous basis, remains the same for matching at virtually all exchanges. The model for the digital exchange of today is therefore something that, in pricing terms at least, appears consistent with practices dating back at least 200 years in the US alone.

Telegraph creates coastal focus, digital unites the world

In the nineteenth century, more than 200 stock exchanges operated in the US. The invention of the telegraph permitted liquidity to flow to a few fixed marketplaces. The telegraph therefore killed all but a handful of US stock markets. Ironically, in the digital revolution some of the walking dead from the telegraphic revolution, such as exchanges in Boston or Chicago who as far as the general public are concerned have been all but hibernating over the past century, have seized the opportunity to exploit digital technology to make them pivotal players in cash and derivatives markets. In the Capital Market Revolution, the capacity of digital technology to bring together all fixed points to another fixed (or indeed floating) point means that the technology of the internet generation will cut a swathe through the world's existing stock exchanges. Fewer than five major stock markets will remain world-wide by 2010. Perhaps two or three of these will be entirely electronic markets which have not yet even been created. No broad-based exchange floor will survive beyond 2005.

Somewhere out there is a bullet with your company's name on it. Somewhere out there is a competitor, unborn and unknown, that will render your business model obsolete.
Hamel and Sampler, in *Fortune* magazine

The big impetus to adopt as slick a method of technological usage as possible will come from a brokerage cost war which will make the already frenzied rate cuts of the past decade look like a mere bagatelle by comparison. It is startling to recall that even such supposed bastions of capitalism as the London Stock Exchange operated a fixed commission market until the mid 1980s. The anachronism of fixed commissions will drive exchanges out of business during the Capital Market Revolution – if any are foolish enough to maintain them beyond the end of 2003. If governments are unable or unwilling to accelerate the deregulation process of financial markets, then deregulated exchanges will simply steal the business from under the noses of the existing bloated cartels that blight a number of economies, most notably in parts of Asia. If the government tries to keep the exchange competition at bay by banning it from existing onshore, it will simply migrate offshore to cyberspace and house its servers in a suitable tax haven. Inefficient brokers and exchanges have nowhere to hide in the information age.

Just as the French revolutionary courts imposed "a reign of terror" with astoundingly bloody consequences, the next phases of the Capital Market Revolution will be a bloody, life-endangering affair for every reactionary bankers' balance sheet. With profits being driven down by decreased revenues, the brokers will have no choice but to sack staff *en masse* in an effort to re-establish equilibrium in the new screen-traded environment. Those brokers whose short-sightedness suggested that getting rid of expensive floor traders would give them respite from the cutting of brokerage rates will find their prospects stymied by an ongoing round of technologically inspired income reduction. The Capital Market Revolution will give the victors great spoils but they will be received only by those who have shown the courage to take risks on innovation. This is not good news for exchanges whose traditional staffers have been used to decision paralysis lest making a choice results in their being singled out for subsequent punishment. Brokers too, need to adopt a more risk-oriented and decision-oriented flexible management structure if they aren't to find themselves being crushed by cost and other disintermediating pressures. Luddites will be doomed. If they have no redeeming skills to be the dealers of the future, then had she been here, we imagine Marie-Antoinette would have offered the suggestion "let them drive cabs." The highways and byways of the county of Essex, east of London, seems to be clogged full of former dealers driving minicabs, following unsuccessful attempts to operate independently from the patronage of large commodity/financial institutions who became unemployed in the first wave of deregulation during the late 1980s. There will be a great many more, for the post-feudal marketplace requires a much broader skill set than many financial markets personnel have ever conceived of.

Already, exchanges are falling by the wayside. Take for instance a commodity which revolves around liquidity, albeit not in the financial markets sense. The London Tea Market enjoyed weekly auctions in the City of London from 1679 until 1998. The decision to close the market in August 1998 was the result of all the key issues which will increasingly afflict the world's other commodity debt and equity exchanges. For a start, there is the question of geography. The London Tea Market was a perfectly sensible venture in the late 17th century when London was the center of tea drinking, the epicenter of a large empire and one of very few economically advanced nations on Earth. By 1998, only the first of these factors was still valid. In the Imperial age, with the product grown overseas in major plantations a considerable distance from London, there was a good reason for the London Tea Market to exist. In 1998, the growers in Africa, India, China and other parts of the world all had access to the internet. They could create their own deals away from the exchange, over the counter. So the market moved electronic. Dealers are no longer obliged to send their representatives to London for the auctions and can transact their tea business from their offices on plantations or at importers and exporters throughout the world. The London tea auction was not a major force in world capital markets. However, the ramifications of the move away from a formal face-to-face structure in a fixed location to a decentralized electronic marketplace will ultimately be felt by every exchange, banker, institution and private individual throughout the world.

The new borderless perspective

The stock exchanges of the future will migrate away from the geographical bounds that the interest groups behind any potential European Stock Exchange seek to retain. Instead of a national view, a sector approach is emerging: for example, investors will not view the market in terms of, say, Germany, Sweden or the UK. Instead, their view will be in terms of pharmaceuticals, IT or forest products.

Per E. Larsson, CEO OM Group

Sector stock exchanges remain a distinct possibility, although to date there have not really been any significant developments. For example, the likes of the ASX in Sydney, or JSE in South Africa could create a global market for resource stocks based around the considerable core competencies of those bourses which list many domestic resources stocks. Similarly, the high-technology stock market for the world essentially already exists. NASDAQ has created a franchise which is still recognized as being a key market for new technology throughout the world, even in the wake of the dotcom collapse, although it has also been trying to expand away from its perceived high-tech niche with overseas ventures in Europe and Asia.

Nevertheless, the problem which faces NASDAQ and all legacy exchanges, is one of opening up their closed systems in a way that prevents their own painful death. This can be referred to as "the Minitel Paradox," after the French information service doomed to ultimate oblivion in the information age. The French videotext service blossomed during the 1980s as a means of gaining information, booking tickets for all forms of leisure pursuit and generally being an excellent tool in the form of a shrunken, less technological version of the internet. However, once the World Wide Web was born, regardless of the French government's natural interventionist inclination to protect their system, Minitel was already in its death throes, even by the time it had finally opened to the rapidly growing internet technology. With financial exchanges, it is precisely the same issue. They simply must obey Drucker's law: "Sooner or later closed systems have to open up or die."

In the late 1990s API (open architecture protocol) mania swept many exchanges world-wide. However, merely allowing anybody to tack a front-end screen to trade your market is insufficient. In the post-feudal marketplace, customers are essentially unconcerned with where they transact their business, rather it will be the marketplace which can marry strong liquidity with good, cheap, execution coupled with cheap, secure clearing that will be of greatest importance. Sadly, the API mania of the late 1990s seems to have led to a bewildering set of different standards. Just as railroads found they worked better in all respects once they found the same gauge, so too the financial markets need to stop arguing over the merits of FIX or other protocols and just get on with producing something which largely fits all markets. Similarly, many exchanges have been spending on technology without realizing that they really need to know just who their clients are. It was all very well for the old-fashioned "clubs" to allow brokers to aggregate their orders to a particular exchange but in the modern era, exchanges need to know better just who their clients are and where they can garner more business. In this respect, exchanges are increasingly going to run into potential conflict with brokers as they must seek to direct large customers to their platforms as cheaply, easily and intermediary-free as possible while brokers of course want to maintain their position in the food chain sacrosanct.

The new merchant princes of capitalism

Clearing members are asking more and more if we need exchanges. Exchanges have every reason to be worried.

John Damgard, President, FIA

For many years clearing houses had little more than bridal status. Even then, they often expected to go to the altar but were jilted before they got there. Yet in the Capital Market Revolution, suddenly clearing houses are the smartest business in town. Interestingly, most clearing houses are already inextricably linked to an existing futures exchange. Major independent entities such as the London Clearing House have truly blossomed in the last few years, by understanding that inclusion and cosmopolitanism are the genuine flavors of the Capital Market Revolution. The LCH's RepoClear may not mean much to the average retail investor but this process has already exceeded all internal estimations and given massive support to the world's government bond markets, by providing solid central counterparty clearing to all players. Such initiatives bind all cash markets with OTC trading and exchange activity. This enables superior collateral management on the part of counterparties and results in lower costs for all participants. A truly virtuous circle born of digital markets.

In olden times clearing houses merely operated what traders regarded as a dull but necessary evil. Clearing houses matched every buyer to every seller and guaranteed that whatever calamities might befall any trader, the counterparty's positions would be safely upheld. Clearing houses guaranteed the standing of locals against the big institutions (and in the case of the collapse of large organizations such as Drexel Burnham Lambert, vice versa). Clearing houses earned a handy stipend for their shareholders but overall their business looked largely unexciting. However, as the effects of the Capital Market Revolution gather pace, it can be seen that in fact clearing houses are about to enter their golden age. In the post-feudal marketplace, the clearing house can act as a king maker in the financial product food chain, adding much-needed credibility in the information age when brands can be created overnight. With the backing of a clearing house, any market mechanism will gain credibility. Moreover, it can be plumbed into the global clearing system without much further ado. It is not all plain sailing; clearing houses themselves are undergoing radical upheaval. Unique amongst existing institutions facing the Capital Market Revolution, theirs is a situation where the market for their services is primed to explode.

At the very core of the stock and futures exchange business, of the leading 20 bourses in the world, at most six or seven will still be independent in 2010. The bulk of this rationalization will have taken place by 2005. Even as this book is being written, a number of merger talks are in process and several more are actively rumored. Although during late summer 2002, it became clear that transatlantic regulatory issues were being blamed for the collapse of serious merger talks between NASDAQ and the London Stock Exchange. Overall, cross-border mergers have been few and far between apart from in Europe, however, the pace of such activity is likely to explode from the middle of 2003 if not before, as the next phase of the revolution starts to see much more blatant open competition for product throughout the world.

I'm not in a position to state categorically which equity or derivatives exchanges will still be in existence by 2010 but I expect the landscape will be radically changed. For one thing, no titan of the open outcry age is assured of survival whether it be the CBOT or the NYSE. The CBOT has made much progress in recent years but unless it can find some new products (or the US government reopens the business of issuing 30-year "long" bonds with gusto), then the exchange may yet be at best a junior partner in a global coalition by the end of the first decade of the new millennium. Certainly, if Chicago loses its dominance as the center of the futures business, the short-sightedness of eschewing common clearing in the late summer of 1998 will likely be seen in the history books as the point where that dominance truly began to unravel. Indeed, in many respects, Chicago has more to lose from the Capital Market Revolution than any other city on earth. Then again, the CME has demonstrated a true determination to innovate in recent years and the fact that all three major Chicago derivatives markets (CBOE, CBOT, CME) came together to create OneChicago as an electronic market for single stock futures, suggests that they all have some understanding of what the issues are affecting them.

The fact that the CBOT spent late 2001 and early 2002 either cutting fees on its open outcry floor or increasing fees for electronic trades, does not give me great confidence that the exchange has yet managed to break the shackles of being held to ransom by floor traders rightly concerned about their future but wrongly trying to stifle innovation. They may yet undermine the CBOT's ACE platform but once business is priced out of the market, it will ultimately just flow to another market, side-stepping Chicago entirely if necessary. The world's last open outcry exchange to survive will probably be the London Metals Exchange. However, it uses a ring system for fixes which are somewhat different from the continuous pit sessions in open outcry. Rather, the "ring" is a single space of some 4000 square feet which is reused constantly for different products. Moreover, the "fix" that results is a sublime piece of global metal market branding which helps make the LME perhaps the best known B2B exchange in history, even though it was introduced some years before the phrase B2B had ever been coined.

Similarly, the New York stock exchange has already essentially been bypassed as the key stock market in capitalism's powerhouse, North America. The NYSE will probably survive with its primacy for some time yet in the aftermath of the dotcom stock froth gradually calming down. However, the future of the world and therefore the future of world stock markets ultimately rests with Microsoft and the other digital media companies. The Dow Jones Industrial Averages served the industrial age. However, the likes of Bethlehem Steel or Boeing are not stocks which can be viewed as the future dynamic equities of the world. They have sectoral significance but their glamour days are long over. The future of American equity dealing lies with the likes of NASDAQ, although as I have already noted, NASDAQ still thinks too much like a legacy exchange. All legacy exchanges need to keep their acts tightly together to avoid being overwhelmed by the new technology and increased promiscuity of exchanges. In the post-feudal marketplace, a complete minnow of a stock exchange will grow to be a world player. It will be an offshore market and it may be in Bermuda, Jersey, Singapore or even a yet to be established cyberspace market with nominal geographical presence in Andorra, Monaco or perhaps a financial center within a high-tax jurisdiction such as the Irish Republic. Perhaps it is in a state yet to achieve independence. Remember, in the Capital Market Revolution the status quo no longer exists. To paraphrase Milton Friedman, "any market, anywhere can become a world leader at any time."

Virtual securities – the single stock futures revolution

Universal Stock Futures represent a revolution in global equity trading. They will be easy, cheap and efficient to trade.

LIFFE Chairman Brian Williamson launching LIFFE's single stock futures products, September 20th, 2000

In a virtual world, the whole concept of virtual securities dealing may yet take precedence. After all, when stocks are being transferred, the priciest aspect to the whole transaction is the clearing and settlement procedure involving transferring titles and storing them in an appropriate depository. Perhaps the solution may be to avoid trading stocks altogether. To date, individual stock futures have yet to make their mark on the capital markets in remotely the size which they ought. However, with virtual dealing in a virtual world, perhaps virtual stock trading (using futures) is in fact the way of the future for many stock traders. After all, the widespread introduction of liquid individual stock futures creates a further form of asset to trade against the option and warrant products, enhancing liquidity in both through greater short selling and spreading opportunity. With dividends increasingly attracting withholding tax at source, investors may become more keen in the offshore dealing age emerging from the Capital Market Revolution to ignore dividends entirely and prefer to seek solely capital appreciation through stock futures. The large equity broking institutions have tended to be trenchantly against individual stock futures (largely out of fear that it could cut their margins on cash stock brokerage). However, the margin on broking equities has already largely disappeared.

Single stock futures

During the decade of the 1990s, the value of the outstanding US debt remained stable at around $3 billion. During the same period, the value of the equity market has gone up to almost $14 billion. This significant increase represents a clear shift from a debt-oriented to an equity-oriented society. It is against this background that futures markets on single stocks have an enormous potential to change the landscape of US capital markets."

Richard Sandor, Chairman and CEO, Environmental Financial Products LLC, Research Professor, Northwestern University

Single stock futures were originally traded as long ago as the 17th century in Amsterdam. Their concept is simple, a contract which allows trading in a forward contract based on an individual share. Their core facets are the same as those for any other futures contract and of course a key advantage is that investors are able to both buy and sell the contracts with equal ease, making them an excellent tool for all-round risk transfer, hedging and speculation.

In essence, the same arguments have been used against single stock futures as were used before against commodity futures, currency futures, interest rate futures and energy futures. There is no reason why these arguments should suddenly be proven correct in this context. Put simply, single stock futures will, like other derivatives contracts, enhance underlying cash market liquidity. They will enable investors and traders to fine-tune their desired outcomes for particular positions and therefore enhance risk management as well as making prices tighter for other related products such as options and so forth. Trading single stock futures provides greater opportunity to exploit easily the different price moves between similar stocks – say two telecom shares, in what are known as "pairs" trades. Such trades can often prove cumbersome in the cash market where shorting is relatively difficult and can be expensive as traders often have to finance stock which is borrowed to make up the short component of the "pair." With SSFs, the trader merely pays a neat margin on each side.

In the US, regulators have argued for some years over single stock futures simply because when the Shad Johnson agreement allowed for the recreation of single stock options in the US during the 1970s, no agreement was ever finalized to permit single stock futures. In the twilight of the Clinton administration, a bill was passed enabling SSFs to be traded and thereafter the twin US regulatory agencies at the SEC (stock market) and CFTC (futures markets and non-individual equity options markets) worked on creating a framework for SSFs leading to the first US trades late 2002, approximately two years after LIFFE had created their groundbreaking international product and Bourse de Montreal had launched the first such product in North America. Nevertheless, markets in various parts such as Australia, Hong Kong, Sweden and South Africa had all listed single stock futures prior to LIFFE.

For those who by now have grown even vaguely cynical of my cries to the world's bourses to mind their management lest they disappear into oblivion, bear in mind that when I first propagated the widespread usage of single stock futures in 1997, it was widely ridiculed by many parties. Yet in 2000/2001, it was my pleasure to work with forward-looking exchanges in London (LIFFE) and Montreal as they introduced the world's first international single stock futures ("universal stock futures") and SSFs in North America, respectively. The single stock futures business has gradually emerged from the shadow of regulatory prohibition in the US where the act of carving regulation between the SEC (equities) and the CFTC (futures and most options) has been a harmful one for capitalism the world over. As has been shown by the lengthy wait for the regulators finally to agree their cross-regulatory structure for single stock futures, the American regulatory system is a dog's dinner of conflicting aims, conflicting rules, conflicting political powerbases and ultimately is harmful to the customer not merely in the US but thanks to America's superpower economy, harmful to clients throughout the world. Nevertheless, whatever the regulatory position, the business of equity trading will be revolutionized itself not merely by technology but also by the increased volume not only of single stock futures but also the unstoppable expansion of exchange-traded funds.

More exchanges, more volume concentration?

While many leviathans will go out of business, there will continue to be a vast expansion in exchanges in the world until the end of the first decade of the second millennium. For in the future, using electronic trading mechanisms, there will be much more opportunity to create exchanges to deal in small global or even regional niches. For example, environmental trading will grow steadily and there are several exchanges staking a claim to this business including the OM venture based out of Edinburgh and the IPE in London, as well as New York, Chicago and Sydney. Equally, weather derivatives are set to be an enormous growth area for the next decade – and ironically, it seems that the "upstart" ICE has stolen a march on all the legacy exchanges in weather trading at the time of writing. In all of these examples (as well as events such as the increasing globalized commoditization of insurance resulting in meaningful insurance contracts by 2005) most product growth is likely to come largely within already existing (if only tiny) markets.

Every new exchange will benefit from a clearing house and with the costs of establishing new clearing houses a major burden to new market structures (which are otherwise remarkably low in capital requirements compared to the old people-dominated structures), the use of an existing clearing house will be a much simpler solution. Nevertheless, that is not to say the clearing houses can expect to have everything their own way. Ironically, telecoms companies became obsessed with 3G auctions just at the moment when they had a much more stable, commoditized opportunity right on their doorstep of core competencies – namely becoming clearing houses. After all, major telecoms companies are little more than a clearing house in many respects. They manage massive numbers of accounts which are administered for relatively modest marginal returns. Indeed, some telcos are already working closer to real time, with monthly or more regular billing – even payment in advance – increasingly the norm for many callback services, etc. Therefore, telcos could yet enter the clearing business with less effort than arguably even some banks! On the other hand, the real impediment to entering the market as a clearing house is in the documentation. However, with US regulation having ensured a clearing house for essentially every board of trade, no matter how small, the opportunity of buying a small player for both regulatory status and its regulations, would be a very feasible way for a left field competitor to enter the clearing business.

Clearing houses will not only be looking within the area of their current business; increasingly they are expanding their remit beyond the futures and options exchanges. New model stock markets will utilize a clearing house to provide central counterparty clearing (CCP – the process of the clearing house matching every buyer with every seller through the clearing house, in other words the clearing house guarantees everybody's trades) to facilitate settlement. The London Tradepoint Stock Exchange established in 1995 which became Virt-X through a venture with the Swiss Exchange in 2000 already employs the London Clearing House in precisely this role, clearing its blue-chip

European stock trades. The London Stock Exchange followed suit in 2001 and many stock exchanges are finally seeing the benefits of reducing counterparty risk even in a relatively short-term clearing environment.

With the power to bestow financial credibility on markets at their whim, clearing houses will increasingly have the capacity to bless financial markets or blight them in a manner akin to the medieval *droit du seigneur*. Meanwhile, there is also the possibility that clearing houses can actually even threaten the very existence of the exchanges they have been serving for hundreds of years. As credit concerns mount across the world, the clearing of OTC traded instruments is already gathering pace (it was first undertaken by OM in Sweden in the 1980s but has made relatively little progress since). Industry jokesters have been known to remark that if the suffix "-clear" can be added to a noun, then the London Clearing House will offer a service in it. With BondClear, EquityClear, RepoClear and SwapClear amongst their many initiatives in recent years, the quip is not too far from the truth. The Basel Accords which set banks' requirements for capital to meet their liabilities is also helping promote the use of CCP, making the world a potentially safer place from certain systemic risks. The net result is the potential to make many more millions of nickels on the nickel and dime clearing transactions which have long been the mainstay of that former Cinderella business, clearing, while all the while helping to make markets more secure places for all types of traders. After all, as those people dealing with Enron directly discovered to their peril, their positions had no guarantees. Whereas, those who dealt with Enron via an exchange had no sleepless nights worrying about how much money they might hope to receive.

Therefore, as OTC clearing takes off then the situation is likely to arise where the clearing house will find itself out selling its services to end users as a competitor (in at least some ways) to the exchanges who wish to get more business on their markets. Frankly, the prognosis in such encounters for exchanges looks bleak. Increasing simplicity of access and more onerous regulation of exchanges has continued to push business onto OTC markets in many financial centers for a decade or more. Settling such transactions through clearing houses will gather momentum as more and more microbanks and other internet-based virtual financial counterparties begin trading with greater gusto.

Silos or separates?

A big issue with the European clearing landscape in particular has been the question of creating separate exchanges and clearing structures. The Deutsche Börse has long been the leading advocate of what is known as the "vertical silo" i.e., everything is processed from the start of the trade through to the settlement and clearing at the same company, in separate parts of the silo.

End users have seemed reluctant to endorse the silo model for fear of being tied to a particular single market. However, the wily Werner Seifert managed to strengthen his hand by taking over a leading European clearing house, Clearstream, in early 2002. While such activity is similar to the US derivatives model where every board of trade has traditionally owned its own clearing house, it is alien to the US securities markets (where DTCC clears every share transaction) and in options where OCC, the Options Clearing Corporation performs a very similar function to DTCC). The leading independent European clearing house, LCH retains a non-profit-making model which despite the largely for-profit ethos of the Capital Market Revolution may yet prove to be a winning proposition in a world where a commoditized clearing utility is a key facet to every marketplace. Similarly, the merger of the UK's depository CrestCo and the European independent depository Euroclear in July 2002 brought together two mutual companies in a single mutual structure.

Ironically, perhaps the biggest challenges for clearing and settlement are not in the much-hyped issues of separates versus silos but in the issue of dematerialization (see Chapter 3), after 09/11, and also the business of actually speeding up settlement. Real-time clearing appears so far removed for cash markets as to be simply a pipedream. Even T+1 settlement (i.e., one day after the trade) is looking a distinctly optimistic proposition to be introduced within the next few years. It seems a little strange that in a real-time world, the supposedly space-age financiers can't actually settle their own trades as fast as many general retailers.

Fulfilling new markets

The battle for dominance in the Eurozone has been the focal point of activity within the EU area for the past several years. In many ways this has been a great boon to the Euro-marketplace but in some ways it has also been detrimental to the clearing business. New markets such as the initial B2B exchange boom were in many ways hampered in their development by the sloth of existing clearing houses (throughout the world, but for varying reasons) to get into their space. In the US, some clearing houses attached to Boards of Trade have sought to detach or at least slightly decouple themselves from their core exchanges and the likes of the CME Clearing House and the Board of Trade Clearing Corporation have worked hard to present themselves as champions of alternative markets. Nevertheless, approach any of them with a proposal to do something with a significant whiff of left field about it, such as sports trading, and suddenly their enthusiasm for the new wanes dramatically. In this respect, the possibility for a new clearing function could be a reality. In the case of sports trading or indeed other customer-related transactions, for instance, it may yet prove feasible for the likes of the TOTE companies (whether in the UK or Australia *et al.*) who have traditionally aggregated betting on horse-racing, to grasp the nettle and become the leading figures for clearing consumer transactions in the new entertainment-related markets which will be the fastest-growing trading activities of the middle to late years of this decade.

Regulators in revolt/at war

Now our basic philosophy is to get out of the way while still providing investor protection.
Arthur Levitt Jr., former Chairman, Securities and Exchange Commission

For the past two decades, financial markets have been a wonderful plaything for governments. Managing economies has become altogether more dangerous and difficult with globalization and the increasing power of the market to decide on politicians' follies. However, in financial markets, governments have been able to do their utmost to provide a structure that makes them feel as if they are doing something of benefit. Occasionally, there have been benefits although in most cases the result has been little more than a strangulation of natural capitalist processes. In London, the salaries for Compliance Officers have soared as companies have had to comply with a never-ending stream of regulatory edicts, many of which demonstrate a palpable lack of understanding of financial markets by the professionals allegedly employed to facilitate a safe and sensible organization – they are known as "business prevention officers" with good reason. The end result has been a sprawling bureaucracy which still doesn't protect investors from determined fraudsters but leaves the innocent majority being largely hamstrung in their attempts to deal effectively. Brokers have been hard hit. With income squeezed through continuing discounting, increased regulatory costs have been an unwelcome burden.

Almost all practitioners would agree that some form of regulation is a necessary evil for financial markets. However, in recent years that regulation appears to have gone too far. Now, it is likely to snap in precisely the opposite direction. For, while regulators may claim that they understand the dynamics of the internet (they don't), that they can operate their regulatory regimes within their geographical boundaries with regard to the internet (they can't) and that their remit will go unchallenged (it won't), the truth is that their very existence is under threat.

The behavior of some regulators towards the virtual world of finance almost defies belief. In the UK, the Financial Services Act of

1985 has been used as a rather crude cudgel against any form of internet-based financing which does not appeal to the UK regulators. One of their more frightening proclamations has been to claim that any investment scheme offered by a corporation beyond a current major regulatory regime, is being specifically targeted at British investors. While English may be the global language of financial markets, apparently this makes it a threat to the UK investors. When a senior UK regulator was asked why he wouldn't amend this ridiculous claim, the tart reply was that it was up to a trading organization to get their counsel to reinterpret the Act and at this stage the UK regulator would look benignly on such an interpretation. Quite why brokers and end users are supposed to spend their money to dig the UK regulators out of a hole of their own digging has never been adequately explained.

The simple fact is that single-nation regulators are largely dead in the water. There will be increasing levels of globalized regulatorial co-operation but the scope and size of domestic regulatory regimes is likely to shrink vastly in the next decade. Frankly, this will be no bad thing. Regulators need to understand the changing nature of the trading business. Alas, their lack of grasp of dynamics thus far suggests there is relatively little hope for most of their bureaucrats. Any heavy-handedness at this stage of the Capital Market Revolution by bureaucrats will merely have massive repercussions. The American government's increasingly swingeing regulations during the 1960s resulted in a massive offshore shift of expatriate American dollars to create the London-based Eurodollar market. Similar heavy-handed pigheadedness by regulators in the modern age will result in a migration to another jurisdiction at the speed of light.

Interestingly, in the US, there have been increasing signs of regulators at the SEC and the CFTC taking a greater interest in softly-softly tactics which seems to suggest that they may have an eye on becoming global regulators for the entire online world. Certainly a very light degree of regulation would be a boon for many firms. However, even with America's status as sole superpower, it will find gunboat diplomacy difficult to enforce in the online world. Certainly, regulators' biggest problem in years to come will be regulatory arbitrage – the process whereby markets move offshore to create a parallel market to the onshore variant. The Swedish OM market did precisely this with the opening of OMLX in the 1980s when the Swedish government played with the introduction of withholding tax on Bond transactions. The OMLX market traded without the tax constraints, the Swedish government had to back down. In the post-feudal marketplace, governments cannot expect to dominate markets as they did with their domestic exchanges.

By 2002, there had been several interesting developments in the regulatory world. The ongoing turf battle between the SEC and CFTC delayed single stock futures for a year from their first inception date and every "i" was bound to be judiciously dotted and each "t" perfectly crossed for fear of either organization being seen to have made an omission subsequently. The market was, as ever, the loser. Likewise, in Australia, the Australian Derivatives Market (ADX) found itself suffering at the hands of a domestic regulator which had not only launched a witch hunt in the aftermath of what had been an unfortunate demise due to a lack of capital, but also the ASIC regulator had been viewed as distinctly culpable for the delay in the launch of ADX in the first place, due allegedly to internal politics within its own organization.

The SEC's Chairman Harvey Pitt seemed to be becalmed in any efforts to help push regulation forward due to his growing feud with the New York State Attorney General Eliott Spitzer over the business of analysts' conflicts of interest in the wake of the dotcom fall-out and the Enron collapse. Indeed, the accounting crises in US companies discovered after the dotcom bubble burst has emboldened interventionism amongst US politicians at precisely the time when tougher regulations may yet drive their stock trading offshore. What America really needs is a coherent single regulator for stock and derivative markets but the ongoing conflict of competition between the SEC and CFTC looks likely to remain for the foreseeable future due to its entrenched nature within the Washington political committee structure (the SEC represents the finance committee while the CFTC is the power plaything of the agriculture committee on account of futures originally being a commodity product).

Trying the new model on the old

London's Stock Exchange appears largely bewildered by the dynamics of the Capital Market Revolution as demonstrated by its stumbling into an alliance with the Deutsche Börse in mid-1998 that even by the low standards of most exchange alliances never went anywhere. LSE subsequently failed to tie up a merger with Deutsche Börse more than anything because it could not stomach being a lesser party to the new entity although DB had more economic clout having retained its settlement arm whereas London had lost the disastrous still-born Taurus project to government intervention in the shape of CrestCo (now merged with Euroclear). The most famous and traditionally powerful bourse in Europe had managed to turn itself basically into an also-ran in the European consolidation game by the time it failed to take over LIFFE in late 2001. Certainly, it would be difficult to have much faith in the London Stock Exchange's policy as it is largely impossible to see what their policy has been for the past 20 years or so. Indeed, the London Stock Exchange could not be clearly accused of having lost the plot, since it's difficult to see when they actually had a firm grasp on the plot in the first place.

On Wall Street, even when the AMEX was absorbed into the electronic NASDAQ, the NYSE still appeared largely in denial at the prospects for electronic trading. Ironically, NASDAQ never integrated AMEX and subsequently placed it up for sale at the end of 2001 having first let NASDAQ float free to make it one of several likely US exchange IPO candidates (along with CME and ISE amongst others).

Towards an invigorating IPO?

Ironically, it may yet be that the process of IPO for US exchanges may truly ignite the touchpaper that sees genuine radical rationalization of the American and global exchange landscape. Both Deutsche Börse and Euronext raised cash piles in IPOs during 2001 which they used to good effect to fund their purchases of Clearstream and LIFFE respectively. If NASDAQ or the CME can really convince investors that they can dominate at least a significant swathe of the world's trading markets then they have a vast opportunity to raise significant funding and set out on an aggressive acquisition trail.

The Capital Market Revolution doesn't take any prisoners but it will see the sort of slashing and burning which has been unknown in financial markets throughout the past three hundred years. Having said that, those who are seeking growth stocks ought to seek to be in the vanguard of the rationalization movement because when the exchanges achieve critical mass then their stock market multiples will reflect their maturity and become essentially a mode of utility pricing as, for example, befell the waves of privatizations in the UK electricity markets during the 1980s and 1990s.

Chapter 5

Power to the People
The Staggering Rise of the Private Individual

As technology empowers individuals, it creates greater opportunities for us all. The marketplace will become even more efficient because of the availability of timely, uncensored information. That will almost certainly put the bureaucracies – both in government and in commerce – out of business. In the Global Paradox – the larger the world's economy, the more powerful its smallest players – it is virtually impossible to overestimate the role of global telecommunications.

John Naisbitt, *Global Paradox*

The global paradox hits financial markets

John Naisbitt, a noted pundit and author of books such as the bestselling *MegaTrends*, understands perfectly the dynamics of how, what he called the "Global Paradox" (the larger the world's economy, the more powerful its smallest players), will affect financial markets. Since the Wall Street crash of 1929, and indeed before, the world's investment markets have increasingly become the playthings of large institutionalized organizations managing billions of dollars. Such leviathans of financial management will find their territory increasingly coming under threat in the post-feudal marketplace.

The problem with large funds is that while big may be beautiful in terms of economies of scale, the ultimate returns tend to be relatively poor. Nowadays, backed up by an array of academic economists, defeatism reigns in many areas of money management. Many funds aim to attain a performance close to the average of some (any) benchmark. Few wish to beat the index as there is a great deal of comfort being amongst the herd. With sprawling bureaucracies increasingly retaining the worst traits of the civil service, the mentality of sticking together and not differentiating has become the norm. In this respect, contemporary large-fund managers frequently resemble something closer to a gathering of water buffalo rather than the leading investment sophisticates their slick marketing claims. True, there are a few fund managers who can be identified as different while still being within the mainstream methods of investing. However, given the many thousands of funds world-wide, they are few and far between. The upside of increased gains has become a huge risk for these fund managers, as it places their jobs on the line.

The modern mass market fund manager is not just a beast skewed away from maximizing returns, it is also an animal which is bloated, bureaucratic and vastly overstaffed. The leviathans of funds management have become huge organizations which cannot move their holdings without affecting the underpinnings of the very markets they are operating in. The stock markets of the world have long lacked liquidity compared to their derivatives cousins. Yet, the big fund managers see being able to deal by stealth as one of the few advantages they have in existing financial markets. If such a lack of transparency is so great an advantage, one is inclined to wonder why fund managers cannot make superior returns. Such a query is fully justified, for there are other more contemporary fund managers who have demonstrated remarkable returns in recent times. The modern large fund-management group is reminiscent of those giant bulk cargo or oil supertankers that require a distance of several kilometers to stop and similarly staggering distances to reverse direction. As the Capital Market Revolution accelerates, such lumbering resource-intensive organizations will increasingly resemble dinosaurs. And in most cases, they too will become extinct.

Online traders

Leave your job, log on and – hey presto! – you too can turn into the newest pariah of America's stockmarkets, an electronic day trader. In the 1980s, it was Wall Street's take-over barbarians.

Today it is the amateurs in jeans and sneakers who sit in front of a computer and trade 40–50 times in a day. Just as they did with Gordon Gecko types in the 1980s, Wall Street's great and good are demonising day traders, accusing them of distorting the stockmarket and causing the volatility in share prices.

The Economist

It was clear that online trading had truly arrived when during 1999 even the rather staid New York Stock Exchange wanted to change its hours to accommodate the online traders by staying open as late as 10 pm in the evening. This move was suggested as a way to take back market share from the preponderance of ECN systems trading after the closing ball on Wall Street.

For once, the relatively slow grind that passes for management innovation at the NYSE worked to its advantage. The dotcom bubble burst, volumes sagged and the first wave of online traders were often forced out of business by mounting losses. While the new breed of day traders demonstrate that the playing field has been significantly remodeled to permit them almost as much access as that afforded to the large professionals who have long dominated stock trading, many day traders were ill-equipped to cope with the gyrations of the stock market.

Now that discount brokerages and the internet have opened up trading to the littlest guy, three distinct classes of day-trading society have evolved; the at-home internet cowboys, the ex-Wall Street pros, and the players who work out of day trading firms. Each group uses different strategies and different financial and electronic tools.

Carol Vinzant, *Fortune* magazine

With the bursting of the dotcom bubble, the more amateurish elements of day trading have tended to find themselves squeezed out – a point I noted was highly likely in the event of a bear market in the original Capital Market Revolution. Nevertheless, as recession has been gripping Wall Street – particularly in the wake of 09/11 – more and more former professionals are joining the ranks of the day traders. This is a good thing for markets as it ought to help add liquidity. Nevertheless, regardless of the casualties during the first phase of the revolution, the simple fact is that day trading is here to stay and will outlast its late 1990s "phenomenon" status to become a fixed aspect of financial markets.

The behaviorist B.F. Skinner would have been intrigued by the phenomenon of day trading. Investors sit at a screen and buy and sell stocks and commodities for long periods. Day traders use their own money and some do 2,000 deals a day. Like Skinner's rats, they get instant reward or instant punishment, profit or loss.

David Cohen, *Fear, Greed and Panic, the Psychology of the Stock Market*

The online traders are evidence of a new stockmarket democracy at work. It may take some years to mature but online trading activity is still gaining advocates by the day – and mostly as I noted above, ex-professionals who have a better understanding of risk. If market makers can't keep their prices up to date, then the online traders will strike mercilessly. This is merely mass market arbitrage and will ensure that only the fittest can survive. For too long market makers and the specialist system has created cosy cartels. Now market makers must truly demonstrate their ability to trade as well as their peers. The fact that many may be sophisticated retail investors, from well beyond the boundaries of the local financial district, only serves to add insult to injury for those proud market makers who have long sniped at the abilities of private clients. After the dotcom collapse, the professionals sneered at the naivete of some retail investors but this was only the dawn of the revolution. There will be more suckers but there will be many more very sophisticated investors too.

By enhancing liquidity with their frequency of trading, day traders make the stock market a better trading environment with narrower bid and offer spreads for all investors. They were also in the vanguard of pressing brokerage levels down in the early stages of the electronic age. However, all online traders need to be aware that brokerage levels in the US are only part of the story. For instance, payment for order flow being given to a broker may result in an order being processed on an ECN or other platform at a disadvantageous price to other markets. This often is a much greater disadvantage than can ever be made up by the ultra cheap genre of $9.99 brokerage rates and similar.

Ultimately, the day trader is here to stay. The sooner the stockmarket establishment realizes that fact, the sooner they can get on with addressing the issues within the Capital Market Revolution which threaten their very existence. Indeed, it would serve the stockmarket establishment much better to identify just how much benefit the online traders bring to capital markets. Just like the online traders in the vanguard of the revolution, many large institutions will not survive unless they begin to understand the big picture of dynamic change affecting all markets. Investors, large and small, now face many of the same difficulties. However, it may take them some more time to realize and even acknowledge that they are ostensibly in the same boat. As *The Economist* has ominously noted:

> Indeed, with their expertise at trading fast and often, when the conflagration comes, [day traders] may prove fleeter of foot than the big, staid institutional investors who have often been bad-mouthing them.

The hedge fund phenomenon

The father of the hedge fund, Alfred Winslow Jones, was born in Australia to an American family and lived a varied life with a spell in the Berlin US Embassy as a Vice-Consul during the 1930s, having previously been a purser on a steamship. Amongst other things, he gained a PhD in Sociology before becoming an associate editor of *Fortune* magazine. It was on his fifth separate career, when 48 years old, that Jones created the first hedge fund with an embryonic structure which balanced:

market exposure = (long exposure − short exposure)/capital[1]

This original ethos of "hedge funds" referring to a fund which buys and sells equal quantities of different stocks so as to remain essentially market neutral, has now largely been abandoned by the largest players. The hedge fund of today is generally a limited partner structure based in an offshore tax haven, which can employ gearing to maximize returns. Hedge funds tend to have two key advantages over contemporary funds. For a start, hedge funds are fast and nimble operations. They often turn around their positions swiftly and avoid illiquid markets where they have difficulty exiting with alacrity when required. Similarly, hedge funds are much, much more aggressive than conventional fund managers. Hedge fund managers usually hold substantial stakes in their own funds. Such a self-interest motive, fuelled by fees being linked to profits, makes the hedge fund managers a lot less reticent about trying to outperform whatever benchmark investors throw at them.

The original and continuing justification for incentive fees in hedge funds is the inherent promise of superior performance − not average performance, not absolute performance, but superior performance. Prudence dictates that investors fundamentally grasp Jones's motivational dynamics and seek to replicate them in the hedge funds they choose.
William J. Crerend (chairman of Evaluation Associates)[2]

Admittedly, some hedge funds carry substantial risks and in this respect, investors need always to bear the *caveat emptor* motto in mind.

Equally, hedge funds tend to be more volatile than their conventional brethren. However, while they suffer greater drawdowns (troughs from highs to lows), overall hedge funds have reinforced the message over the years that they can and do regularly bounce back from their periods of famine into renewed, and exceptional, periods of feast.

Hedge funds are the glamour boys of the funds management industry. Anybody arriving at a cocktail party who announces that they are a "hedge fund manager" cannot be regarded as anything but rich. After all, hedge funds are those ultra-sophisticated practitioners of high finance. So far ahead of the ball game compared to the pedestrian folk managing mutual funds, they must have difficulty not passing themselves just getting into their office elevators. And of course their offices are opulent. True, some might be a touch on the kitsch side, but the important thing to remember is that hedge fund managers are just so damned incredible that, for them, controlling a fund about three times the GDP of a small African potentate is about as simple as ordering a bagel for breakfast to the rest of us.

Hedge funds, to put it mildly, are moving so fast and their managers are such glitterati of the industry that it is obvious that the only inviolate factor in the world of high finance – and the worlds of not so high finance, positively mediocre finance and finance so low grade that covering it is about as sexy to the average investor as wrestling in toxic waste – is that one thing above all must be clear. Hedge funds are now so firmly established as to be here to stay in exalted permanence, one of the holy trinity of big-league financiers along with the world's great proprietary traders and the most leveraged of the M&A men.

New math, new risks: the foibles of avarice

The fact of the matter is that there are brainy people and superb corporations throughout the world. There is no shortage of fools and suckers either.

Professor Robert Sobel

An intriguing issue with the hedge fund business is the lengths to which its detractors will go in order to sully its name. Perhaps it is merely jealousy at the perceived vast wealth of the managers themselves. It is perpetually disappointing to see many figures in the mainstream media lapping up the miserable messages from conventional funds while simultaneously taking the advertising dollars of these dinosaurs. Likewise, the hedge fund industry is perpetually reported as being little more than an expensive punting operation. The failures of funds are perpetually dragged out in the first instance in an attempt to undermine the hedge fund industry. Yet, nobody seeks to discuss the banking industry in a mature fashion by first looking at the spectacular failures of that industry. And the truth is that the past few decades have been littered by spectacular banking failures on all continents, such as, BCCI, Chase Manhattan and Credit Lyonnais to name but three.

Of course there are those hedge funds that will be seen to fly Icarus-like too close to the sun and find the burnt wax on their wings causes their feathers to fall off and lead to a sickening plunge back to earth. However, overall returns in general stock market funds tend to be pale facsimiles of the results achieved by most hedge funds.

Long Term Capital Management was in many ways a fairy story example of a hedge fund. Its principals all had extensive financial backgrounds. The senior partner was John Merriwether, a former chief dealer at Salomons. Amongst the remaining partners were no fewer than two Nobel laureates, Myron Scholes and Robert Merton, plus a former US Federal Reserve Vice-Chairman David Mullins. The fund raised a staggering US$1.25 billion when launched in 1994, then a new fund record. The minimum stake was US$10 million.

In late 1998, the Long Term Capital Management organization suffered the humiliation of being bailed out by a syndicate of banks organized by the US central bank, the Federal Reserve. LTCM had fallen apart at the seams with losses of virtually all its capital. In many ways this looked like a classic example of high finance squeezing extra returns from the mathematics of rocket science. While the collapse of LTCM is precisely an example of the foibles of the Capital Market Revolution at work, in fact the reasons for LTCM's collapse were much more the result of the age-old problem of greed overstretching itself. Investors in hedge funds employing gearing (the vast majority) need to realize that just as gearing can be terrific when conditions are propitious, the fall-out from losses arrives a great deal faster. Hence the problems of over gearing with inaccurate risk management. There is a limit to the point where gearing becomes useful. Once this level is surpassed, the added gearing rapidly endangers the fund's wellbeing with remarkable alacrity. In the case of LTCM, gearing often reached staggering levels of 50 times capital or more. At these sorts of levels, the slightest bump in the carpet can send a whole fund careering into oblivion.

When a consortium of banks launched their bail out, the *Financial Times* noted that Merriwether's fund was "using a system so complex and erudite that it was thought that nothing could possibly go wrong." In other words, LTCM was the unsinkable investment, the *Titanic* of hedge funds. The foibles of avarice had resulted in the management forgetting a simple precept of trading. Risk management involves thinking the unthinkable. Many market observers were wont to repeat the old hedge fund maxim: "You don't know who is swimming naked until the tide goes out." To discuss all the aspects of the LTCM management's failings falls largely outside the scope of this volume. The simple fact remains that LTCM's mathematics were impeccable. Unfortunately, in practice, the real world has some flaws.

A shock to the system?

Ignore the continuing newspaper headlines throughout 2002 and thereafter predicting doom. As things stand, the outlook is gleaming for the hedge fund industry. Expansion is so substantial and apparently accelerating to such a degree that, during my research for this book, various luminaries weren't even willing to put a number on just how many funds there might be. True, some of the founding fathers of the hedge fund boom during the past thirty years such as George Soros and Julian Robertson (Tiger Fund) have opted to take a lower profile in investment terms, if they have not retired altogether. However, such a natural turnover ought to be seen as healthy for the industry. Ambitious journalists have tried to make a name for themselves in the past few years by repeatedly calling a top to the hedge fund boom, yet this is itself to misunderstand entirely the forces at work. The pensions and investment management business is itself being revolutionized by technology. Scale and scalability of hedge funds make them the new all-rounders of the investment business. Their maneuverability enables them to run rings around the bulk carriers of the dinosaur funds.

Similarly, things couldn't look brighter on the horizon. For a start, the industry is being helped by vast flows of speculative cash into the system, bloated by US baby boomers determined to ensure that they have adequate pension provision for the day they retire. The profile of hedge funds is high. Everybody, but everybody, seems to know what a hedge fund is, even if they haven't got the remotest clue what they actually do – apart from their founders frequently being predisposed to donate money to their own charitable foundations and occasionally argue with Asian Prime Ministers. Everything looks good in the hedge fund domain, and a good few incentive fees are being paid by happy clients. Indeed, the very fact that a hedge fund manager could come under attack from the Prime Minister of a sovereign nation (Mahathir Mohammed on George Soros during the 1998 Asian crisis) just goes to show the presence which this industry has gained during the last 20 years.

The fact is that for the past few years – probably longer – the sun has shone. The hedge funds have been able to bask on the beach in the glow, occasionally taking a brief dip in the balmy waters, before retiring to their beach-side haciendas smug in the knowledge of another profit in the bank. By 1969, everything was looking rosy in the hedge fund world. For a start, equities were strong and getting stronger, the economy looked good and it seemed that little could affect the bounteous profits to be found all over Wall Street. But after a long-lived and vibrant bull market, the bear struck. And this time it struck hard. The tide went out. Abruptly. From 1969 to 1974, the Value Line Composite Index (a good measure of the broad market) declined by over 70%. During 1969–70, the S&P500 fell only 5% if dividends were reinvested, but the broad market fell some 43%. Then stocks bounced for two years, before the bear reasserted itself. The Oil Crises of 1973–74 pushed prices vigorously south. During this phase, blue-chip stocks fell 37%, while the broad market was smashed by some 57%.

Naturism – or at least skinny dipping – was evidently highly popular for the hedge fund fraternity. The community dwindled and all but died out. The 28 largest funds in the end of 1968 survey by the SEC suffered (both from losses and withdrawals) a decline in their assets of some 70% by the end of 1970. By the end of 1974, most funds were dead. Only a few resourceful managers including Jones himself – and, of course, the likes of one George Soros Esquire – survived to fight another day. Meanwhile, many of the hedge fund practitioners went off to work in the fast-developing world of private pension management, which was then being deregulated by the US government.

Looking at the current situation in the hedge fund industry, many folk see an uncanny similarity. Certainly, given the rapid expansion of the hedge fund industry, new talented fund managers are in short supply and quality concerns over some new funds remain. Nevertheless, capitalism is a competitive business and some folk will always fall by the wayside regardless of the business. Look at the UK where a veritable titan, Equitable Life was brought to earth with a dizzying bump by what was simply a flat-earth investment strategy in the age of three-dimensional ones. Dinosaurs are just as precarious as hedge funds and in the event of market difficulties, there will always be some casualties in the hedge fund industry. However, a few entrants falling by the wayside does not mean that the entire marathon entry is therefore in danger.

After all, the growing gap in pensions means that short of having high double-digit growth in stock markets year on year for several decades, there is simply no way dinosaur funds can hope to plug the gap in pensions liabilities. The ageing population is acute not just in Europe, but Japan as well. In Germany and Italy, the proportion of the voting age population who are retired will increase by 30% and 60% respectively (again by 2030). Overall, 25% of the entire German population will be drawing pensions. In Italy, this will be 34%. (All the usual caveats regarding linear statistics should, naturally, be inserted at this point.)

If they are to avoid a huge crunch at some stage, Japan and even the most reactionary of European governments must bring more capitalism into the provision of pensions. During 2002 the UK regulator, the FSA (Financial Services Authority) was not alone in warning that younger adults were simply not making sufficient provision for old age. This is already resulting in widespread deregulation which will dwarf the equivalent process in the United States during the early 1970s. If the hedge fund industry hits trouble, its refugees may end up being employed in the same way as their counterparts in the previous cycle, only this time the pension reforms will be in Europe. Or is that just too neat a scenario – even for hard-bitten, cynical contrarians such as this author?

A hedge fund pullback may take place but in the quest for alpha – absolute returns, the relative advantages of hedge funds will be enormous. The hedge fund industry is here to stay regardless of what some misinformed journalists and dinosaur fund managers may claim. Ironically, while many teenage scribblers in the journalistic fraternity fret that hedge funds are about to collapse, many invariably defend real-estate price increases as being a bubble impossible to burst. Naturally, any reasonable contrarian would start to look for the price movement in precisely opposite directions.

The fact is that for all the precision of mathematics, the world retains certain minuscule imperfections. The increasingly mathematically oriented fund managers amongst the hedge fund ranks must understand that even as the Capital Market Revolution reaches fruition and the new playing field is functioning smoothly, the dangers of man's arrogance over the elements will remain the greatest risk to investment losses. Risk management is the most important aspect to any form of trading. Indeed, many of the best alternative fund managers often utilize fairly mundane order-entry procedures but expend huge amounts of research resources on attaining the best exit points from all trades, both loss-making and profitable.

New alternatives

The Commodity Trading Advisor or CTA has been very much a phenomenon of the last 20 years. Such advisors are frequently small (often just one- or two-person) businesses, trading primarily exchange traded derivatives. Clustered together with hedge funds, CTAs are some of the most exciting new fund managers around. The whole CTA business allied with hedge funds is creating an enormous new industry of specialist fund managers grounded in the most volatile markets on earth who will provide significant advantages to returns when a judicious degree of money is invested, with their approaches as a fillip to the conventional fund management industry.

But do we really need conventional funds?

Actually, this question can be answered with an emphatic yes and no. The existing CBD-based large sprawling bureaucracies will increasingly lose ground to a wide-ranging array of cyber fund managers operating off much lower cost bases with fewer staff, cheaper overheads and all the advantages of less regulation and tax-free location which offshore status provides. The only remaining large-fund managers will be some national-oriented superannuation funds, investing the pension funds for those "wage slaves" who find themselves still trapped under the influence of an over-intrusive government which has failed to grasp the post-feudal marketplace.

Government influence over all areas of life is already being significantly weakened in the electronic age, but even government's paying lip service to PFM will maintain a degree of stranglehold over physical assets within its boundaries. Thus, pension funds saddled with large quantities of property will find it more difficult to move seamlessly offshore unlike their hedge fund and alternative investment cousins. Of course, governments grabbing their super funds more firmly around the neck will not merely strangle their own fund managers and encourage faster offshore movement but will also hemorrhage their wider economy. Whether or not Cyberbusiness and Cyberfinanciers have to migrate offshore is a key issue. The mere threat of moving to a more competitive domicile will be sufficient in many cases to maintain flexibility and competition between regimes. Therefore many companies may stay onshore but they are already increasingly hedging themselves by keeping offices in various tax havens as an insurance against a government which loses the plot and tries to enforce monopolistic taxation. Meanwhile, individuals will also find themselves increasingly incentivized (and able) to move assets offshore as the power of government to trade transactions declines.

The new model fund manager

The investment management industry will be increasingly polarised between the whales and the goldfish. The big investment management firms will become increasingly cumbersome, converging on passive investment strategies while more talented managers split off to set up more nimble and entrepreneurial structures.

Paul Marshall of Marshall Wace Asset Management Ltd. (quoted in *Investing With the Hedge Fund Giants* by Beverley Chandler)

Conventional methods of fund management will of course still exist. However, they will increasingly exist in cyber form.

By the time the Capital Market Revolution has reached its zenith, an investor (regardless of jurisdiction, regardless of investment aims) will be able to click onto a website and select a model balance for their portfolio in seconds. The core of a portfolio for most investors will probably be the exchange traded funds, an innovation so deliciously simple that it ultimately will kill many dinosaur fund managers by being cheaper, more flexible, more liquid and more transparent. Such funds are designed to follow market indices precisely, while some variants can also lock in profits, using derivatives, as they are accumulated at various points (say every 20%) regardless of whether the market subsequently drops back. Such funds can be increasingly automated. The old-style fund managers, with the emphasis on large numbers of employees, will find their margins evaporating as cheaper online alternatives grow. In the cyber age, payment on results is also likely to become more common. The old established ways of fund managers taking large chunks of money, both up front as an entry fee and following that, significant fees for management regardless of returns, are already being wiped away. Five hundred basis points was common for many mutual funds in the mid-1990s, especially in Europe. Nowadays, even 50 basis points (0.5%) is seen as increasingly excessive. Why? Because ETFs can perform the same function much, much cheaper. As I will discuss further in the next chapter, the Capital Market Revolution and indeed the dawning of the information age are all examples of "the new meritocracy." A huge upside to the information age is to give all hues of investor better, cheaper, faster access to any financial market and financial market data.

ETFs: the people's derivative

Exchange-traded funds (ETFs) are the most important – and potentially the most versatile – financial instruments introduced since the debut of financial futures some 30 years ago. Like other newcomers to the financial stage, ETFs are finding some starring roles, other roles where they will be an important part of an ensemble cast and, of course, others where they will have merely a "walk-on" part to play.

Gary Gastineau, ETF pioneer, in *The Exchange-Traded Funds Manual*

ETFs (Exchange Traded Funds) were simply the neatest innovation in equity products during the 1990s. The ETF was born in the US, first listed on the AMEX stock exchange and has been pioneered by several leading investment banks world-wide. They are now available on all the major US exchanges and ECNs as well as the vast majority of European and Asian markets. An ETF is a packaged fund tracking a particular index. For investors, there are many wonderful aspects to investing in ETFs:

- ETFs are cheap – no more vast entry and exit spreads, you just pay the equivalent of a normal bid/offer spread according to order flow/market maker prices.
- ETFs are transparent – you buy or sell on the stock exchange of your choice according to the price you see on the screens. No more disputes about getting what you feel is a disadvantageous settlement price agreed under some arcane settlement procedure.
- ETFs are liquid – you can buy and sell as long as the exchange is open.
- ETFs are flexible. Major issuers and major index providers can offer a multiplicity of indices from all over the world.

Furthermore, thanks to the way that investment banks and other organizations can package shares into fund units, supply is ultimately unlimited, so long as each index component company has enough shares available for purchase. In practice, ETFs are more scalable, without cost to the end user, than any retail investment product in history. Exchange Traded Funds are simply a brilliant innovation for every investor whether large or small, retail or institutional who wishes to track any index. In this respect, ETFs deserve the moniker: the people's derivative.

With ETFs at the core of every portfolio in the digital age, future fund management clients will have the capacity to skew their investment returns according to their preferences. Therefore, a simple basket of ETFs may be skewed to a particular national market or have a slightly higher weighting assigned to a sector of the market (local, national, regional or global) all at the click of a mouse. Then the client will be able to decide into which additional funds he or she wishes to invest the remainder of the funds. Here there will be a panoply of alternatives. Indeed, the increasing commoditization of financial products means that in future, investment alternatives will be extensive. Obviously, investors will have to choose between those that offer the potential of significant returns for their personal time horizon coupled to the clients' established risk profile. Liquidity issues will also be important. While real-estate funds may show good returns, investors will also need funds which can be more liquid, just in case they must withdraw funds in the event of an unforeseen need for cash. Equally, the "onshore" nature of most prime real-estate means values may be threatened by an increasing move offshore by many sovereign individuals while the fund may also be endangered by future predatory government activity.

Hedge funds and CTAs are already becoming increasingly homogeneous. In addition there will also be a panoply of new specialist funds with scopes ranging from the very, very narrow right through to the broadest imaginable. Already, the sports and leisure boom throughout the world has led to a series of funds being established with narrow focuses such as investing only in soccer clubs. Such funds have been created as mutual funds, and even hedge fund structures. The classic mutual fund will still find itself struggling to survive within the next decade despite radical reductions to their fee structures in recent years. In the Capital Market Revolution, entitlement fees for management will be radically downsized. Performance is being emphasized by all parties with incentivized fees being the result. An up-front mutual fund entry fee looks increasingly anachronistic. Such fees are being gradually eliminated as increasing numbers of new (often offshore) cyber funds find their much lower overhead bases allows them significantly to reduce and ultimately eliminate such up-front loadings. Ultimately, where an index must be tracked, passive fund managers will be replaced by ETFs. Active fund managers will need to be as flexible as the better hedge fund managers if they are to survive. For those funds not traded on exchanges, redemptions will be increasingly available online, with a commensurate reduction in the often substantial bid/offer spreads current in many mutual funds. Nevertheless, even online, the days of the mutual fund, except for certain specialist niche funds, are numbered.

The new funds

The small will flourish in this new environment because they have always been at the periphery and they have economies of scope and the ability to make quick decisions. They have speed. In the old economy speed was not so critical. Today it is everything.

John Naisbitt, *Global Paradox*

In the digital age, the reduced costs of entering the funds management markets will increasingly bring in a vast array of new marketplaces and hugely innovative new means of managing risk and providing portfolio returns. The most exciting innovations will be offshore. This will be a largely unregulated (or at most very lightly regulated) market unless regulators manage miraculously to lose their plodding heavy-handed approach (commonplace in domestic markets) and suddenly understand the benefits of soft regulation, bureaucratic speed (if that isn't a contradiction in terms which strikes at the very heart of regulators' ethos!) and a new-found capacity to make fast decisions. In other words, the post-feudal marketplace is an enormous threat to regulators. I will examine this in more detail later.

Those investors who seek regulatory protection will be able to deal onshore but it may cost them a significant premium. Admittedly, dealing offshore will bring some greater risks due to the relatively lax regulatory regime. Having said that, the offshore locale which manages to provide an even-handed and relatively simple to administer regulatory regime offshore that gives some protection to investors without hampering investment managers will be poised to reap huge rewards for their island or state. In the Capital Market Revolution, regulators are under threat of extinction unless they learn fast how to evolve away from narrow nationalistic borders.

Time zones, taxes and the regulatory regime are the only impediments to investment nowadays. Borders no longer exist.

Paul Davis, Fund Manager, Tech Invest

Onshore funds, saddled with extra regulatory burdens will still exist but their costs of doing business will be significantly higher. Such costs will have to be borne by investors who prefer the comfort of regulation.

In the Capital Market Revolution, funds to invest in all sorts of markets will be possible. Geographical specialization is already commonplace, although this will increase as even tiny regions are targeted by specialist niche managers. The old narrow nationalist borders will increasingly shrink from many investment horizons in line with Paul Davis' "borders no longer exist" thesis. In the future, one will not merely invest in Italy, but rather in the Prato textile region, or even the development of Liguria. Similarly, there will be funds devoted to investing in the technology of racing cars. Indeed, I am not alone amongst those who have produced draft prospectuses for funds to invest in classic cars in recent years. In the mid-1980s, a leading classic-car dealer, Chris Drake almost succeeded in listing a vehicle to invest in classic cars on the London Stock Market. Ironically, the venture would have shown staggering returns in the subsequent classic-car bubble of the later years of the decade.

"NewVas" will result in funds devoted to everything from the very largest industry groups right through to micro operations. The venture capital business will be hugely affected by this enterprise as we will see later. All these bells and whistles will be instantly available to an online trader through the web. Switching funds will become sheer simplicity. Already many single functional operations are available. However, in the future, investors will be able to do all their personal financial applications and their investments online, with a capacity to move their mortgage and other debt financing back and forward as and when they need, to add duration to their portfolio or append some form of gearing. In fact, any feature of fund management, investment or stock brokerage will increasingly be available from a series of one-stop shops on the internet.

Tied agencies are dead

In retail financial services, thanks to the Capital Market Revolution, integration just got serious in a way nobody would have conceived of ten years ago. Similar to the NewVas broker models within derivatives and stock markets, the new-age financial services salesman will become a much more sophisticated animal, advising a much broader array of customers. Increasing commoditization of all policies (including life insurance, assurance and endowments) will be simpler to buy (and indeed resell in the after market). The increasing commoditization of such products will have a very significant impact on commissions. Brokers will see their returns dwindling on each sale, as increased cross-border competition pushes broker returns down. Such dwindling returns will also prompt financial services retailers to adopt much leaner organizations with far fewer staff. There will be many more customers per salesman (thanks to allowing the customers increased access to electronic decision-making tools via the internet). This will also bring the commissions payable for many insurance products down dramatically, as increased competition kills the old-style tied agents.

Equally, the old-style insurance and financial planning salesman will be able to offer much more extensive services at little extra cost. Depending on the regulatory regime they operate under, a financial services retailer will be able to add a stock, bond, commodity, futures and options brokerage overnight, by simply signing up to a brokerage franchise plan. Similarly, where before there were often significant fiscal advantages to being tied to one of the old localized leviathans of fund management, the new retail broker will find the need to be fast and flexible in line with the NewVas model. Brokers will want to pick and choose from a vast array of global financial services, many of which are provided by small boutique operations. This is one area where disintermediation of financial services may be seen to operate in reverse. However, the costs of such intermediation will be so slight for customer and vendor that the returns will hugely benefit both parties. Similarly, tiny boutique fund managers will now be able to market to the world through their own websites and a network of agents all signed up with a minimum of fuss on a *pro bono publico* basis. Regulators will initially attempt to lash out at such activity via the internet as they see their turf being virtually invaded but ultimately they too must reform or die.

Indeed there have already been several websites launched which refer to themselves as "funds supermarkets." However, to date most such operations are really the product of just one fund management company. In the near future, all such closed systems will find themselves under increasing pressure to open and embrace the full range of investment possibilities or find themselves withering on the web and dying. Just remember: a supermarket that sells only meat, is a butchers.

Bottlenecks in the system

The demand for hedge fund operators with innovative new ideas and a track record of substance means that such people are already becoming increasingly difficult to find. A new format for ascertaining good money managers will have to be utilized within the industry. At present, many fund allocators are themselves alarmingly little more than sheep in the allocation process. The demand for vast swathes of statistics to justify decisions has led to a large skewing in favor of traders who can trade entirely automated methods. While system traders will continue to grow within the post-feudal marketplace, thanks to the continuing growth in computing power, the fact remains that the best money managers in history such as Warren Buffett (Berkshire Hathaway), Julian Robertson (Tiger) and George Soros (Quantum),[3] *et al.*, are invariably discretionary managers who take decisions based upon a system to their design but one which contains a vast array of variables and is implemented by human inputs rather than automated on computers.

Commodity pool operators (CPOs) and other hedge fund allocators need to rethink their own way of doing business with new and smaller funds if they are not to find a chronic undercapacity of managers with a severe oversupply of funds trying to find its way into the CTA/hedge fund programs. Similarly, the money allocators will have to get away from what seems to be a continuing fear of investing with (discretionary) global macro funds. Global macro funds management in an era where communications are so far superior to anything yet seen in history, will be a significant aspect to the whole rise of the new money managers. Allocators need to stop eschewing such advisors, as they will doubtless end up finding different niches across the world from many of their counterparts. Plus, ultimately, the absolute best returns in history have been achieved by global macro managers. To eschew this whole area of investing due to allocators being concerned about risking their jobs by moving away from the herd, is frankly farcical. This area of the allocation business needs to be addressed and reformed rapidly. Those who do so fastest, will find themselves in pole position to get the best choice of the new wave of fund managers in an era of unprecedented growth.

The hedge fund growth splurge will be simply explosive during this decade, although naturally no market follows an entirely linear path up. The explosive rise in alternative fund managers will precisely mirror the crumbling decline into almost total annihilation to be experienced by the existing conventional large money managers whose stranglehold on investment had looked like it could be a 1000-year Reich. Some will survive. Many brands will probably be snapped up by cheeky hedge funds seeking to add to their marketing muscle through a household name. However, the giants of investment management as they stand today are largely doomed to oblivion and national obscurity in the future.

Regulation – always close to the surface of the problem

A second problem already perfectly visible to observers and practitioners alike concerning the "new alternative money managers" is the issue of regulation. Several CTAs with perfectly plausible track records have already been forced to rethink their business (and indeed in several instances, forced out of business) by the regulatory regime, where bureaucracy is seen as a way to save everybody from risk. The reality is that small onshore CTAs are often being stymied by excessive quantities of paperwork, a situation made worse for European CTAs by the EU sticking its nose in through various investment directives during the late 1980s and early 1990s. Stories of European CTAs spending half their day's business dotting "i"s and crossing "t"s to satisfy faceless bureaucrats are commonplace. Such a situation is farcical and is in fact a danger to the good operation of a CTA. Unless a fund manager can be free to research and trade with as little input from regulators as possible, the CTA business will die.

Despite the foibles of the LTCM débâcle, regulating hedge funds is, in reality, little more than regulators seeing their remits dwindle and making a last-ditch grab for new turf. Increasingly, the large allocators will insist on more gearing transparency from the hedge funds which will largely eliminate the concerns raised by LTCM. It is such lone allocators who have the leverage to achieve more prudent fund management; a degree of influence one can only envy. Meanwhile, the CTA and smaller hedge funds will increasingly find themselves being nurtured offshore. Already, several organizations have been working on creating hedge fund incubators in various parts of the world. Above all else, the influence of the big fundamental money managers will never regain the near-monopoly position of financial assets they attained in the late 1980s and early 1990s.

Bottlenecks will occur amongst the ranks of the new alternative managers. Nevertheless, the future upside for the alternative money managers is awesome. Their scalable capacity for managing up to and beyond hundreds of millions of dollars each using compact flexible management teams is the way of the future. If stock markets are not sufficiently liquid for such funds to invest then they will seek ways to replicate holdings through derivatives, or some other methodology which affords an easier investment. Some funds will specialize in holding such illiquid investments. However, in the information age, it is more likely that a lot of funds will hold smaller parcels of stock in companies on transparent exchanges. Stock market liquidity will also be aided by the biggest change of the post-feudal marketplace, the vast move away from corporatizing assets through massive fund managers with a significant quantity of funds flowing back to the control of private client traders.

The remarkable rise of the private client

Ironically, communism has long promised but invariably failed to deliver "Power to the People". Now capitalism, and free-market capitalism in its essentially undistilled form,[4] is giving the individual the chance to shape their financial destiny, with better flows of information and access to markets, than has ever been witnessed at any previous time in history. The Capital Market Revolution provides private capital with all the tools it requires to take on large institutional funds and beat them. It won't be a walkover but at least now the deck is becoming less and less stacked against the individual. In other words, the private individual will become a more pivotal figure thanks to PFM than has ever been seen before.

There have been ebbs and flows of mass involvement in the stock market before, such as in the 1920s when the public largely lost out in the great crash. Even in the aftermath of the Capital Market Revolution, investors will still have to be talented to exploit their newly acquired advantages to make healthy profits. The rise and fall of the first, overambitious and uninformed wave of online investors and day traders in the dotcom bubble, was a salutary lesson that digital markets don't make investors any more intelligent. Nevertheless, the democratic opportunity for everybody to invest profitably is here to stay.

Throughout the post-war era, the increasing intervention by government in financial markets has seen the tax system skewed to favor massive blundering investment corporations while the public has largely been brainwashed into thinking that these self-same large funds are the best way to gain an edge in financial markets. As I have already detailed, their results overall are generally somewhat woeful – especially if one recalls that these were the results made by the so-called professional experts! The fact of the matter is that investors have grown increasingly suspicious of large-fund managers, who seem to demand extortionate up-front fees for little reward and a considerable amount of risk.

Nowadays, teleworking, freelancing and other forms of working from home are becoming increasingly popular. Self-employment is becoming a norm amongst those who wish to be financially secure. It will have all the usual concomitant risks but the wages to be earned from onshore wage slavedom will be increasingly less attractive as desperate governments squeeze the bourgeoisie "until the pips squeak." Equally, the number of early retirees (some voluntary, others enforced by the incapacity of many corporations to see the benefits of employing experienced, mature citizens because they aren't as cheap as less educated, less experienced youths – the increasing desperation of government to get youth unemployment down while letting the more mature citizens flounder plays a part here too) with some pool of capital acquired through a working life and topped up by redundancy, will add significantly to the potential pool of funds to be invested. With time on their hands, such individuals are already honing their investment skills. Moreover, as adults live ever longer, they will likely turn to greater investment in their dotage.

The new playing field for financial investment has become far more level than ever before. It allows vast quantities of information to be disseminated to any trader anywhere in the world within seconds. Paper-based publications are already seeing their margins eroded through the rapid accessibility of electronic media. With total immodesty, I am happy to draw readers to the attention of my own titles, via http://www.erivatives.com – available for free. It is difficult to think of a better price to pay for information. What's more, the information is not merely free, it is global the instant the new issue is published on the first of the month. Paper publications can typically take days to reach even local addresses, and may take weeks to get to the other side of the world. Aside from being free, a good part of the reason my magazines have readers in over 130 countries world-wide is due to their instant dissemination to all corners of the globe.

As with monthlies, so too with hard news. Admittedly, information flow is only as good as the reporting and in third-world countries getting information out will remain an imperfect art for years to come. Indeed, the same is true even of some advanced nations such as Italy where financial news traditionally percolates around a network in Rome for a while then gets projected to the Milanese banks and finally breaks out of the cycle of going from bank to bank after maybe a few hours. Such information seepage will probably continue amongst those nations with the least perfect governance, but the internet means the timings are being increasingly reduced before an announcement is made official.

Market access is now becoming ever simpler for all manner of products across the globe. Equally, the increasing needs for derivatives brokers and clearing agents to entice more business on account of electronic trading providing lower margins will lead to increased access to all manner of commodity markets for any individual with the cash to enter this market. Now it will be possible to beat the big guys in a David and Goliath struggle. However, it won't be easy.

The amazing ascent of the online broker

Technology has dramatically reduced the cost of executing a trade. Suddenly, broker expertise might not be as valuable as brokers want investors to believe.

Andrew Klein, founder Wit Capital Corporation

Born in the US, online investing was a massive growth business until the dotcom bubble burst. The much lauded late 1990s projects of two-thirds of all brokerage commissions being earned online proved illusory as online brokers peaked in market share in Q2 2000 with 27% of transactions. By 2002, the ongoing negativity hanging around the stock market kept online commissions somewhat muted. However, the key issue to bear in mind with online trading is that while the initial froth was largely created by the first enthusiastic but often unskilled day traders, the key investing demographics of internet investors suggest that they are richer and more successful than the bulk of investors still using those brokers who "smile and dial."

Gradually, as the stock market picks up and as stock brokers become better able to offer a NewVas service (see below), thus encouraging their clients to move online, the future of brokerage will be exclusively via the internet with likely net dominance by the latter years of this decade, bear market or no bear market. For one thing, the cost of keeping human brokers is vastly greater than that of having a few client advisers who provide advice and leave order routing to the computers. If the stock market improves, more investors will probably move back online as they become more comfortable with underlying conditions once more. Similarly, if the bearish conditions of recent times worsen then brokers will be forced to reduce costs, retrenching staff and encouraging their clients to trade online. Whatever happens, online dealing will win the day.

The NewVas paradigm

Financial Services firms are not good at coping with rapid change.

The Economist

Different types of customers have different needs. Large institutional traders will look for value added from their brokers in the form of access to liquidity, anonymity, information dissemination and ultimately efficient order matching. These services will reduce the friction and slippage in their trading day. As markets evolve this will become a bigger and bigger issue as we see open outcry go electronic. Side-by-side trading and the eventual migration to the equity model of centralized clearing and competing ECNs, will cause liquidity fragmentation which will put large aggregators of order flow in a value added position enhancing the value of our services to the trader.

Brokers will act as an overlay to the exchanges creating price discovery. Smaller retail customers will use electronic systems but the value proposition from the broker is evolving into mainly an advisory capacity with more of an asset-gathering portfolio management approach, for example, advising on which asset managers or CTAs to invest in while being compensated through commission.

I see increased use of technology for retail investors being combined with broker interaction. The main focus will be in the investment advisory capacity wrapped into brokerage service.

Joe Murphy, CEO Refco

Nowadays, brokers need to be smarter, more conversant with a broader range of product areas and have more global knowledge than ever before. With a diversified client base, linguistic skills will remain at a premium. While English is undoubtedly the global language of financial markets, clients like being spoken to in their own language. As the broker's job becomes less that of an order gatherer and more of a dynamic client liaison person, the man who can speak to his customers in their domestic language will remain highly prized. The successful brokerage must be capable of providing "new value added services" (NewVas). NewVas means being more in touch with every aspect of a client's business. The old days of a broker who merely regurgitated a few lines of research and then spent the day shouting orders into markets at a clients' behest while providing heavily price-driven information are already long over. In many respects, the broker's job is becoming one akin to a trainer or coach. The NewVas broker therefore will need to be well read, creating his own ideas with a vast array of understanding of the markets, as well as more traditional broker "savvy." The old-style "wide boy" which London's East End exported to the world is going to face extinction unless he can learn a great deal more about how and why markets function on both a micro and macro level. His role as a glorified trade processor is already under death sentence and will not last beyond the next five years.

Discounted broker ... but not discount brokers

The key to winning in online brokerage is harnessing state-of-the-art execution technology to the essential analytical and sales capabilities of the best existing brokers. Even with all the advances of modern technology, people still matter.

Mike Stiller, Managing Director, Global Direct Dealing (GDD) AG

There is one enormous misperception that existing brokers just don't get about the process of brokerages going online. Many "full-service" brokerages erroneously (if not contemptuously) have lumped online trading firms together with traditional "no frills" discount brokerage operations. In fact, the two are entirely separate. Discount brokers are providing a cheap service without any added extras. On the other hand, online brokerages are merely exploiting the technological apparatus of the Capital Market Revolution to offer a scope of potentially extensive breadth and depth of analysis, data, research and brokerage quotes/prices and ultimately direct market trading access which no full-service broker can ever hope to provide via one broker.

Ultimately, the full-service brokers face annihilation as most execution goes electronic. Similarly, brokerage offices will become relative ghost towns as the number of staff shrinks commensurate with the need to remove salaried bodies from the food chain.

Who owns the money?

One of the most significant issues to the business of building a cohesive strong global brokerage will be the issue of who owns the money. Being a "distributor" (i.e. taking a large number of orders and processing them through your own funnel to a broad range of different markets) is a key issue for every truly significant brokerage in the information age. However, if you don't hold the cash, then your prospects for survival are limited. The idea that successful intermediaries are "technology" companies is of course a red herring. Brokers and exchanges are no more technology companies than MTV or CNBC. The simple fact is that if my money goes into an account that both my broker and I can use to settle my trades (aka a bank account of some denomination), then that broker is infinitely better placed to survive than the broker whose relationship with his client is more tenuous in terms of money held.

Pitfalls of avarice

All of us think of ourselves as rational beings even in times of crisis, applying the laws of probability in cool and calculated fashion to the choices that confront us. We like to believe we are above-average in skills, intelligence, farsightedness, experience, refinement, and leadership. Who admits to being an incompetent driver, a feckless debater, a stupid investor, or a person with an inferior taste in clothes?

Peter Bernstein, *Against the Gods*

In *Seeing Tomorrow – Rewriting the Rules of Risk*, Ron Dembo and Andrew Freeman quote the behavioral economist Meir Statman, bluntly addressing the risk facing the private investor when he enters the ring after some amateur bouts to contest a few rounds with the professionals:[5]

> Most investors simply cannot see that they are the suckers in the game. The real suckers are the ones who think they can divine inside information from the *Wall Street Journal*. For example, they might read an article about ageing baby boomers who need bifocals and think they can make a buck by buying shares in an eyewear company. But they are usually just observing something that lots of other people already know.

The private investors who will survive the grueling pace of professional investment will need to be trained like Samurai in the art of investment. In many respects the online trader casualties of the dotcom boom were entirely as a result of their believing they had some unique insight into markets – a process reinforced by continuing bull market profits which was more a reflection of what the market was doing than any particular skill on their part. Therefore the need to be suitably educated will of course be helped by an increasing range of training courses and seminars put on by the successful pros. Alas, there will also be a lot of substandard material, peddled by those affectionately referred to as "snake oil" vendors by many trading professionals. Certainly, a worrying aspect to the internet stock boom of the late 1990s was that so many private client traders looked alarmingly like they were being driven more by the "greater fool"[6] theory than anything else. Nevertheless, those pouring money into simple, boring old-fashioned courses need to be aware that in the digital age, with attention spans always being attacked by other more exciting images, the point of education must be that it is an entertainment issue rather than a lot of boring Powerpoints displays or paper courses. Education needs to be entertaining. In many ways customer education needs to happen by stealth.

Certainly, many private clients will need a considerable amount of application to be in a position to trade with the experts. However, given how many months it will take to study to cook like a cordon bleu chef in all foodstuffs, the road to being a competent trader in many (if not all) markets is probably somewhat easier. What's more, only the truly exceptional cook can become a genuine cordon bleu chef. Armed with a judicious dose of discipline and reasonable application, just about any reasonably capitalized individual has the opportunity to make it as a professional trader.

A new blueprint for a new local

Locals can and are beginning to use electronic systems effectively.

Roz Wilton

Open outcry works as well as it does because of the locals. They are the ones that supply the bids as the market looks for a bottom. They are the ones that scalp the market, providing the liquidity, keeping the spreads in line.

Why are locals willing to do that? Why do they take those risks? They do it because they make money at it. The reason they make money is that they have an advantage by virtue of the fact that they stand in the pit. They see and hear and feel things traders away from the floor can't sense. The successful locals can turn this extra information into enough of an advantage to make a living.

Wendell Kapustiak, Director of Global Futures Operations, Merrill Lynch

Ms Wilton's statement dating all the way back to mid-1997 when she was MD of transaction products at Reuters, demonstrates one aspect to financial markets which has been of some concern to many individuals and institutions alike. Indeed, even today in Chicago, many floor locals simply refuse to believe that there are independent traders profiting from screens. Of course, there are, but they employ subtly different approaches to those required for successful floor trading. Independent traders on the floor of an exchange – "locals" as they are referred to – are as old as the trading floors themselves. The local has traditionally provided liquidity in exchange for being able to trade on the floor. The local garnered certain advantages from this geographical proximity to the market which helped him profit. For locals, one great advantage was the capacity to watch order flow entering the pit and then be able to trade in the direction of the orders. In a way this was a sort of "front running" to the market, but it still gave an advantage to the faster institutions and penalized the slow which after all is the core competitive Darwinian dynamic which sport and trading are all about. Locals were fortunate in that pit orders could not be precisely prioritized as to the time they arrived in the marketplace. Therefore, locals could simply lift the offers to buy the market as they wanted when they needed to be aggressive and move the market (or vice versa) when they wished to sell. This lovely advantage has been removed by electronic systems where the exchanges are imposing a first-in, first-out order execution system. For locals trading in an electronic age, the cream has gone. Accepting things will not be the same again remains a key reason why the locals are flirting with oblivion not just for themselves but all the legacy US open outcry exchanges, every time they drag their feet on closing their beloved floors.

The evolving local *Realpolitik*

Many folk have tried to say that locals are written off. Most of them are abjectly misinformed, the rest tend to be institutional employees who feel acutely jealous of the fortunes accrued by the best of the independent pit traders. The fact is that locals now have a tremendous opportunity to profit from the post-feudal marketplace. However, they will have to modify their styles of dealing and their thought processes substantially. Those who cannot manage such fundamental re-engineering will find themselves out of business. However, there will be others who will readily fill this space. The e-locals will flourish in the new environment, especially as they will be able to diversify risk and explore new opportunities in a vast array of different markets, all of which can now be traded electronically from the comfort of wherever they wish to be.

The trading arcade concept that the likes of Fastrade US and Transmarket have popularized in Chicago, Kyte futures in London and organizations like LQuay and Traderspace in Sydney, Australia have created in recent years will be a core meeting place for those locals who enjoy a degree of social side to their trading. Otherwise, one downside to trading alone at home is that it can be a remarkably solitary experience. The experience at LIFFE for instance will be mirrored when the US trading floors close. At first, the clustering was dense around the old exchange floor above Cannon Street station in the heart of the "square mile." Then as traders realized they had sufficient data available at the click of a mouse, new trading arcades sprang up outside central London, for instance, at the junctions of the M25 motorway around London – especially to the east, and in Essex where many former LIFFE floor locals live. Equally, arcades are already proving popular in tax havens where locals can keep their profits away from rapacious, reactionary governments who have yet to understand what the post-feudal marketplace means for them. A similar process of moving out of town will happen in Chicago where in a few years time new trading arcades will be established such as Evanston and other suburbs and dormitory towns as opposed to just within the loop where they began clustering in recent years.

Interestingly, when MATIF first went electronic, the exchange actually found itself initially adding capacity from locals soon after the move to screen-based trading. Local volume moved from 15 to 20% of exchange volume totals, when comparing the initial electronic trading period to the latter months of open outcry. In fact some 20 new locals joined the exchange to trade exclusively electronically soon after the market closed the floor.

The data revolution

Just as the whole process of the new multimedia age assists the smallest independent traders, so too the whole ethos of the information age may have significant effects on the finances of existing exchanges. In the late 1990s the Chicago Board of Trade typically received *circa* $50 million in revenue for the sale of its quotes to dealers throughout the world. Exchanges have habitually charged a fee via the data vendors such as Reuters or Bloomberg for any market to which a trader has sought access. Indeed, when computer archiving was more expensive during the 1980s and early 1990s, historical data was traditionally a rich resource which could be resold by vendors for significant premiums. Alas, the increasing digitization of common (and readily transferable) formats of data storage are already radically changing the way data is sold.

While in the interim, exchanges have clung on to selling their real-time data to bolster post-demutualization profits, ultimately this revenue will be under threat with continued outright competition for market share in competing products. In an environment where a niche exchange can spring up via the internet within a matter of months, there will be increasing numbers of contracts competing for the trader's attention. True, some core dealers will invariably focus on particular markets and will be willing to pay the appropriate data fees. However, with markets increasingly needing to keep the liquidity providers happy, there will be many independent traders, e-locals and the like who will tend to look at contracts where they are given free access to the real-time feeds.

Similarly, with the cost of disseminating such prices falling all the time, exchanges have been offering limited live quotes via their web-sites since the late 1990s. Such free vending of quotations will continue to grow exponentially and will wreak havoc with the existing structures of established exchanges. In the case of some exchanges, fees on contracts to members and users have been kept artificially low for the sake of placating the membership but this cross-subsidy from selling data is about to become extinct. Then again, the CBOT demonstrated an interesting sense of proportion in early 2002, by raising fees for electronic trade in what many onlookers sensed was a hamfisted method of trying to protect the floor from the electronic a/c/e platform the CBOT had itself created.

Data fees may survive until 2010 but I expect only those exchanges with strong niche monopolies will be able to get away with this. In capital markets where barriers to entry are low, free data will increasingly be the norm after 2005. There may also be small charges for certain precious pieces of archived data but this too will be a fraction of the cost of such services in the 1980s and 1990s. After all, online front-end trading systems for futures markets are not paying quote vendor fees for the data their clients use to trade with. The question must soon arise, why will a quote vendor continue to charge merely to look at such data when those using it for trading are getting it free? The Capital Market Revolution blows holes in existing exchange cash flows. Nowhere is this more graphically apparent than with regard to data vending fees. However, most exchanges will try to patch over this until they can at least get their IPOs out of the way.

There may be some new sources of revenue available to exchanges, such as increased returns from those outside issuers of OTC or on exchange products linked to particular indices (index tracker funds, etc.) where a fee will be paid for the use of the exchanges index, etc. However, even these are unlikely to make up for the losses to be suffered from exchanges who find that in a truly competitive market, data cannot be sold at the sort of monopolistic prices which became a habit for some large markets during the 1980s.

Survival skills for the revolution

In many respects, the Capital Market Revolution is likely to become a huge destroyer of jobs. As is typical of all revolutions, existing interests will not be well served by this process.

For those who are currently employed within and around the securities industry, the risks provided by the ongoing waves of the Capital Market Revolution are massive. Having said that, the upside for those well placed will be quite stunning. Nevertheless, all practitioners will need to make some sacrifices, or at least amendments to their lifestyle, if they are to succeed in the information age. Of course, the one prerequisite everybody needs is naturally enough computer literacy. Then again if you don't already have this, one is inclined to wonder which cave you have been living in this past decade or so. But what else can you no longer ignore?

1. Language skills   Even in a world where translation skills mean that it will soon be possible to speak Mandarin at the touch of a

button during a telephone call thanks to an online translator, Naisbitt's "Global Paradox" still applies – the more global things become, the more the influence of the individual increases. Foreign language skills will remain prized assets for financial practitioners – especially as the NewVas broker is likely to spend considerable amounts of time travelling to client liaisons in their home countries.

2. Geographical flexibility   Nobody can expect to work in New York and live upstate in the commuter belt any more. The best jobs will often be in foreign countries and frequently offshore ones at that. The employee who limits his home to a narrow geographical area (even one so globally relevant and cosmopolitan as New York or London) will find their prospects severely diminished. Note how New York remains the financial powerhouse of the US but with much of the computing power in California. Financial power in and around Silicon Valley will continue to grow especially as the post-dotcom bubble world of internet-related computing starts to become profitable.

3. Market knowledge   It will be critical to learn more about as many markets as possible. Stockbrokers are already amongst the least employable of those made redundant during the Capital Market Revolution. Why? Because they have the narrowest focus of any major brokerage group. They tend to understand how to sell securities only within narrow fields (in the new globalized market even the whole American stock market is a narrow field compared to the vast array of investment opportunities soon to be found at one-stop shops online). In the futures markets, while a large number of relatively narrowly focused, execution-oriented brokers remain, their days are numbered. The post-feudal marketplace suggests that the brokers who succeed will be an informed, globally literate, cognitive elite. For stockbrokers wondering how to break out of their niche, gaining an understanding of futures on single stocks and from that index futures as well as related index and individual stock options and warrants is a very good way to start. The single stock futures

business will likely take about 18 months to reach critical mass but it will ultimately become a pivotal aspect to the entire securities industry.

4. Think global   The virtual world is one where the entire market will be available at the click of a mouse. Specialization in one narrow locally focused sector is already insufficient to maintain employment at many leading institutions. Brokers, analysts and traders need to think macro, with an eye on the micro, when it comes to research and trading. The old concept of simply trading a particular share because it holds a niche in one small national market is over. In the future, the market will be more niche-bound than ever but those niches will be regional and global, rather than provincial.

Whoever you are, whatever you do, wherever you are involved in financial markets, the Capital Market Revolution is already making an impact on your business. The keys to surviving and prospering in the revolution require some application but to the victor the spoils. To the losers go the keys to the taxi cab.

Notes

1. *Hedge Funds – Investment and Portfolio Strategies for the Institutional Investor.* Editors Jess Lederman and Robert A. Klein, Irwin, ISBN 1-55738-861-X.   This original hedge fund methodology was hugely successful for AW Jones. Indeed, Carol J. Loomis even wrote a feature for *Fortune* magazine headlined "The Jones Nobody Keeps Up With".

2. Ibidem.

3. The position of Soros in managing Quantum can be to some degree debated that in fact while Soros himself has a prodigious capacity for managing money, his key attribute actually lies in picking the right people (such as Henry Druckenmiller) to manage the Quantum coffers at appropriate stages of the investment cycle.

4. That is, bereft of meddlesome politicians trying to carve a niche for themselves by interrupting the money flows, usually in the interests of protecting a cartel which to a greater or lesser degree usually seems to include the politicians themselves.

5. *Seeing Tomorrow – Rewriting the Rules of Risk* by Ron Dembo and Andrew Freeman, Wiley 1998, ISBN 0-471-24736-7.
6. The "greater fool" theory states that any investment is a good one provided you can always find a "greater fool" to buy it from you at a profit. Ultimately, when one runs out of fools to pay higher multiples then the market must collapse.

Chapter 6

The Microbanking Manifesto
aka How Very Small Can Be Beautiful Too

A whole industry is shifting from the physical world to the virtual.

The Economist

London: As one walks across from the Bank of England in Thread-needle Street, one passes the incredible front of the Royal Exchange. Nowadays a magnificent Georgian structure housing a swish shopping arcade, dealing operations have taken place at this site since the Middle Ages. More recently, the LIFFE futures market began within its beautiful shell. Approaching Mansion House as one crosses the end of Cornhill, the amazing history of the City of London is everywhere in evidence.

Crossing King William Street and just beside the Mansion House – the magnificent ceremonial headquarters for the incumbent of that most famous of civic positions, the Lord Mayor of London – one reaches a rather anonymous looking Georgian building. Inside, "One Lombard Street" is a magnificent restaurant, occupying a wonderful banking hall long since rendered redundant by the march of technology in the financial industry. In its heyday, this long white-walled chamber complete with domed ceiling leaving the interior bathed in natural light was used by many great bankers of the Empire. Now the wheeler dealers of the electronic age increasingly congregate for splendid dining within an austere yet magnificently charismatic environment.

Similar gastronomic ingenuity has transformed the likes of the former Reserve Bank of Australia Hall in Sydney's CBD into a wonderful fine-dining restaurant appropriately called "Banc." Throughout the world, banking rationalization and mergers have left many grand premises unoccupied. With the Capital Market Revolution further driving staff numbers down, those that do house restaurants may ultimately find themselves also forced out of business as financial districts struggle to come to terms with the stunning changes being wrought throughout the capital markets. In the world of banking, retail and wholesale, the changes will be no less stunning. It may be worth noting that as glorious banking halls increasingly become restaurants and bars the world over, perhaps the word bank may ultimately be applied to some form of eating reference. After all, banks themselves derived their name from the word for the benches at which moneylenders sat and transacted their business in the days before banks were formally organized.

The only matter of consequence silicon produces are relationships.

Kevin Kelly, editor of *Wired*

For the past decade, the world of banking has been increasingly transfixed by the ongoing merger mania at the very top end. To be a serious bank, one had to be a serious global player. To be a serious global player, one needed to be in as many physical locations as possible, not just for retail banking but for investment banking and related functions too. Global megabanks are probably here to reign supreme for perhaps a decade or more before a wave of rationalization befalls them. Meanwhile, the banks which will have the greatest effect upon the world at large will be entities that are a fraction of the size of the megabanks. Microbanks will become the massive success story of this century. They will be tiny institutions, with staffs smaller than most existing megabanks' IT departments. Yet such institutions can still be global, with only token offices in more than one jurisdiction. They will be capable of handling vastly complex banking transactions from almost any part of the globe and yet they will exist almost entirely in cyberspace. A virtual bank servicing a virtual world. Nevertheless, the megabanks will remain the biggest focus in onshore finance the world over, thanks to their retaining core brands in the main retail marketplaces. To the microbanks will fall the niche spoils thanks to their specialization and flexibility in approaching new markets.

In the post-feudal marketplace, any bank can operate anywhere, regardless of the banking statutes in force. Indeed, whereas the US has often had a relatively open policy towards the creation of new banking institutions, many European countries have traditionally been loath to accept new banks being established unless they have staggering quantities of capital available. Some of the few new banks to be established in the UK during the 1990s were all owned by supermarket chains. The existing banking industry was incredulous that businesses skilled in stacking shelves, shuffling produce into a network of stores ahead of impending sell-buy dates and providing a wide choice of consumer products for the customer, were intending to enter the "specialized" business of banking. If nothing else, the moral indignation of existing bankers at the government for permitting such new competition only served to demonstrate just how mollycoddled banks had been and just how far removed from reality the banking business had become. And of course, the fact that big brands could enter banking without much prior experience of the process but with the power of their brand and consumer businesses to bring in custom, is itself another clear indicator of just how "left field" players can still enter the marketplace for any financial service, including the exchange business as I have already discussed.

A premium on incompetence

Online banking puts further strain on the established clearing banks with their antiquated notions that it takes three days to clear a cheque – in an age of real time, 24-hours a day, global transactions this simply will not do. Digital cash systems – micropayment schemes – will not only create the largest market in the World but also – because of the attraction of issuing proprietary digital cash – threaten the very foundation of established finance – and point towards a disintermediation of many of the financial institutions that have emerged since the Industrial Revolution – maybe even the disintermediation of national governments.

Bob Cotton

Bankers are almost universally unpopular. Given their often aloof, incompetent, uncommunicative ways of dealing with customers, it isn't difficult to see why. Banks have had a lovely cartel for too long. If a client disliked being a captive client of one bank, they could switch to another and be treated with the same cavalier disregard. Banks knew that they were the only safe guardians of money and that their audience was essentially trapped into doing business with them. In other words, banks treated their customers with the same blithe disregard as governments treated their citizens. No matter how bad their service was, people would still need banks and with only limited competition in most jurisdictions, banks knew they could stay in business thanks to government restrictions on new entrants. Nowadays, there is simply no reason why it should take ten days or more for a payment to leave a bank account in London to reach a bank in the Mediterranean – yet that is one of the shorter time periods I have experienced during 2001 and 2002. If everything else can go real-time, why can't banking?

Micropayment – the key to new banking

Banks traditionally make their money from fees charged for transactions as well as holding money for periods of time during transactions when it is legally owned by a client. Such clearing services are increasingly farcical. Transactions beyond national borders are costly and frequently incompetent. The SWIFT system supposedly offers three-day transfers between, for example, UK and Italian banks. In reality, the process can easily take a fortnight. When a customer tries to discover what has gone wrong, both banks shrug their shoulders and point the finger of blame at the other. Even within domestic markets, lodging checks often takes a three-day wait before the money is actually lodged to an account. Information as to where the payment actually is in the system is not available to the client. In the information age, where other businesses are increasingly adjusting to improved information flow, the banks seem to be setting their computers the task of making transactions easier to charge for without adding any value to the service.

With the Capital Market Revolution already destabilizing their financial market transactions, the core banking business of holding money and moving it from one place to another (at which banks appear singularly incompetent in many instances), will be revolutionized. To date banks have been arguably poorer than their exchange cousins in understanding just how flexible they need to be to achieve online success despite most of them trying to pay lip service to the benefits of the internet. Eventually, banks will be unable to expect fat fees for minuscule effort. In the information age, the commoditization of banking will result in increased facility of transaction and remarkable drops in fees. Micropayments will become the order of the day for banking transactions, even though they are currently seen as a rare animal despite being much touted during the dotcom boom. Transaction costs will drop to a few cents for what is today regarded as a "sophisticated" cross-border wire transfer. Furthermore, transactions will be in real time. Banks will lose the capacity to rape their clients through fees and the withholding of their funds. Without massive adjustments to their overheads and dealing practices, correspondent banks will wither and die. The banks have fought to keep cybermoney at bay and have been reluctant to embrace cheap cross-border transactions. However, the common Euro currency region is already being undermined to some degree by the fact that transferring the Euro from one Eurozone country such as Germany to Spain can be prohibitively expensive. When the proposed cheap alternatives from the likes of Visa are fully functional, banks will find their networks being challenged for the first time.

Using cybermoney, there will be a huge new market for tiny transactions. Microroyalties will be increasingly payable online for information. A single article from a newspaper will be purchasable for a few cents, the bank will receive maybe as little as a fraction of a cent for facilitating the transaction. Increasingly, parallel forms of e-cash will compete for transaction dollars. Online, many currencies will be corporatised, owned by institutions with either the enabling technology such as Microsoft or the commercial reputation of a global brand, for instance McDonald's. Ultimately, if governments are seen to have done a poor job, it will be virtual cash which becomes the currency oiling the world's economy and its financial markets in the aftermath of the Capital Market Revolution.

Indeed, the basic economics of cyber banking have not changed since the birth of the internet. Arguably online transactions have become slightly cheaper over time but even as long ago as 1998, the statistics were unequivocally demonstrating that something must give in the banking hierarchy when Frost and Sullivan calculated relative costs of simple cash withdrawals in 1998 (all costs are in US dollars)

Personal over-the-counter transactions	1.95
ATM transactions	0.80
Telephone banking transactions	0.60
Internet banking transactions	0.30
Internet credit card transactions	0.20
e-cash transactions	0.01

E-cash in some shape or form is inevitably destined to beat the banks. However, first it needs to establish a credible foothold in customers' wallets. While the concept has so far moved slowly, it nonetheless has had some interesting moments to date.

At present online banking is largely cumbersome, user unfriendly and pernickety. The banks need to understand how to create a way to hold customers' cash and manage it to the best possible benefit of both banker and client. At present, apart from isolated experiments such as Zebank (discussed below) there have been few attempts to do anything other than move traditional bricks-and-mortar banking online. As the *Financial Times* noted in February 2002, UK high street banks were increasingly losing their wealthy customers to online financial services and overseas private banks who could offer online account information, etc. The bond between the local bank manager and his clients has long since been broken by the high street banks themselves as they sought to increase profitability. Now, the wealthier clients (as we saw previously also more likely to be dealing online in shares) are also happier with leaving their money in online bank accounts too. In other words, the smart money is already moving online. How long before they start to demand more and more intriguing services? In the digital world of the 21st century, there is nothing to stop banks creating their own benchmarks for investment and indeed money as a store of value.

New currencies

E-cash will be the money of the future. Banks will predominantly be based offshore – or at least in very reasonable onshore regulatory environments. They may even operate in parallel locations to stop predatory policing by increasingly desperate large nations throwing their weight around. Dale Davidson and Rees-Mogg neatly described how an investor will place all assets "in a cyberaccount in a cyberbank that is domiciled simultaneously in Newfoundland, the Cayman Islands, Uruguay, Argentina, and Liechtenstein. If any of the jurisdictions attempt to withdraw operating authority or seize the assets of depositors, the assets will automatically be transferred to another jurisdiction at the speed of light."[1]

E-cash will revolutionize banking. Electronic cash will not merely be equivalent to existing currencies such as the US dollar or Japanese yen, it will increasingly take on a life of its own and indeed will ultimately subsume many, if not all, national currencies.

The end of fiat money?

A more advanced stage will mark the transition to true cybercommerce. Not only will transactions occur over the Net, but they will migrate outside the jurisdiction of nation-states. Payment will be rendered in cyber-currency. Profits will be booked in cyberbanks. Investments will be made in cyberbrokerages. Many transactions will not be subject to taxation. At this stage, cybercommerce will begin to have significant megapolitical consequences of the kind I have already outlined. The powers of government over traditional areas of the economy will be transformed by the new logic of the Net. Extraterritorial regulatory power will collapse. Jurisdictions will devolve. The structure of firms will change, and so will the nature of work and employment.

This outline of the stages of the information revolution is only the barest sketch of what could be the most far-reaching economic transformation ever.

James Dale Davidson and William Rees-Mogg, *The Sovereign Individual*

Of course, investors will need an incentive to invest in such digital money. Initially, consumers will hold small quantities of virtual cash in order to facilitate online transactions. However, as the virtual world develops, the prevalence of online transactions will increasingly encourage investors to move their money online. Governments' increasingly desperate clampdowns on assets left onshore will serve only to accelerate the process. In the end, the best stores of value will win. Since the end of gold standards and the collapse of the Bretton Woods agreement, the era of "fiat" money (i.e. money with no underlying value apart from a guarantee of the solvency of the central bank and government) has been with us. In the event of somebody wishing to create asset-backed currencies online, fiat money may well find itself suffering intense competition.

Like all market structures, a wide array of currencies will exist in cyberspace although increasingly a small number will gain widespread acceptance. In this respect, I believe the currency of the future will be asset-backed. One of the more frightening aspects to the finances of the late twentieth century was the common use of worthless fiat money. While it is true that the system still exists, a future financial crisis has the power to demonstrate clearly just how worthless this fiat money is when operated by increasingly out-of-touch governments. In the future, currencies will revert to being asset-backed. Digital cash will equate to quantities of silver or gold and other precious metals.

Interestingly, no less an economist than Friedrich von Hayek argued in *The Denationalisation of Money* as long ago as 1976 that the implementation of competing private currencies would be an effective weapon in reducing, if not entirely eliminating, inflation. Privately issued money must retain its value, or investors will be attracted to a different currency which can safely maintain its valuation. In the information age, digital money issued by a wide range of organizations on a huge number of different bases will increasingly bring Hayek's dream to reality.

Money will increasingly take on other characteristics as well. With increasing commoditization of financial processes, it will be perfectly feasible to use a vast array of fungible versions of electronic transaction units (ETUs) which will take an infinite number of forms. ETUs will be limited in their construction only by the ingenuity of humans to develop them. In a wired world where real-time valuation is a fact of life, anything can be instantly traded. Use of ETUs will be dismissed as barter by governments but it will increasingly be impossible to discern what is really money and what an asset. In the online world, real-time valuation makes all assets instantly transferable.

Typical early examples of ETUs will probably include equity-linked money where the cash is collateralized by share values. Thus, such cash will be backed by the assets of a company and valued as a function of the stock price. Instead of having to sell stock, the online consumer will be able instantly to buy household goods, or a car or property online with payment in stock notes. The vendor will be able instantly to transfer the value of the ETU into the digital cash of his choice (for a minuscule transaction fee) or hold the ETU in its current form as he wishes. Of course, such quasi-barter may not appeal to tax authorities but then again the virtual world will remain an ostensibly tax-free zone. Taxes will accrue according to the jurisdiction in which an individual or a company wishes to locate.

Other forms of ETU will include securitized notes based on bank loan portfolios, or mortgages, insurance policies – any form of financial asset. Ultimately, the realms of ETUs are limited only by the imagination. I expect that there will be ETUs issued based around such relatively esoteric concepts as the success of sports clubs. What more imaginative way could soccer fans be invited to fund their football team's new stadium or player acquisitions than by inviting them to buy discounted ETUs which rise as the club gains points in the league or wins domestic or international competitions?

In the old days, companies and sports clubs had to issue bonds through complex offering memoranda governed by securities laws. In the near future, bonds will become ETUs. ETUs will be essentially cash (thanks to instantaneous 24-hour-per-day valuation on electronic markets) and be readily transferable for goods and services in a way which has not been seen for several centuries. In the future, the whole business of money will become a core focus of our everyday lives. The cyber traders and e-locals who go online early in the revolution will be well placed to capitalize on the enormous change in business, commerce and domestic lifestyle.

The story so far

There have been several experiments to date with cybercash although none has really managed to create a measure of traction. Perhaps the most publicized to date was the Beenz project which went bankrupt in 2001. While the management blamed the costs of transferring cash to their own online currency, in reality Beenz was fundamentally flawed from the moment it was christened. The public doesn't want money called "Beenz" any more than it expects to deposit funds with the Bank of Toytown. Nevertheless, the issue of keeping a cost-effective currency is key. However, just as exchange traded funds can create vast index trackers for fractions of cents on the dollar, so too a well-engineered new currency can operate in a similar fashion – although of course it cannot be too reliant on expensive bank networks (as Beenz was) to offer an alternative product.

There are some interesting online payment methods using the existing government currencies such as PayPal which have increasingly grown in popularity, although their ability to become global solutions is still somewhat hampered by cross-border regulation. Nevertheless, that is changing. Also, the need for a central clearing service could yet be a boon for utilities in telecoms, gas and electricity who may be able to morph into quasi-banks of some denomination through being already accustomed to providing commmoditized low-cost services. Likewise, Amazon has edged into the same field through the provision of payment systems for certain online subscriptions and their own second-hand book-selling service. Surprisingly, there is already a poten-tial ETU which is readily understood by the population and which could certainly transform itself into huge units of cybercurrency; perhaps even adding to profits at companies which were at one stage facing widespread oblivion as recently as the first half of 2002.

The future of cyber currency: all up in the air?

In 1981, American Airlines launched Aadvantage, the world's first mileage-based frequent-flyer program. By 2002, some 100 million people around the world belong to at least one such scheme (excluding those for hotels and so forth such as Starwood's excellent Preferred Guest Program). In the beginning, they were a reward for loyalty and a chance for airlines to garner information on their most regular users, providing essential marketing information about the airlines' most profitable customers. According to the *Economist*, nowadays almost 50% of air miles are attained without ever leaving the ground. Various means such as credit cards, telephone calls, grocery shopping with the likes of hotel rental and share trading offering further opportunities to top up air mile accounts. In 2001, American Airlines frequent flyers occupied some 10% of total passenger flying miles, up from 8.4% in 2000. That said, some airlines are more difficult to redeem miles with, as many passengers will readily attest.

The key problem is that without restrictions to fly some airlines could be bankrupted by the existing quantity of their miles in circulation. And what is a mile worth anyway? Well, if you can redeem enough for a first-class ticket, it can be around ten cents. Some airlines sell miles to credit card companies for about two cents per mile and from 2001, some American airlines were selling direct to customers for three cents per mile to top up their existing accounts. Of course, one issue for all frequent flyers is that their miles are not freely tradable. On the other hand, perhaps the airlines have not realized just what a huge opportunity they are missing. Never mind the relative merits of going faster in the mooted Sonic Cruiser or the existing "Speedbird" Concorde as opposed to using Jumbo Jets or the Airbus A380, what airlines ought to consider is creating their own cybercurrency. By allowing their miles to become more popularly used to shop online, it may alleviate the overhang of miles that threaten so many airlines as well as the continuing threat of a widespread air mile devaluation. Such a move might help equate supply/demand differences for flights but risk alienating a public who have worked so hard to accumulate this second currency in the first place.

After all, the pressure upon air mile systems is growing daily and without a new avenue for their utilization, the airlines face deep difficulties. The website http://www.webflyer.com, has some alarming statistics. For instance, the total number of miles awarded in the past five years has doubled but redemptions have increased by only a third. During 2001, the *Economist* notes, "over four times as many miles were earned as awarded. At the current rate of redemption, it would take 23 years to clear this liability even if no new ones were issued." There were something like eight trillion miles available for redemption across all frequent-flyer schemes at the end of 2001. Airlines could help themselves, and indeed create a wondrous boost to online trade, if only they have the vision to become the masters of the one electronic trading unit that vast swathes of consumers already know and appreciate. Of course, such currencies may have significantly greater impact on specific regions. British Airways Air Miles may be largely a UK-related currency with Singapore Airlines' KrisFlyer miles more widely accumulated in Asia.[2] Having said that, relative mile pricing between different cyber currencies would be a simple calculation for most automated payment web sites.

The prospect for frequent flyers of taking online commerce into orbit is wonderfully intriguing. With the currency underpinned to a degree by the value of air travel, the currency itself has arguably more net worth than fiat money. And as a wider means of exchange, the possibility for them to become tradable units would reduce the pressure on the airlines, as well as providing them with a potentially lucrative franchise as currency issuers.

However you look at it, sooner or later new means of exchange are going to enter the marketplace and on the internet, while the US dollar may be king at the present moment, it nevertheless has a fairly fragmented share of the total trade. Likewise, owning the money will be a key process (just as with investment) and indeed in that respect eBay taking over PayPal in July 2002 was a key transaction. EBay, arguably a stalking horse brand for all forms of transaction capitalism, took over a company already heavily reliant on it for revenue but added to the eBay network the fundamentals of its own payment and arguably banking and currency issuance service. Remember, who "owns" the money (in whatever form) is a key facet to the Capital Market Revolution. Likewise, branding is also vital.

Increasingly, consumer entities seen as providers of a "good deal" to the public have been entering financial services. The British billionaire Richard Branson for instance. Similarly, in late 2001, the British easyJet discount airline founder Stelios Haji-Ioannou announced plans for an "easyMoney" credit card brand. Just like in the exchange business, banks are sufficiently unpopular world-wide that consumer champions in all regions of the world have the potential to usurp them in the digital world not just in banking but also investment products.

Governments lose power

As governments find themselves increasingly pushed out of the monopoly provision of currency issuance, they will doubtless endeavor to destroy the early forms of digital cash and ETUs when they first begin to threaten their existence. By then it will be too late. Cries of anguish that the whole system is unregulated by government intervention will be true. The inference that the system is more dangerous as a result will undoubtedly ring false. After all, banking systems have often flourished without government intervention or the questionable benefits of government guarantees on deposits (which throughout history have tended to become little more than a government charter to foster banking inefficiency or excessive risk taking). Private currencies competed successfully in Scotland for much of the first half of the eighteenth century without any form of Scottish central bank. Private bankers (free to enter the market) took deposits while issuing their own currency with backing of gold bullion. As Michael Prowse has noted in the *Financial Times*:

> There was little fraud. There was no evidence of over-issue of notes. Banks did not typically hold either excessive or inadequate reserves. Bank runs were rare and not contagious. The free banks commanded the respect of citizens and provided a sound foundation for economic growth that outpaced that in England for most of the period.

This is not specifically to endorse the Gold Standard. However, in a world where arbitrageurs and investment bankers can instantly parcel up a unit of exchange traded fund for a negligible cost with perhaps hundreds of separate components, then there is no reason why their ingenuity cannot also be used to create interchangeable stores of value related to other stocks, or commodities such as gold. The rights to such units can then be easily transferred online through smart cards at the click of a mouse.

Microbankers will encompass a whole new league of small-scale private banks and investment banking operations somewhat similar to the vast number of firms established in the nineteenth century. Their unique brand of direct capitalism threatens entirely to undermine attempts by rich governments to regulate markets during the past 50 years. In the nineteenth century, comparatively small banking institutions such as Barings, Lazards and Rothschilds were able to lend monies across the globe both within and beyond the broad reach of the British Empire. Banking will in many ways return to this sort of relationship in the new millennium. Banks will be able to handle millions, even billions in deposits, transactions and loans with only a minuscule number of staff. Once again, the established interests have a huge amount to fear from the Capital Market Revolution as nimble new players will be able to run rings around their massive bureaucracies. With public key encryption (as used for instance in ATM transactions at large commercial entities) now commonplace, the advantage is increasingly shifting in favor of the cyberbankers/cyberfinanciers. In the future, established onshore banks will become little more than facilitators of mortgages for onshore investment and owners of ATM machine networks for those few transactions that actually require paper money. Indeed, physical coins and notes will be largely defunct by 2020.

Meanwhile, the cyberbankers in the new era will be faced with the wonderful opportunity of providing a global service to customers throughout the world from the comfort of tiny offshore offices (perhaps several in parallel). The offshore regimes which swiftly offer the best terms for banking licenses will increasingly tap into a hugely profitable market as more and more companies congregate in offshore banking colonies. They may still have token offices in the old world's financial centers such as London, New York or Tokyo for appearances sake but the future banking centers of the world will become city states like Bermuda or Singapore. True money laundering may remain a concern but overall in the digital era, the ability to follow electronic transfers has improved sufficiently that the genuine criminals can ultimately be tracked down via their transactions regardless of where that business originates. After all, for every dollar that flows through some of the less reputable offshore islands in this day and age, it is clear that a great many transactions are also routed through major financial centers. Ultimately, banking clients are investors and they will all ultimately seek to be the guardians of their own fate (even if that entails picking money managers). The age of TOMBIS ("Total Online Management by Investor Solutions") grows closer by the day.

To accommodate the new world of fluid money and related customer services, the whole ethos of banks will have to change if they are to have a chance of prospering in the microbanking arena. Zebank (originally founded with backing from Bernard Arnault's Europ@web) may have ultimately been sold to the UK online bank, Egg, at the end of January 2001 before it reached maturity but it has outlined intriguing new possibilities for just what revenue model a bank must follow. Entirely online with no branch network, the bank was in fact more a broker than a conventional banker. Aside from a modest loan book for managing overdrafts, all deposits were netted off on the money market at the end of the working day and Zebank took a small "haircut" on the net interest rate. Similarly, if clients wanted a loan, they simply went to the providers recommended on the Zebank site and chose one of the preferred suppliers who then paid Zebank a small introductory fee. The same was the norm with all the other conventional banking services. Zebank acted as a central cash depository and provided cheque books and credit cards but the financial risk was all held by other specialist organizations. It was an intriguing model, devised by Olivier de Montety who had earlier

been a pioneering figure in European online trading, helping to
develop the Fimatex system for a Société Générale subsidiary.

The venture capital revolution

Clamour from small investors who want venture capital returns will alter how companies fund
themselves, and perhaps alter the nature of ownership.

The Economist

In the past, venture capital has been a curious business in many
respects. A bureaucratic operation with its own conventions. Venture
capitalists typically tend to seek so much equity for the financing they
inject that they are nowadays routinely referred to as "vulture
capitalists." Outside of America, they command relatively little
respect, although some firms such as the British-based 3i have been
very successful. However, it is the American culture that has really
embraced successful venture management. In Europe too many
organizations balk at the initial sums of money required rather than
valuing the potential upside. Essentially, America is simply more
entrepreneurial. A failed idea in Europe can lead to venture capital
ostracism; in America, there is no indignity in a failed venture for
either party. Indeed, such has been the culture of capitalism that in
California, some legal and other service firms have become rich
during the past decade on investments in companies as a *pro bono* for
services rendered. In Europe, accountancy and law firm partners tend
to go weak at the very thought of giving up income for any form of
investment.

Nevertheless, in Europe and indeed anywhere beyond the more
freewheeling and dealing shores of the US, the whole concept of
venture capital has been one which has largely failed to make major
inroads into the sort of business it could have had. One cannot blame
existing venture capitalists for their desire to cherry-pick the best deals.
However, at the same time, many projects have floundered in their
attempts to succeed or have been severely constrained by the relative
lack of funding available. The Capital Market Revolution will change
all of this. The opportunities afforded by it within the next decade will

be enormous. New businesses will be able to find funding and existing businesses be able to expand in a way unprecedented since the Industrial Revolution.

The downside, however, may be felt by existing venture capital firms. With traders increasingly able to take control of their own destiny and with the internet reducing the cost of accessing capital, the entire venture capital industry will see its core markets rendered much more competitive as companies increasingly use new, cheaper middlemen (or even go directly online under their own auspices) to raise capital. The key to this whole aspect to the revolution will be the increasing commoditization and globalization of investment and industrial/business markets. New pools will spring up to invest in technology or other specialist applications companies across the globe. The trading in the after market of shares and holdings in small companies will be radically amended. Of course such dealing will be risky but the rewards will once again be concomitantly vast.

In the new era, the smart venture capitalists will be online. They will not require huge numbers of employees to monitor investment opportunities. Rather a great deal of the work will be contracted out to third-party specialists, expert in geographical and industrial sectors and other appropriate niches. The whole process of seeking investing for a business will be greatly facilitated by being able to go online to seek out a venture capital broker who can offer your business the best service to help it expand, survive and prosper in the new reality. The simple process of utilizing contemporary multimedia for presentations will radically help promote business throughout the world and will help entrepreneurs find finance without having to take to the road to waste tedious amounts of time travelling between presentations to city houses in their offices. Regardless of headquarters, increasing globalization will permit ever simpler valuation of companies according to industry sector (although some small regional disparities may remain). However, the more business is transacted in cyberspace, the more such companies will be valued on the same premises.

Contemporary venture capital is a mix of specialist funds (such processes will increase due to the various processes I have already outlined with regard to funds growth in Chapter 5). Equally, those who organize venture capital funding through networks of interested parties, will in future be online networks. At present, such networks tend to be heavily localized. In future, such networks will be global. Pools of investors may be ready to invest in projects at the click of a mouse, hugely speeding up the whole venture capital process. For entrepreneurs, the revolution will be a godsend.

The disintermediation process will permit more and more entrepreneurs to go directly online to seek the funding they require. The modern venture capitalist will probably cluster around his website which has built up a reputation for quality deals. His fees will be much lower than currently sought by many investment banks even presuming they would actually organize the funding in the first place. With their margins for organizing funding under threat, only the swift will survive. Having said that, the prospect for those venture capitalists who can adapt to the new reality are, as ever, enormous. With an increasing pool of professional investors drawn from the ranks of e-locals and those retired, and prematurely retired, who manage their own funds, the pool available for direct venture capital investment will grow significantly.

There are amazing prospects for the big winners in digital finance who can create a new system of banking that is genuinely able to help clients as well as profiting from commoditized returns. Sophisticated securitization techniques have opened up the possibilities of Martini banking "anywhere, anytime, anyplace" (as the Turinese drinks manufacturers advertisements classically stated) and indeed 4A currencies "anything, anytime, anywhere, anyplace." Branding is as key an issue as it is anywhere and the good news for left field players is that customer satisfaction with existing bricks and mortar players – even many of the ones with online subsidiaries, is remarkably lukewarm – to put it mildly.

Notes

1. In *The Sovereign Individual*, 1999, Touchstone Books (US), 1998, Pan (UK).
2. For the benefit of disclosure, the author is a member of various frequent flyer programs including Singapore Airlines and British Airways.

Conclusion
The Winners, the Losers, and the Future of Finance

History never looks like history when you are living through it. It always looks confusing and messy, and it always feels uncomfortable.

John W. Gardner

The physical network of financial market dealers has given way to the virtual. To stay still is to await death by a thousand cuts. As I have outlined in this book, the Capital Market Revolution has had a lengthy history already. However, the real impact of the revolution is on the verge of crystallizing as I write. The major winners and losers will soon become evident.

The marketplace as such is not under threat. Indeed, freedom to price dynamically is a right effectively enshrined by the internet. The concept of an exchange will survive although it will be as a commoditized customer-oriented business rather than the old-fashioned clubs which are gradually being swept away. Unless the CBOE and CBOT *et al.* reform their practices and close their expensive floors within the next three years, they will be dead, swept away by cheaper, faster, more flexible competitors – quite probably ostensibly new entities emerging from left field. Even the venerable NYSE will need to reorganize soon – no operation can be sensibly managed as a commercial entity with a 24-person board of directors. Once upon a time the London Stock Exchange seemed as impregnable as NYSE. Now, the LSE will be lucky to limp home in the final running of Europe's rationalization as an independent entity, unless it can find a remarkable way to turn around what has been decades of management neglect.

Markets are unemotional, although floor traders have sought to make the business of closing their floors an emotive one. Acts of flag waving or rallying protectionist policies against even their own exchange's electronic alternatives will only harm the legacy markets foolish enough to believe they can hold back the tide of revolution. There are a lot of budding King Canutes in financial markets who felt they had stopped the tides of revolution engulfing them when they posted significant volume increases in futures markets during 2001. However, nothing can stop the revolution now. Even if the US government sought to maintain the floors, it would ultimately find that regulatory arbitrage had quietly moved the business to another financial center.

Brokers of most financial products also feel they are going to survive forever. Yet, apart from a handful who can garner "processor" status and maintain highly commoditized networks surviving on regular nickel and dime cashflows, there is little or no hope for brokerage organizations. There will be survivors who will gain enormously in the "winner takes all" environment which favors those who have the capacity to build global networks. However, at the end of the process, barely a half dozen global brokerages having a major influence on all asset classes are likely to exist.

The downside for incumbents is quite severe. That said, for those willing to grasp the nettle, the opportunities remain enormous. With markets like single stock futures, ETFs and sports trading all set to explode, the world of the online trader is going to get more and more exciting throughout this decade. Legacy providers need to be as radical as possible as swiftly as possible. Seize the day, and you may yet be able to save your organization.

These days the name of the messenger is derivatives products, virtual finance. He carries his news through computers. In the past, the messenger used telegram, cable or carrier pigeon! In this respect it is quite amusing to note how short people's memories of financial affairs can be.

Eric Briys and François de Varenne, *The Fisherman and the Rhinoceros*

The digital world is and will remain a derivatives world. The process of securitization permits just about anything to become a traded market whether it is the outcome of the next Superbowl or the rainfall patterns of Dade County, Florida. Derivatives themselves are now employed by the World Bank to help bring price stability to farmers in some of the world's poorest regions. The day of derivatives being seen as an alien concept for only a few highbrow boffins is passing. Just as almost every citizen can understand how to work a computer, so too more and more people are able to follow just what derivatives can do for them. After all, nobody barring the most foolish would go to a golf course and expect to play a good round with only one type of club. Through judicious use of electronically traded options, futures, warrants and ETFs *et al.*, investors and traders can create for themselves a whole new world of possible pay-offs.

The new markets

Most "new" products are already in existence but the overall extent of growth is likely to be enormous for markets such as bandwidth and various energy products as continued deregulation takes hold. That said, the largest growth of all will be in the ultimate consumer-to-consumer marketplace.

The biggest traded market in the world by 2010 won't be in stocks, bonds or foreign exchange. Nor will it be in venture capital or commodities. Rather the securitization of sport is already beginning to revolutionize the world of gambling and trading. The rise of sporting exchanges (where you can both bet and lay off risk) creates a morph whereby previously the bookmaker was an all-powerful monopolist on prices. Nowadays, any investor sitting at home can decide on a multiplicity of different trading strategies in fixed odds and spread markets. Indeed, soon many people will start trading from the games themselves using PDAs with mobile phone connections.

The online gambling industry will increasingly overlap with the trading business – more so than even today. The hedging of political risks using "spread betting" (essentially a price system rather than a direct odds basis as such) will be seen as attractive for many corporations and bankers. Moreover, the concept of centralized exchanges for sports betting and trading where there is no core bookmaker, but where traders can face off against each other, are going to grow enormously in the next few years. In 2000, I was a founder of Intrade, (http://www.intrade.com) which launched the following year as the world's first fully fledged sports spread trading exchange. Based around core spread betting concepts, winners of events are traded on indices ("PIX") where the winner expires with a value of 100 and the losers expire at 0. Naturally, for closely matched sports, the excitement and volatility of trading can be largely unrivalled even in the existing financial world.

For those who wish to trade their passion in the US, the first such exchange was TradeSports (http://www.tradesports.com) launched in 2002 using the technology pioneered on Intrade. If you prefer making markets or trading using traditional fixed odds, Betfair (http://www. betfair.com) provides a remarkable range of sports from all over the world. During the soccer World Cup in June 2002 and with the English flat horse-racing season well under way, Betfair was already matching some £45 million of trades every week, A simply staggering sum for a nascent market only two years old. The other Dublin-based exchange (in addition to Intrade and Tradesports) is http://www.betdaq.com, created and controlled by the noted Dublin entrepreneur and horse-racing enthusiast, Dermot Desmond. Ultimately, the world of sports trading has the potential to dwarf the business of financial market trading in a decade's time. Certainly, sports trading will be the biggest growth market for the rest of this decade. The US market will be a key battle ground, although question marks hang over the regulatory position. Ultimately close regulation will be broken down, but it remains a moot point just how rapidly the US government will understand that the world is moving towards transparent sports pricing.

Ironically, in a similar vein but going in the opposite direction, fixed-odds betting on financial markets will also gain in popularity. Several intriguing sites offering simple odds transactions (http://www.bluesq. com) through to more interesting – and indeed sometimes highly complex – bets from the likes of Xodds (http://www. xodds.com).

One key issue with the online sporting exchange business is how it mimics its online investing cousin through having a significantly higher overall net wealth of the average user. The off-track betting shop with its somewhat seedy reputation will remain the first choice for those wishing to have a simple flutter, especially in blue-collar areas. However, the smart money in betting will increasingly be seen online. As things stand, there is already strong anecdotal evidence that the bookmakers themselves are using online sports exchanges to lay off (or "hedge" as they say in capital markets) their exposure to particular sporting outcomes. Make no mistake the opportunities in sports trading remain utterly enormous.

Amongst the other key developing markets during this decade will be the following. Intriguingly, none are particularly new segments or sectors but there is room for significant expansion in all sorts of areas. However, as the first paragraph notes, it is the digital processes enabling securitization which is making markets so much more feasible in just about any form of tangible or indeed intangible asset.

Securitization

A moderate niche for many years, this process came of age in Europe and the US during the 1990s. With capital adequacy requirements to be met, many banks have found it easier to take loans off their balance sheets through securitized bond issues (on just about anything, car loans, mortgages, credit card receivables). Equally, there have been securitizations of properties and even pop-star royalties – such as David Bowie. With increasing commoditization of securities markets and the greater facility for packaging such products in ever smaller quantities cost effectively, I see securitization as a big growth area. Microbanks will become massive users of securitization processes, as a means of maintaining their modest staff size and flexibility of management, thus accelerating the securitization process further. Indeed, securitization is at the very core of the Capital Market Revolution, as it enables a great many of the sophisticated growth products of the internet century to be created, whether it is exchange traded funds or cybercash electronic trading units.

Islamic finance

With the growing importance of the Muslim world, the prospects for Islamic finance are increasing rapidly. Interpretation of this financial genre tends to differ from country to country. (Malaysia, for instance, interprets Islamic finance differently from some more fundamentalist countries in the Arab world.) Nevertheless, Islamic finance will continue to grow in importance, a process which will be accelerated if the Muslim world comes closer to harmonizing its financial practices. In the aftermath of 09/11, the business of legitimate Islamic finance was in many ways given a massive push forward as the US and its allies have sought to root out the dubious Islamic financiers with terrorist links and a history of laundering money. In this respect, Islamic finance is probably going to grow very rapidly during the period 2003–2005 as western bankers increase their efforts to engage more closely in such financing methods.

Equity derivatives

In the equity markets, derivatives remain the key growth area. Single Stock Futures and related products such as Contracts For Difference will grow exponentially during the decade. Likewise, the business of exchange traded funds is set to explode. ETFs will increasingly morph away from their original base in equity markets and encompass commodity markets as well as other hybrid products. ETFs will form the backbone of every major investor portfolio by 2010. Likewise, the hedge fund industry is going to continue to record significant growth throughout the decade as it becomes a key (if invariably niche) part of every smart investor's portfolio.

Weather trading

Elsewhere, the developments of the late 1990s will continue to be implemented. Markets such as weather will become increasingly mainstream. By 2005 every smart restaurateur with outside seating will be perusing the futures and options related to their local climate and rainfall with a view to hedging their potential exposure to a poor summer. Interestingly, the US ICE exchange managed to be the first market to establish good regular volume in their weather futures contracts by mid-2002, beating off the initial efforts of legacy exchanges such as the CME and LIFFE. Any event, from the village fête to the Indianapolis 500 motor race, will increasingly be subject to weather hedging by the organizers seeking to keep their events as profitable as possible come rain, hail or shine.

Electricity

It may not be the most popular of markets thanks to the aftermath of Dynegy, Enron, Reliant *et al.*'s somewhat dubious trading practices on occasion. Nevertheless, properly deregulated energy trading remains the best opportunity for the consumer. A nascent market but one which, when combined with oil and other energy products and linked to weather derivatives, has enormous potential. Coupled with the related weather market (producers need to make more electricity for extremes of climate whether to heat radiators or power air-conditioning units for instance), power producers and large industrial consumers will propel the growth of this market with smaller businesses increasingly able to enter the market by 2005 and thereafter.

Credit

The emergence of credit derivatives in the mid-1990s was a revolutionary force in the business of risk management. I expect an increasing move towards cleared credit derivatives of both OTC and exchange traded contracts by 2005. (so removing the theoretically minuscule but nonetheless tricky, stumbling block of counterparty risk in the guaranteeing of a separate counterparty risk!). Credit derivatives may seem to many onlookers like the most boring product imaginable but for those who had suitably hedged themselves against the risks of WorldCom or Enron in the aftermath of the burst dotcom bubble, the benefits were enormous. In an increasingly global marketplace, hedging credit risks will be increasingly significant not just for multinational corporations but also for small and medium-sized enterprises exporting or importing around the globe.

Emissions

This is the final cog in the chain linking all forms of energy, along with weather and financial products, to the by-products of the industrial age. Emissions trading has been slow to build momentum thanks to the machinations of the bureaucrats at the various Earth Summits. However, with governments increasingly impotent in so many other ways, and with emissions being a global problem, I expect that market solutions will be seen as the most efficient means by far, rather than relying on state subsidy (which governments will increasingly find impossible to resource anyway). As the Kyoto protocols (or indeed any subsequent protocols) are introduced, expect to see more market-based solutions for emissions trading coming to the fore. The Chicago Climate Exchange (CCX), brainchild of Doctor Richard Sandor, is poised to become the market leader in climate related markets.

Insurance

Interlinked with weather, insurance will become a huge growth business. The insurance industry itself is likely to become more open to niche companies underwriting specific specialist policies which ought to enhance competition and create lower premiums for many policyholders. In addition, the use of insurance derivatives will increase the exchangeability of insurance policies, so leading to much lower prices for purchasers, as well as the likelihood of insurance products reaching a more consumerist audience through cheaper, simpler policies. The internet opens competition for insurance to be more international than ever, thus helping create a better level of protection than has previously been seen. The insurance industry may have been rocked by 09/11 but it has weathered the storm and can look forward to significant opportunities in future years.

Bandwidth

Exchanges like Band-X trading fixed telecommunications bandwidth are relatively aged in internet terms having first opened as long ago as 1997. Telecommunications is the oil that lubricates the information revolution, and the prospects for traded cash and futures markets based around telephone lines is simply enormous. Perhaps the most intriguing of the telecom ventures has been the London Satellite Exchange, the first bandwidth market which trades satellite capacity for all possible applications including television and radio as well as pure telephony. In a dealing room reminiscent of a

NASA mission control room (right down to the team uniform resembling space agency officials), a team of brokers and dealers are constantly creating deals through a purpose-built online system.

Growing derivatives

There are also many other potential areas for growth. Like those listed above, they will be heavily reliant on trading in derivatives products. While there are many sadly misinformed Luddites who seem to believe that derivatives magically create risk, it will increasingly become good business practice to employ derivatives. In the 1990s, millions of people in the developed world benefited from stable mortgage rates fixed for months and even years in advance thanks to smart use of derivatives products by banks. In this decade, thanks to World Bank programs involving purchasing existing exchange commodity options contracts to hedge farmers' outputs, the developing world will benefit from the derivatives markets too.

In the post-feudal marketplace, the flexibility of derivatives products will be increasingly popular for investors, traders and hedgers. There will be many areas of large growth in existing products – I especially like the look of stock-related products as private share owners become increasingly sophisticated in their quest for maximizing returns. Equally, if food-oriented protectionism and subsidization can be broken down then new and exciting commodity markets look likely. Rice is potentially the biggest, but at present the market is fragmented and overly protected by government regulation in big producer nations such as Japan, precluding a global contract, although some regional trading takes place in the US.

While I expect the largest financial marketplaces to become increasingly unified over the next decade, there will be a continued flowering of tiny niche microexchanges covering very narrow product lines which, thanks to the low cost of creating an online exchange mechanism, will be created in increasing numbers. Likely markets will include such diverse choices as essential oils, PC chips, fine wine and essentially any other product whose price provides sufficient volatility to interest speculators and attract hedgers looking to gain price stability.

More professional traders will be self-employed as the revolution continues and banks and other intermediaries find themselves constantly pressed to reduce their headcount and become more flexible entities. The self-employed traders themselves will be helping create liquidity as banks come under increasing shareholder pressure to stick to fee-earning business and not rely on relatively unreliable proprietary-dealing profits. A great many of these traders will have started out on the exchange floors – as is already the case in Europe and Asia – although similarly a great many others will not make the transition. For the individual investor, the freer access to markets and information provided by the internet remains a huge boon. However, investors also have to temper that with the fact that they need to understand markets better to truly profit from them when they are allowed to play alongside the professionals. The day trader will return to prominence in due course, although ultimately only the most market savvy will survive.

Outright competition has bubbled under the surface of the exchange business for several years. During 2002 it was becoming clearly evident that many exchanges were set for a direct land grab of competitors' turf. This outright competition approach will be utilized by exchanges in tandem with an acquisition policy – although only those with a significant asset will find themselves being acquired. In the end, the vast majority of exchanges will be losers in the rationalization game. A few key markets will become the leaders in each region and by 2010, expect to see only a handful of major markets in the entire world – if not fewer.

While brokers and exchanges must become bigger, more commoditised, preferably global entities if they are to survive, the Capital Market Revolution is also very much about the opportunities for the "micro" provider. Microexchanges will continue to grow and thanks to relatively cheap software providers such as COMDAQ, there will be hundreds of such markets added to the surviving B2B exchanges over the next few years as price discovery hits markets as disparate as essential oils and quite feasibly human organs (although the latter will obviously provoke a public outcry and operate at least initially from a relatively obscure offshore locale). Literally any commodity that can be priced and traded will migrate to an exchange platform, whether continuous trading hours or a simple form of auction, within the next few years. The B2B exchange has been written off in many quarters. Ironically, it has only just begun to provide significant benefits for people throughout the world.

The post-feudal marketplace will continue to evolve dynamically in years to come and some enterprises which appeared so important during the revolution will themselves disappear. ECNs remain a sideshow, a symptom of the problems of old-fashioned club markets rather than a genuine solution in their own right. Those who have not managed to change into proper exchanges will remain as carbuncles on digital markets for a few years and then gradually die out. The Capital Market Revolution at its core is all about paring down markets and becoming a much slimmer, fitter system of dealing as opposed to the old-fashioned people-intensive methods of capitalism's feudal age. In that respect, any extra mouth in the food chain which can be rendered unnecessary – whether human or, like ECNs, electronic, is ultimately going to be swept away.

Naturally, there is much pain in the wholesale transfer of any industry from the physical world to the virtual. In the case of capital markets, the events of 09/11 were felt throughout the industry and have had a marked effect on management strategy since. Many previously highly populated brokerages have been heavily digitized – not in any way as an insult to the dead – but rather when it came to rebuilding after the tragedy, there was simply no alternative. Similarly, 09/11 showed up many flaws in the disaster recovery mechanisms as well as demonstrating just how floors have become a liability as a target in many respects. The central business districts of every major financial center will survive but in a very different form. Unless it is essential to have staff meeting their counterparts every day, then those bankers will gradually be migrating to the suburbs and "declustering" significant swathes of the corporation to lower-cost environments on the edge of the big cities.

Enron in many ways provides some salutary lessons for the entire industry. A great deal of *Schadenfreude* has been employed to ridicule the company – yet the folk now so openly contemptuous of Enron were predominantly those terrified of its rise to prominence. Certainly, Enron demonstrated how to build brand swiftly and how to create new markets. Alas, they were held hostage by their own greed and ultimately to some extent the greed or stupidity of their clients. Monomarkets (i.e. one provider of services to many clients) are in many respects just glorified bookmakers. You are placing a bet not only with the organization but you are also to a considerable extent betting that the organization itself will be around long enough to pay your winnings. Monomarkets can have their place in certain niches – such as areas of gambling as I mentioned above. However, true markets must be "polyglot" structures – all human life must be there and involved in the price discovery process.

Contemporary digital markets increasingly do price discovery better than anybody else – freer access is available from throughout the world, traders can indeed place their prices directly. The market is not being "discovered" by a cartel of privileged members through which all trades must basically flow. Rather, digital markets are clear, open and democratic. The more polyglot they can be, the greater will be their pricing efficiency. Initially, Enron demonstrated that left field competition could be highly predatory and make a serious impact on wrong-footed legacy exchanges. However, the big lesson which was alas learnt by many people only after Enron had collapsed was to recall just who "owns the money." Centralized clearing processes through bona fide clearing houses are key to orderly financial markets and the sooner clients realize just how much risk they are undertaking when dealing bilaterally with relatively poor credit rated companies, the safer shareholders will be.

Of course the clearing process itself must rationalize, in order to permit customers to use their money more efficiently and reduce administrative overheads. Likewise, the clearing organizations need to keep running in the medium term just to keep up with the many new opportunities afforded to them by the ongoing growth of microexchanges and so forth. In the clearing domain perhaps it is most difficult to see genuine left field competition emerge – but it is not impossible. A great many cash-cow utilities could move into the clearing business if they had the inclination. With the US clearing field likely to begin rationalizing soon, acquiring the human assets and core documentation of the US minnow commodity exchanges may yet prove a handy way to bootstrap into clearing for a left field player. Meanwhile, those who still disbelieve that left field players can emerge suddenly and make an impact on digital markets need only remember two acronyms: ICE and ISE. The former has become a powerhouse commodities market predicated on energy-related products while the latter is gradually destroying the oligopoly open outcry stranglehold of Chicago, New York, Philadelphia and San Francisco. Neither of them were in existence before AD 2000. New brands will emerge and old franchises will learn the hard way that nobody really cared for them in the first place (the LSE and NYSE run the biggest risks here). Similarly, managements need to readily realize that in the intense competition which will follow, one key strategic error or indeed a single trading error which is badly handled may yet spell the end of their independence and thus remove them from the game of trying to become one of the exclusive members of the global champions' league of markets.

Categorizing the winners and losers is a difficult task – some might argue a foolhardy one. However, in the spirit of this book, I have no qualms about assessing the risks and opportunities for a variety of players in the capital markets game. And in so doing, one can see certain key maxims which can be applied to give a good idea of who will win and who will lose out in the ongoing machinations of the Capital Market Revolution.

Overall, in management terms the truly skilful players need to have the soul of the entrepreneur, although in the exchange business the ability to have the patience of a mandarin is a distinct advantage when going through regulatory processes. For instance, the Euronext, LIFFE and LSE managements all appeared before a British Parliamentary Select Committee when LIFFE was taken over. Exchanges (even derivatives ones – a sound demonstration they have now come of age) have that curious "national flag carrier" aura that makes them a somewhat emotive sort of business to take over. Doubtless this will further affect predatory managements' attitudes in deciding to attack head on or take over smaller legacy exchanges. The business of running a club for fixed interests is very different from that of running a business for outside shareholders. In that respect, there are few inspiring exchange managements who have seen the transition from club to corporate through. Indeed, with the bare exceptions of Werner Seifert and Jean-François Theodore, there are essentially no others. True, some exchanges have subsequently taken on sound CEOs, such as Jim McNulty at CME and Tom Kloet in Singapore,[1] but overall legacy exchanges with legacy managements are ill-equipped to cope. The new breed of exchange management are people like Rudi Ferscha, the multilingual Austrian ex-Goldman Sachs investment banker who is equally at home in London, New York, Frankfurt, Vienna or any of a dozen other capital cities. The US exchanges in particular look vulnerable.

Even where new management blood has been injected, there is evidence (e.g. at CBOT) that perhaps the CEO (ex-Bank One Deputy Chairman David Vitale) may not always be in as direct agreement with his Chairman as the glowing conference speech tributes suggest. So, in many ways, the "wolf in sheep's clothing" metaphor holds good for the modern exchange manager (and indeed the modern intermediary manager). Sir Brian Williamson appears every inch the British establishment insider yet beneath the classically tailored suits beats the heart of an absolute radical. At home in the corridors of power (Williamson seemed absolutely at home in front of the Commons select committee) yet capable of far-reaching radical decisions to reshape his marketplace, the modern intermediary manager needs to be a veritable chameleon.

Of all the indicators of coping with the revolution, an organization that is able to talk the talk and walk the walk of technological acronyms is usually the least useful. Rather, in searching for likely winners, look at management structure, and the core skills sets of management. Increasingly, exchanges and all other successful intermediaries need a range of skill sets not usually found only within those markets. The US Refco futures brokerage has been radically reshaped through the arrival of Joe Murphy (who has an investment banking background). By exploiting the Refco brand, judiciously acquiring competitors and ruthlessly exploiting new technology, Murphy has radically reshaped Refco into an excellent example of a cutting-edge digital brokerage. So, as I have already said in many ways the key facet for a leading intermediary manager in the post-feudal marketplace is the possession of the mind of a mandarin and the soul of an entrepreneur.

Utilizing such indicators, among other tactics, one can already categorize the likely winners and losers within the exchange world as the revolution develops. In the predators and prey tables on pages 207–215, I have provided three basic categories which ought to be reasonably self-explanatory:

"Predator" (i.e. looking to acquire other markets whether through direct acquisition or indeed outright competition);

"Prey" (i.e. awaiting takeover or perhaps just hoping to be taken over rather than finding their key markets under siege from a competitor);

"Roadkill" unlikely to find itself surviving the revolution, there are probably already vultures swooping around waiting for the animal to stop wriggling so they can extract any juicy tidbits from the carcass.

So, to the victor the spoils and the losers eternal damnation from the capital markets. This is a winner-take-all market (regulation notwithstanding). Only a handful of major players at most will still be standing in five years time. And indeed, some of the world's largest exchanges are not in the table of predators and prey, as I have excluded the upstart betting exchanges – but if it continues as it has begun at least one of them will be a top-ten marketplace within this decade.

Fortune favors the brave and investors may find some interesting value propositions as markets are effectively auctioned off like LIFFE was in late 2001. At the time, many folk complained that the value of LIFFE was simply unsustainable. However, to keep Jean-François Theodore's Euronext in the game of European platform domination, it was surely a small premium compared with facing elimination. The LSE has had plenty of time to reflect on what might have been had it but been able to raise a few dollars on its own market and present a more coherent management strategy in the wake of its humiliating failure to acquire LIFFE. Once the strong man of Europe, by mid-2002 it faces being an also-ran unless it can pull a rabbit out of its hat.

Revolutions are all about upsetting the established order and in that respect those facing the greatest risks are the biggest incumbent franchises. The NYSE may yet emerge the new global powerhouse of capitalism in the post-feudal marketplace. However, while NYSE is capable of talking the talk, to date it has conspicuously failed to really grasp the revolution. New floors that won't be built fail to impress. Pondering how to create ivory towers, particularly after 09/11, is utterly *passé*. The specialists have had their day, so has the idea of a stock market floor on Wall Street (or any other street for that matter). Few revolutions are concluded with the same world order as they had before they began. In this respect, the Capital Market Revolution will be no different. The totality of possibility is opened by a revolutionary act. In capital markets, the opportunities are enormous – then again so are the risks to the legacy players.

You see things, and say why? But I dream things that never were, and I say, why not?

George Bernard Shaw

Predators and prey – a brief exchange guide

American Stock Exchange (Amex)	Prey
Put up for sale in January 2002 by parent NASDAQ.	
Athens Stock Exchange	Prey
Australian Stock Exchange	Prey
ASX seems to have gradually given up the idea of becoming an Asian leader and look increasingly willing to succumb to a bid to be an Asian hub for a European or American predator.	

Bangkok   Roadkill

Unlikely to be the focus of much attention in the medium term, ultimately will be driven out of business by the dominant Asian markets.

Borsa Italia   Prey

Borsa Italia will ultimately fall prey but the canny strategy of ex-McKinsey consultant Borsa CEO Massimo Capuano to bulk up what remained of one of the few strong independent liquidity pools in Europe outside DB/Euronext/LSE through acquiring the Monte Titoli clearing/settlement organization in mid-2002, means that Borsa Italia retains the ability to be a Kingmaker in the ongoing European domination race.

Boston Stock Exchange   Predator?

Certainly, the relatively tiny Boston Exchange isn't going out without a fight. It has launched BOX with Bourse de Montreal and leading market maker Timber Hill to provide more options and related products on a new market in the near future. Getting to the top of the big league looks like a daunting task but at least they're going to make a splash *en route*.

Brokertec   Predator

The core cash bond business of Brokertec was being taken over by leading OTC broker ICAP as this book was being concluded. The original investment banking conglomerate that started the exchange will retain Brokertec futures which is the major threat to the US Bond complex at CBOT. CBOT has a relatively divided management, being pulled hither and thither by the members. Brokertec futures has a strong management consisting of career investment bankers. The CBOT thinks it has the game won, but with ICAP adding its support to Brokertec I wouldn't bet against Brokertec. Even if it fails in Bonds, it will likely morph into another business sector. Certainly, for ICAP's brilliant supremo Michael Spencer, the addition of the cash Brokertec business is a masterstroke which places him in a leading position to make ICAP the world's most prominent money market intermediary in an era when his competitors are increasingly facing extinction.

Chicago Board Options Exchange (CBOE)   Prey

Having built an electronic system that the members don't want to be used during the "sacred" floor hours, CBOE faces a quandary. If it doesn't stand up to its members, it faces extinction - a long and lingering strangulation at the digital cortexes of the upstart ISE. In fact, without significant action by Q4 2002, CBOE will have gone from industry leader to a road kill rating in record time. CBOE is a great example of an incumbent entering the revolution and then failing to believe that its own dominant franchise could be even remotely harmed.

CBOT   Prey/Roadkill

How the mighty have fallen. CBOT is the first organized futures exchange of the modern era, with over 150 years history as a commodities exchange. True, but the really worrying issue about CBOT is that few people seem to appreciate just how acute its problems truly are. In 2001 the exchange was often dogged by rumors of money problems which management assured us had been cured by mid-2002, although the downgrading of the partnership with EUREX to essentially a vendor/client one in July 2002 emphasized that many more costs needed to be trimmed. Nonetheless, the once invincible market at 141 West Jackson, finds itself in a fight for its life. The lack of Treasury Bond issuance coupled with competitors in the arena has left the CBOT's volumes looking somewhat lackluster compared to key competitors. The market's electronic trading system appears to be actively discriminated against by the exchange's own pro-floor transaction pricing policy – yet will it be enough? CBOT is in danger, have no doubt about that and unless its members realize they cannot control the game, the CBOT will end up as roadkill.

Chicago Stock Exchange   Prey

The CHX could easily be a predator once more in the changing tides of the revolution, as it is small enough to be sufficiently flexible to change its spots. Overall, however, CHX is probably too small to be taken over but it could yet form an interesting angle of a killer Chicago combo if the Windy City's exchanges can get their acts together.

China
Closed

China is game-on for exchange-based capitalism but likely to remain closed to foreign investment in exchanges until the revolution has progressed at least a few more years.

Deutsche Börse
Predator

There are predators and then there are predators. DB and Euronext are the only truly proven predators at the time of writing. Werner Seifert's pipe-smoking persona belies his ability to be a ruthless predator. Seifert can operate on both the takeover trail and besieging liquidity simultaneously. His EUREX subsidiary is another helpful business and his silo-clearing operations ought to be a veritable cash cow for future acquisitions. DB will be a leader in the Eurozone with Euronext by the end of 2003 at the latest, at which stage I expect to see Seifert switch his attentions overseas.

EUREX
Predator

While 80% owned by DB and 20% by the Swiss Exchange, EUREX is in fact a fascinating, somewhat separate predator in its own right. The exchange has mastered the art of stealth attack (e.g. in European equity options markets) having first taken the Bund from LIFFE during a war of attrition where ultimately digital dealing won the day and propelled the Capital Market Revolution forward. EUREX will operate as a very pragmatic sibling to the DB parent but it will undertake its own campaigns to ensure that EUREX maintains its position as the world's biggest derivatives marketplace.

Euronext
Predator

Under Jean-François Theodore, who may have the bearing and cunning of Napoleon along with the empire building skills of Charlemagne, the Dutch/Belgian and French bourses (along with the LIFFE derivatives powerhouse and latterly Portugal's exchange too) will be the other competing duopolist alongside DB in Europe. Theodore has the air miles under his belt and the experience in doing deals that even the likes of the NYSE's Dick Grasso lacks. Expect Theodore to look beyond European boundaries as soon as the key remaining markets (Italy, Spain, Switzerland and of course LSE) are accounted for in some way, shape or form.

Hong Kong   Prey
Sooner or later the Chinese will find a way to absorb Hkex into its domestic capitalist infrastructure.

Intercontinental Exchange (ICE)   Predator
Jeff Sprecher is the only US exchange official with a takeover deal under his belt in the modern age. From zero to hero in a couple of years, Sprecher has the drive to create a truly global enterprise and with London's IPE, he already has diversified significantly from his original Atlanta base. Expect fireworks here and don't be surprised if he ultimately takes over NYMEX. Nevertheless, ICE can take business both ways.

Instinet   Predator
Instinet's strategic purchase of fellow ECN Island added management strength and strategic opportunities to the Reuters subsidiary's advantage. While not an exchange (yet), by buying Island, which had been actively working on exchange propositions in cash markets and futures, Instinet has the opportunity to morph across markets and asset classes, and in the process provide a potentially awesome competitor to the US and overseas stock exchanges. Instinet may not be registered as an exchange yet but it is already shaping up like one – and a predatory one at that.

International Securities Exchange (ISE)   Predator
ISE is simply the best example of how to take business straight from your competitors' mouths through using computers instead of people. ISE has leapt from nowhere in 2000, to being close to market leader in US equity options by mid-2002. ISE is unlikely to take over a competitor simply because it won't want to be saddled with the legacy exchange's problems. Rather, ISE's competitive advantage as it strives to be dominant in equity options is in straightforward competition for market share. If ISE then wishes to expand beyond individual equity options, it may seek acquisitions in the medium term. Whatever happens it is a pure play predator.

Japan	Closed

Foreign investment or take-over is highly unlikely in the medium term in Japan's markets. Likewise their focus remains strongly domestic based.

Jakarta Stock Exchange	Closed

Unlikely to be sought after, insufficiently large to consider being a predator.

Johannesburg Stock Exchange	Prey/Roadkill

The JSE has a long and noble history. Alas, the lure of London has been robbing it of many leading stocks (e.g. Old Mutual) in recent years. JSE needs to stop the hemorrhaging but it probably will be best served doing this as part of a bigger entity. With technology services from LSE, this might seem the easiest strategic fit but then again, JSE is probably too small to be a key focus for LSE when it needs to do a major deal which will assure its shareholders that it isn't at best an also-ran.

Korea	Closed

The KSE and KOFEX derivatives marketplace has already become a major equity derivatives powerhouse in Asia although its clientele is predominantly local. Whether Korea can become a capital market powerhouse for Asia really depends on how the economy is opened to outside competition. For the moment it remains in a state of "splendid isolation."

London Metals Exchange	Prey

A unique franchise, but with probably nowhere to go but into another organization. Independent and dominant in most metals markets, the LME has a unique system of dealing in the rings giving it the likely opportunity to be the last open outcry exchange in the world. Nevertheless, its niche is too small to truly leave it with much option other than to be rolled into a major commodity marketplace in the near future.

London Stock Exchange	Prey

It seems staggering to suggest LSE can be prey after several hundred years of history as the biggest market in the

European region (and indeed for a long time, the world). However, if you manage badly enough for long enough, anything is possible. If LSE can do an overseas deal, it can survive. If it can't, it must undergo the ignominy of being swallowed by the sort of predator that ten years ago it would barely have deigned to negotiate with (DB and Euronext naturally lead the pack here).

Malaysia

Closed

No sign of any big changes here, too weak to be a predator and unlikely to elicit much interest from overseas for take-over even if the government showed any interest in foreign capital taking such an interest in the local markets.

Manila

Closed

Much like Malaysia and the other Asian minnows, insufficiently attractive for take-over, unlikely to do any itself.

NASDAQ

Predator

NASDAQ is a predator as its various overseas ventures, such as NASDAQ Europe, NASDAQ Deutschland and NASDAQ Japan, show. However, none of these has exactly crossed the threshold of success and therein lies the rub. NASDAQ has commonly promoted itself as the engine of new technology investment yet its own management pace is described by competitors and allies alike as "glacial." NASDAQ thinks it can win the day thanks to a great brand and the arrival of SuperMontage. In reality, it needs to become a nimble operator and at present there is little sign of that. While a predator on paper, NASDAQ runs the risk of being prey if it doesn't slim down its management style.

New York Board of Trade (NYBOT)

Prey

The NYBOT has survived with various commodities and assorted second-tier financial markets for some time. Nevertheless, the fact that the first task was to rebuild the floor after 09/11 demonstrated that NYBOT either hasn't seen the light or its members still have the control but not the vision to move the market. NYBOT logically ought to be rolled up by NYMEX, although sometimes things aren't quite that logical.

New Zealand Stock Exchange   Roadkill

Located somewhere on the edges of the capitalist map, with
a bare handful of key stocks, NZSE vacillated in merger talks
with ASX. ASX or some other predator ought to consider a
direct attack on the liquidity at an early juncture.

NYMEX   Predator?

NYMEX was originally a predator, having stalked the London
IPE for years only to have the exchange snatched by the
audacious Jeff Sprecher. The untimely death of popular CEO
Pat Thompson coupled with the departure of Chairman
Danny Rappaport left the exchange feeling its way during much
of 2001. Nevertheless, NYMEX has muscle and a good core
product base in energy and metals products. It may yet
emerge as the buyer of LME in the medium term but it also
needs to shore up its defenses against the tenacious ICE.

OM   Prey

The OM exchanges are undoubtedly prey, indeed OM itself
was trying to sell them late in 2001. Similarly, the exchange
technology business of OM might yet find itself part of a major
roll-up strategy with an exchange which is looking to go
electronic. Nevertheless, the likely future for OM's technology business will be as an independent entity. The closure
of the retail-oriented pan European Jiway venture in October
2002 was a blow to OM's exchange ambitions although given
lackluster volumes after a launch, unfortunately timed to coincide with a slump in equity prices during 2000, it was hardly
an unexpected one.

Pacific Coast   Prey

Having partnered with Archipelago, the San Francisco-based
market may yet emerge to be a predator but I suspect it will
still find it hard to battle against total upstarts from left field and
the power of the major legacy franchises. Electronic trading
for options may help keep volume away from the ISE but it
may also be implemented too late to make much difference.

Philadelphia Stock Exchange   Prey

Ought by rights to have been dead years ago, yet CEO Sandy
Frucher has managed to keep "Philly" in the game. However,
for how long can it simply hang on? The exchange needs a

fillip to get somewhere and rumored tie-ups with second tier markets like Hong Kong really don't seem to make much sense. On the other hand, Philly losing its floor and tying up with a major left field player could be a very exciting proposition and lead to a "predator" upgrade.

Russia   Closed
Not sophisticated enough and still regarded as too speculative to see meaningful exchange infrastructure outside investment for the time being.

Singapore Exchange   Prey
The success of Singapore is in its leveraging from a small population base (roughly 3 million people) to become a credible stock market at all. On the other hand, it's difficult to see what the market can do to enhance its size. Therefore, ultimately it will be prey but probably not for some time yet as the Singaporean government will be unlikely to rubber-stamp a deal which does not involve Singapore emerging on the winning side.

Swiss Exchange   Prey
With the stake in Virt-X (created from London's Tradepoint and SwX's overseas trading) based in London, the Swiss Exchange has a variety of options, which will probably in the end maximize value, but the Swiss market will still ultimately end up being rolled into one of the major Euro-bourses. On the other hand, with half the board seats on EUREX, even though it owns only 20% compared to DB's 80%, it is difficult to see how SwX can be sold lock, stock and barrel to anybody but DB. Or at least DB needs to secure the remainder of EUREX anyway to avoid what could be a tricky management situation in the interim. Whatever happens, the business won't go cheaply, as it has European King-making potential along with various kickers such as the EUREX stake.

Sydney Futures Exchange   Prey
The SFE has already all but begged for ASX to be allowed to take it over in a press release of October 30, 2001. The only problem is that it probably doesn't hold a lot of attraction for an overseas bidder who would likely want to acquire ASX first.

Note

1. Kloet did not renew his SGX contract and left the exchange in late 2002 for personal reasons.

The Revolutionary's Lexicon

As a quick primer, I enclose a guide to some key words and phrases which will come to dominate all discussion concerning the Capital Market Revolution.

B2B: the Business to Business transaction process. It climbed like Icarus and melted the wax on its wings in the initial dotcom boom but behind B2B there remains the ongoing possibility of vast cost savings and efficiency improvements in markets of all shapes, sizes and formats.

Broker assisted: yip, I feel a hybrid moment coming over me. It may be cool to claim that everybody will deal digitally direct but for a few years yet expect to see some new markets in particular enjoying a degree of client "spoon feeding" as old-fashioned phone brokers help coerce them into becoming digital traders.

C2C: the cousin of B2B, customer-to-customer transactions may be frowned upon by those who fear disintermediation but for the millions of punters at Betfair, eBay, Tradsports *et al.*, C2C is a wondrous revolution democratizing everything from auctioneering to sports gambling.

Cognitive elite: those who will thrive in the eye of and in the wake of the Capital Market Revolution. They are cosmopolitan and likely to feel equally at home on several continents.

Cyberfinance: digital markets, a digital world, cyberfinance is the collective term for everything that is a networked financial product in the 21st century.

Cyber cash: electronic money, delivered by smart cards and when asset backed, known as ETUs (see below).

Dematerialization: if every transaction can be digital, then why do we end up with so much paperwork? Dematerialization holds the key to true virtual dealing once we have removed cumbersome certificates and other paper baubles from the transactional food chain.

Derivative: at once both an offshoot of modern finance but also in the digital age, essentially the hub around which all other markets gravitate. Literally, a product derived from a cash market.

Disintermediation: the process of being bypassed by the food chain. Not a word to bandy around in front of nervous brokers or insecure exchange officials.

ECN: much hyped, much discussed, much misunderstood. Remember, Electronic Communications Networks never solved anything. They aren't the answer to the creative destruction of the Capital Market Revolution, rather they are a symptom of the old problems of "club market" mentality.

E-local: an independent trader speculating regularly (usually intraday) on any of the world's major exchanges.

ETF: abbreviation of exchange traded funds, the central building block of modern investment strategy. Why bother with simple mutual funds when a simple ETF structure is so much more cheap, transparent, simple and efficient to deal in?

ETU: electronic trading units, i.e. cybercash. Specifically, ETUs will likely be asset-backed by stock, securitized assets or plain old-fashioned glittering resources, both precious metals and the fluid stuffs too.

Facilitator: anybody who can still rightfully claim the right to intermediate. Trading screen providers undoubtedly facilitate business, few brokers or exchanges will be able to rightfully claim to be facilitating business unless they can adapt to the new reality with gusto.

Fiat money: crummy banknotes which never held their value. Governments used to palm them off on citizens until ETUs stopped that sort of profligacy.

Floor exchanges: once upon a time there were great empires owned and operated by the likes of Britain, France and Belgium. Once upon a time floor traders reigned supreme on their floors. Nowadays, most people have forgotten that great empires ever existed. In Asia and Europe, they have already largely forgotten about floor exchanges too.

Food chain: the string of folk involved in any transaction. From the client through a voicebroker to a gang of floor traders and back again, the old-fashioned marketplace was verging on the labyrinthine. Nowadays, the food chain is much shorter, and the market increasingly digital throughout.

Free agent: any independent individual who is operating beyond his national borders. Many E-locals epitomize the free agents' spirit, offshore, enjoying a more relaxed level of regulation and quite probably existing tax free too.

Friction: digital markets have much less friction, fewer folk in the food chain, resulting in less possibilities of a bottleneck with your order.

Knighthood: if you want to risk an already considerable reputation by being quite possibly the only capital market revolutionary who will successfully rescue an exchange from almost certain extinction in the face of certain death then the Queen of England may give you one of these. Sir Brian Williamson will probably be the only revolutionary to be so honored, then again he will probably be the only revolutionary to rescue an exchange from oblivion.

Left field: is NYSE really the brand we all associate with great and wonderful frictionless capitalism? Or is it Wal-Mart? Forget the legacy exchange catfights, it's a whole big brand from the wonderful world of mercantilism which can yet win the day as the world's exchange.

Legacy exchanges: the guys who started the game, spent a few hundred years as clubs and now have gradually emerged blinking into the sunlight of open competition. Thrust to the epicenter of capitalism as competitive entities, suddenly a lot of them don't look quite so sure-footed as they did when you could measure their success by the size of their headquarters' Georgian colonnades.

Leviathans: the real leviathans of the future will be the guys who manage to emerge as the key players in the new markets – whether existing markets digitized or new players from left field. There will be at most three leviathan exchanges by 2010 in the stock markets of the world, with dealing on several continents, 24 hours per day.

Luddites: the managers who reckon full-service brokerage isn't affected by online brokers, the exchange supremos who believe that open outcry is the only way to trade, the trader who wants to phone his orders to his brokers, the locals who think their floor will survive.

Microbanker: the new, most dynamic form of digital banker. Operating with a tiny permanent executive, the small but perfectly formed microbankers will come to dominate much of the banking business on every level. A similar bounty awaits the microbroker, who will often be directly affiliated to the microbanker.

Microexchange: not everybody believes that small is beautiful. On the other hand, there are those who wish to create centralized marketplaces on the tiniest of commodities (N.B. a billion a year can be small in these terms) and they are busily creating a subdivision of B2B transactions on their microexchanges to prove the benefits of scaled-down digital commerce.

Monomarket: a market where there is one provider of prices and liquidity to many end users. Enron is the example that most easily springs to mind, although monomarkets aren't usually run in such a cavalier fashion. Conventional bookmakers are a good example of the genre in the world at large.

NewVas: short for "new value added services", the process which brokers must embrace if they are to succeed in the new reality. Remember: the old ways are the ways of the dead.

New Capital Market Revolution: the Capital Market Revolution began in the late 1990s. A reaction in the wake of the dotcom bubble bursting suggested there might yet be more space in the food chain for intermediaries. Now we have reached the crucial second phase, where the winners and losers will be decided. Only a handful of intermediaries have the necessary qualities to survive. What are they and who might/will they be? Read on, carefully.

Open outcry: really, the open outcry ought to be just why so many (particularly US) exchanges ever thought they could tough it out against bits, bytes, servers and fibreoptic cable and remain masters of the (exchange traded) universe. In reality, open outcry is a somewhat intriguing process resembling the processes of racecourse "tic tac" men. Used to operate floor trading remarkably efficiently. Then somebody invented the microchip and sooner or later the whole floor trading bandwagon ground to a halt. Not that a good many folk in New York, Chicago and other locales were willing to admit it by the time this tome was published but it was all over (including the shouting) in Europe already.

OTC: remember, the upstairs classes are where the game is truly at. Yes, the exchange folk may still make a spectacle to help CNBC make TV programs but for the time being most big institutions are distinctly bilateral, trading with each other on the over-the-counter marketplace.

Polyglot market: monomarkets are where one person believes they have the God-given right to tell everybody else the price they must trade at. Polyglots on the other hand are the true markets of the future. "All human life is there" to quote Paul Gallico on baseball games. Lots of folk can deal freely and easily with lots of other folk and in a digital world they can be based anywhere in the world, trading to anywhere else in the world with a minimum of friction using a marketplace that can itself be based somewhere entirely different.

Post-feudal marketplace: once upon a time those clubs all existed in a fashion not dissimilar to the Seignors of feudal states, or perhaps even Emperors from antiquity. Nowadays, we have moved ahead but before anybody starts feeling all modern, democratic and contemporary, let me just add that yes, this is a whole new, much more level playing field but the management of intermediaries has just about hit the middle ages – a classic era but nonetheless one which is post-feudal but hardly modern.

Screen-based trading: the preserve of big blokes and wimps alike, indeed folk of any sex can apply. No need for brawn or a desire to be stood upon and wrestle shoulder to shoulder with a heaving mass of other pit traders. Welcome to the more democratic modern version of markets thanks to digital technology.

Single stock future: ironically the Dutch traded these several hundred years ago. Then again they healed things with essential oils a millennium before anybody had ever heard of California. Single stock futures are a pivotal new product as the equity derivatives revolution continues apace.

Sports trading: where the action is. In ancient Rome they had gladiators and the politics of the age were dominated by ensuring *panem et circensis* (bread and games). In the modern age, the markets that will genuinely attract the interest of much of humanity will involve speculating on their favorite sporting action.

Spread betting: once it was all a question of fixed odds. Nowadays, you can also digitize those positions and trade just like a stock market – except Manchester United, the New York Yankees or the Ferrari Formula One team will surely always arouse more passion than anything listed to date on NASDAQ?

Smart card: the lovely little bit of plastic which allows you to hold currency which isn't necessarily issued by a government. A device which can produce money, allow you to make purchases, and even better, give you access to your trading terminal in the quest for a few more cyberdollars.

TOMBIS: not to be confused with Tombeau, which is a lovely genre of baroque music composed by the likes of Couperin, Lully and Marais, TOMBIS is short for "total online investment management by individual solutions." "TOMBIS" means individuals taking total control of their assets.

Throttling: the process of orders being pressed into some sort of bottleneck when they ought to be allowed to proceed freely. Typical examples of "throttling" include insufficient bandwidth somewhere between an order being sent from the end user terminal to the exchange, or a brokerage that, having failed to grasp the Capital Market Revolution's central tenets, insists on placing some form of human intermediation in the path of an electronically transferred order.

Trading arcade: a center for traders to operate from *en masse*. Usually operated by an exchange affiliated clearing agent or a brokerage.

Virtual aliens: those guys doing your back office paperwork and computer programming from New Delhi, India. They feel just like your colleagues in the New York office but in fact they're manifesting the global digital economy.

Voice brokers: they might be enjoying a brief renaissance in the broker-assisted markets out there but then again, how long do we really expect to have to give any orders to a dulcet-toned creature at the end of a phone line? I'll take that direct digital order entry routing any day.

Further Reading for Revolutionaries

By the same author

Capital Market Revolution, 1999, FT Prentice Hall, 0-273-64232-4.
The Promiscuous Investor, 2002, erivatives.com, ISBN 0-9542361-0-6.

Various articles, most notably in the magazines (see below) published by http://www.erivatives.com

By other authors

Briys, Eric and de Varenne, François. *The Fisherman and The Rhinoceros*, 2000, John Wiley & Sons, 047188961X.

Carlson, Charles, B. *The Individual Investor Revolution*, 1998, McGraw-Hill, 0070120498 (updated paperback edition, McGraw-Hill, 0071357858).

Chandler, Beverley. *Investing With the Hedge Fund Giants*, 1998, FT Prentice Hall, 0273632434 (2nd Edn, 2001, FT Prentice Hall, 0273653806).

Chernow, Ron. *The Death of the Banker*, US Vintage Books, 0375700374; UK 1997 Pimlico, 071266646X.

Christensen, Clayton M. *The Innovators Dilemma*, 1997, Harvard Business School Press, 08785845851.

Cobban, Alfred. *A History of Modern France*, Volume 1: 1715–1799, 1979, Penguin Books Ltd.

Cohen, David. *Fear, Greed and Panic, the psychology of the stock market*, 2001, John Wiley & Sons, 0471486590.

Davidson, James Dale and Rees-Mogg, William. *The Sovereign Individual*, US 1997, Simon & Schuster, 0684810077; UK 1997, Macmillan, 0333662083.

De La Vega, Joseph. *Confusion de Confusiones*, 1996, John Wiley & Sons, 0471133124.

Dembo, Ron and Freeman, *Andrew. Seeing Tomorrow – Rewriting the Rules of Risk*, 1998, John Wiley & Sons, 0471247367.

Gastineau, Gary L. *The Exchange Traded Funds Manual*, 2002, John Wiley & Sons, 0471218944.

Hama, Noriko. *Disintegrating Europe – The Twilight of the European Construction*, US 1996, Praeger Pub, 0275955818; UK 1996, Adamantine Press, 0744901225.

Hibbert, Christopher. *The French Revolution*, 1980 (reissue 1982), Penguin Books, 0140049452.

Jones, Colin. *The Longman Companion to the French Revolution*, 1990, Longman Books, 0582494176.

Kelly, Kevin. *New Rules for the New Economy*, US 1998, Viking Press, 0670881112, 1999, Penguin USA, 014028090X; UK 1998, Fourth Estate, 1857028716, 1999, Fourth Estate, 1857028929.

Kuhn, Thomas S. *The Structure of Scientific Revolutions*, 1996, University of Chicago Press, 0226458083.

Lederman, Jess and Klein, Robert A. (eds). *Hedge Funds – Investment and Portfolio Strategies for the Institutional Investor*, 1995, Irwin, 1-55738-861-X.

Lee, Ruben. *What Is An Exchange?* 1998, Oxford University Press, 0198288409 (updated paperback edition 2000, Oxford University Press, 0198297041).

Leer, Anne (ed.). *Masters of the Wired World – Cyberspace Speaks Out*, 1999, FT Pitman, 0-273-63559-X.

Melamed, L. and Tamarkin, B. *Escape to the Futures*, 1996, John Wiley & Sons, 0-471-11215-1.

Nairn, Alasdair. *Engines That Move Markets*, 2002, John Wiley & Sons, 0471205958.

Naisbitt, John. *Global Paradox*, US 1995, Avon, 0380724898; UK 1995, Nicholas Brealey, 1857880501.

Sampson. Anthony. *The Money Lenders*, 1988, Coronet, 0340486155.

Sculley, Arthur B. and Woods, W. William *A. B2B Exchanges*, 1999, ISI Publications, 962-7762-59-8 (updated paperback edition 2001, HarperCollins, 0066621089).

Tapscott, Don. *The Digital Economy*, 1996 (new edition 1997), 0070633428.

Taylor, A. J. P. *Europe: Grandeur and Decline*, 1979, (new edition 1990), Penguin Books Ltd., 0140136029.

Vlasic, Bill and Stertz, Bradley A. *Taken For A Ride*, 2000, John Wiley & Sons, 0471497320 (updated edition 2001, HarperBusiness, 0060934484).

Selected periodicals

appliederivatives	http://www.appliederivatives.com
erivativesreview	http://www.erivativesreview.com
The Economist	http://www.economist.com
The Financial Times	http://www.ft.com
Technology Review	http://www.techreview.com
Wired	http://www.wired.com

Acknowledgements

Since the first appearance of *Capital Market Revolution* which has since been expanded, modified, sympathetically restored and indeed has grown significantly to become *The New Capital Market Revolution*, I have a vast number of people to thank for their input. Despite being unpopular in certain quarters for the frankness of my views, I am delighted to have met and enjoyed the acquaintance of so many people throughout the world during my 15 plus years in capital markets, many of whom have helped shape my opinions and have a hand in creating this book. Nevertheless, Beverley Chandler still deserves pride of place as the Godmother of the Capital Market Revolution.

Writing as it were from the front line of the revolutionary battlefield has undoubtedly made things difficult as the firmament has been changing as fast as I could write about it. If anything is missing, it is my omission but I hope readers will understand that I have truly challenged the limits of patience and indeed publishing possibility with TEXERE in my strenuous efforts to make this book as up to date as possible on publication!

The whole Capital Market Revolution project remains most exciting and one which I hope you will find suitably illuminating, concerning an upheaval which is simply so enormous in its ramifications as to be difficult to contemplate. I can only hope that within this relatively slim volume, I have given you sufficient inspiration to be able not merely to understand, but also to survive and ultimately profit from the revolution.

The New Capital Market Revolution was written with some alacrity by myself, on the template of *Capital Market Revolution* which I originally wrote in 1999. This edition has been edited by David Wilson who has been a firm supporter of the CMR concept and I have found it a pleasure to work with the professional team at TEXERE, including "le Patron" Myles Thompson who I hope will have recovered from the cost of our first breakfast at the Grosvenor House by the time this is published. Stuart Macfarlane has been a patient and indefatigable manager of the production process.

It often startles people to hear me refer to erivatives.com as my "front company" but it is from here that I draw a lot of my front-line experience and it is with thanks to my colleagues, the indefatigable Seana Lanigan as well as Hilary Redmond and Emily Saunderson (before her departure for a legal career) that I must turn first to acknowledge their work at keeping erivatives on track without which support my time could never have been spared for *The New CMR*.

On my roving travels a number of folk have generously provided accommodation, internet access and sustenance during the genesis of this book. In particular, I would like to thank my very good friends Charles Sidey and Gabby Leiders who are amongst London's most generous hosts, closely followed by Seana Lanigan (again) and Marcus Ackworth whose trivia machine remains an excellent way to unwind after a frantic day in the big smoke. Thanks must also go to Harry and Anne Graham, Jeff, Sharmaine, Alf Guadagnino, and Ruth for putting up with what has undoubtedly been an entirely self-absorbed houseguest on occasion! Raymond M. "Kip" Cheseldine remains perhaps the most gregarious, generous and absorbing host I can recall, whichever continent he seeks to provide hospitality upon!

Throughout the writing of *The New Capital Market Revolution*, I have been delighted to call upon various very good friends who have been happy to while away many an hour informing me of areas of their specialist technological expertise or debating the finer points of the post-feudal marketplace. In particular, Rory Collins has been a complete star with endless piercing insights and amusing anecdotes. My dear friends Jeremy and Julie Braithwaite have been hugely supportive and enthusiastic about this project from its birth and their unstinting forwarding of appropriate cuttings is greatly appreciated. I am also delighted to report that having been soundly thrashed at

Grand Prix 2, Grand Prix 3 and Grand Prix Legends, I finally managed to get a few stages over Jeremy on Colin McRae Rally 2!

In the past few years, I am delighted to have had my researches aided and abetted by some marvelous conferences. Everybody at IFSA made my first visit to Brisbane highly memorable – even if I didn't bring a suitable space outfit to wear at the gala dinner, and my trips to South Africa, particularly with the Banking Council, were a fantastic experience. Every reader ought to stay at the Chateau Montebello at least once, preferably during the Montreal Exchange's annual conference! My good friends Paul-André Jacot and Paul Meier, ably supported by Carol Gregoir continue to organize the best annual derivatives conference at Burgenstock and I hope they will invite me back for as many years as I am capable of chairing their Crossfire session! My trips to INSEAD in recent years have been great fun, if nothing else thanks to the stimulating debate provided by Europe's smartest MBA students and my thanks go to Professor Herwig Langohr and Professor Jonathan Story (whose book *Frontiers of Fortune* is utterly brilliant by the way) who have provided a great deal in the way of intellectual stimulus.

On the way through revolutionary times, one cannot help but acquire some intriguing new friends and associates. To that end, it has been a pleasure to spend time discussing the revolution and its many facets with the simply brilliant Sir Brian Williamson. I am delighted to have been privy to much of his thinking in the past few years and I truly cannot think of anybody else who could have taken LIFFE from intensive care back to being a powerhouse of global capital markets. Perhaps the only thing more entertaining than dinner with Brian remains dinner with both Brian and the brilliant Doctor Richard Sandor. He, in so many ways, helped shape the derivatives game which we are now able to play. As a relative upstart on the scene, it has been an honor to get to know such titans whom I am sure the history books will record in a century's time as having been pivotal in the development of our industry.

Meanwhile, I would like to extend my thanks to a group of key supporters whose input has been so appreciated these past years. They include but are not limited to: Luc Bertrand, Patrick Birley, Paul

Bowes, Phil Bruce, Ray Cahnman, Mike Charlton, Joe Cross, John Foyle, Rich Friesen, Gary Gastineau, Scott Gordon, Ina Hanisch, David Hardy, Bernard Horn, Martin Mosbacher, Joe Murphy, Jimmy Oliff, Bob Paul, Juliette Proudlove, Simon Raybould, Clive Roberts, Jim Sherman, Steve Smith, Mike Stiller and Richard Ward. My fellow directors of erivatives.com, Brendan Bradley and Giuliano Gregorio deserve a special mention. Indeed, Brendan deserves plaudits for pointing out my omission of the changing of European regulations following Maastricht which permitted the then DTB (now EUREX) to place screens in the EU beyond Germany. Andrew Stanton and Luellen Triltsch are just two avid erivatives readers whom I would like to mention, as their input and discussion has been hugely stimulating for many years; thanks for all your input. Kate O'Regan has been a constant source of encouragement, as has Heidi Wulfers while I struggled to bring everything together in *The New CMR*. Finally, Iain Cain deserves huge plaudits for managing to ensure that I never became a totally obsessed author by judiciously ensuring highly memorable social evenings to keep me reasonably sane while producing this tome.

While it pains me to include a mere list given their input into the project, alas to even remotely acknowledge everybody who has helped would probably occupy a fair-sized paperback book in its own right. Therefore, a representative selection follows with the caveat that not being on this list in no way negates my gratitude to those not mentioned for their input to *The New Capital Market Revolution*.

Anyway, my thanks therefore (in some semblance of alphabetical order) go to: Bob Aalam, Gwen Annee, Walter Allwicher, Jarrid Anderson, Gilles Antoine, Jim Austin, Graham Ayre, Mamdouh Barakat, Adam Bailie, Katie Barry (and the delightful Nora), Ron Bernstein, Basil Bourque, Lesley Boxall, Didier Bouillard, Diane Brown, Phil Bruce, Xavier Bruckert, Bill Burnham, Nick Carew Hunt, Raymond Cheseldine, Mike Charlton, David Chin, Sally Clarke, Will Corry, Richard Cook, Bob Cotton, Jonathan Cowan, Peter Cox, Joe Cross, Geoff Cutmore, Antoinette Darpy, Paul Davis, Gary Delany, Caroline Denton, Robert Dischel, Karen Dixon, Bill Doyle, David Dancox, Matt Docherty, Malcolm Donaldson, Danielle

Dycus, Marc Faber, Jackie Farnish, Rudolf Ferscha, John Fitzgerald, Hugh Freedburg, Stuart Frith, Sir Peter Froggatt, Richard Froggatt, Clive Furness, David and Sue Ganis, Judith Gantley, Maria Gemskie, Alan Genn, Grant Graham, Lewis Graham, Lindsay Graham, Sammy Graham, Luca Giovannetti, Giuliano Gregorio, Olivier Gueris, Kristina Halvarsson, Noriko Hama, Richard Hanson, David Hardy, Chris Hartley, Andrew Hilton, John Hinge, Simon Hobbs, Martin Hollander, Fiona Hoppe, Bernard, Shirley and Rachel Horn, Colin Howard, Richard Humphrys, Trevor Jarrett, Katie Jones, Daniel Jones, Jack Kelly, Andrew Klein, Grant Klein, George Kleinman, Julia Lampam, Seana Lanigan, Jim Lee, Andre Lewis, Luca Lombardo, John Lothian, Janelle McKimm, John Mackeonis, Michael March, Jeff Marsh, Sean Matthews, Olivier de Montety, Nick Neubauer, Stuart and Deborah Newby, Maurice Newman, Philip Nixon, Peter and Marlene Panholzer, Bob Paul, John Parry, Juliette Proudlove, Arthur Rabatin, Simon Raybould, Tony Redhead, Clive Roberts, Simon Rostron, Angus Richards, Laura Rigby, Paul Ritchie, Julian Roche, Riccardo Ronco, Lamon Rutten, Gustaf Sahlman, Pascal Samaran, Emily Saunderson, the ladies of the SFE library, Laura Shumiloff, Lutzifer Lor Matisse Shumiloff, Charlie Sidey, Mark Sieff, Guy Simpkin, Jean-Yves Sireau, Steve Smith, Carol Spagg, Scott and Norah Stark, Mike Stiller, Rob Sucher, Mark Thornberry, Luellen Triltsch, Manfred Unger, Liz Valentine, Sophie Van Straelen, Tim Van Doorn, David Vitale, Fredrik Wahlman, Suzanne Wallace, Linda Walrad, Colin Walsh, Lucie Wang, Richard Ward, Ross Westgate, Max Whitby, Brian Williamson, Steve Zwick,

To everybody who has assisted in the creation of *The New Capital Market Revolution*, my thanks to you all, and apologies to anybody whom this list may have inadvertently omitted.

Finally, my thanks to Sharon Maguire who remains the doyenne of financial book selling and has been a constant supporter of *The Capital Market Revolution* from day one.

Patrick L. Young,
Monaco, October 2002

Index

About TEXERE

TEXERE seeks to become the most progressive and authoritative voice in business publishing by cultivating and enhancing ideas that will illuminate the global business landscape. Our name defines the spirit of our vision: TEXERE is the ancient Latin verb "to weave." In an increasingly global business community, we seek to create an intersection where authors and readers can share the best thinking and the latest ideas. We want to leverage the expertise and insights of leading thinkers by weaving them with TEXERE's capability to deliver them to the marketplace. To learn more and become a part of our community visit us at:

www.etexere.com
and
www.etexere.co.uk

About the typeface

This book was set in 11/15 Sabon. This elegant typeface is a descendant of the types of Claude Garamond and was designed by Jan Tschichold in 1964. The Roman design is based on a Garamond specimen printed by Konrad F. Berner, who was married to the widow of another printer Jacques Sabon. The italic design is based on types by Robert Granjon, a contemporary of Garamond's.